Experiencing the Body and Blood of Christ:
Communicating Biblical Truth
to Late Millennials and Generation Z

ENDORSEMENTS

"As each generation seeks to discover spirituality, Christian Communion offers participants an authentic experience with the living God of the Bible. In his book, Andrew provides key insights into the perceived spiritual experiences of representatives of late Millennials and Generation Z in the celebration of Communion, held to the light of biblical truth and church history. The insights that Andrew provides will serve ministry practitioners very well in their work among students."

DeLonn Rance, Ph.D.
Director of the Melvin L. Hodges Center
for Pentecostal Missiological Research
Chair of the Global Mission Department
Professor of Intercultural Studies
Mobilizing the Church to the Mandate and Equipping
the Called

"A fascinating study in how to communicate ancients truths to new audiences in a world as tumultuous and changing as the first century Roman Empire, Andrew Fox shows us how to bridge gaps with people looking for the truth about reality but unsure where to find it and who to trust. Belief is hard at the best of times, but this book shows us to get past barriers both old and new."

Samuel Gregg, D.Phil.
Research Director,
Acton Institute

"For a postmodern generation with a post-Christian worldview, a lived experience during Communion can become transformative. From thorough research in biblical, historical, theological, and sociological perspectives, Andrew shows the practice of Communion is essential in communicating an authentic message of faith, and challenges leaders to infuse its celebration with the redemptive story and creative liturgy. What Andrew develops is fascinating and yet simply applied."

Carol Peters-Tanksley, M.D., D.Min.
Dr. Carol Ministries, Georgetown TX

"The potency of this book has the potential to transform leaders and impact the lived experience of Millennials and Generation Z as they participate or observe the practice of Communion. This ancient practice of remembering Christ through bread and wine can be a deep personal spiritual experience. Andrew's research opens the door widely into our understanding of how ancient practice and contemporary culture are both hungering after a missing spirituality. For those of us who have a deep interest in people coming to faith in an authentic way amongst younger people we are left with some intriguing options in the communication model Andrew creates."

Ian Green
Coach, Author, Speaker, and Global Network Connector
Bedford, UK

"Andrew's research has yielded yet another 'ancient' pathway into effective evangelization of postmodern generations with a post-Christian worldview. His thorough research and discoveries will have significant impact on helping all of us understand that starting with the experience and communal aspect of communion and moving toward biblical truth could yield a better starting point than the other way around. Thanks for the reminder that sometimes people 'belong before they believe!'"

Michael Cuckler, Ph.D.
Southeastern University, Lakeland FL

"Communicating the Gospel in meaningful ways to Millennials and Generation Z, with tech-shaped worldviews vastly different than most current church leadership, has Christian leaders deeply concerned. As central as Communion is to the Christian tradition, it has rarely been unpacked with a view towards Gospel communication. Andrew has listened carefully to the voices and experiences of the young and helps ministry practitioners see how the ancient practice of Communion can become a key vehicle for carrying biblical truth to those who value spirituality but not formal religion."

Alan Johnson, Ph.D.
Assembly of God Theological Seminary, Springfield MO

EXPERIENCING THE BODY AND BLOOD OF CHRIST

COMMUNICATING BIBLICAL TRUTH
TO LATE MILLENNIALS AND GENERATION Z

ANDREW K. FOX

ABSTRACT

This book recognizes the preservation and practice of Communion as a Christian celebration throughout church history and the current need to communicate the redemptive story through it to individuals and communities with a postmodern/post-Christian worldview. This book explores lived experiences of college students that represent Millennials and Generation Z with a postmodern/post-Christian worldview. The qualitative method of interpretative phenomenological analysis (IPA) was used to reveal what those experiences were, and four interpretative lenses were used that revealed how the perception of those experiences can be understood during Communion.

The research involved 425 students from St. Edward's University in Austin, Texas, in addition to selected faculty and staff. A total of 49 religious affiliations were represented on campus, of which 38 incorporate Communion into a church service. Their participation helped me discover what the students experienced, explained in their own words, in their own way, and with the meaning they associated with it. Their participation also helped me discover what can be understood from a lived experience during Communion.

All of the students encountered who they identified as a supernatural God; however, what the students perceived as an encounter with God was not informed by historical or biblical contexts. Consequently, this book also examines the ways in which participants in Communion experienced Christ as described in church history and in the biblical text. Emerging across the research were key discoveries towards understanding how celebrating Communion can communicate biblical truth to postmodern communities similar to Millennials and Generation Z with a post-Christian worldview by retelling the redemptive story. Such understanding informs ministry practitioners how people, like those at St. Edward's University, associate a Christian celebration with meaning making or sense-making.

Summary: This book recognizes the preservation and practice of Communion as a Christian celebration throughout church history and the current need to communicate the redemptive story through it to individuals and communities with a postmodern/post-Christian worldview. To that end, the book explores lived experiences of college students that represent late Millennials and Generation Z with a postmodern/post-Christian worldview.

Scripture taken from the Holy Bible, NEW INTERNATIONAL VERSION®, NIV® Copyright © 1973, 1978, 1984, 2011 by Biblica, Inc.® Used by permission. All rights reserved worldwide.

Publication date: March 2020

ISBN Print: 978-1-7340733-0-0
ISBN eBook: 978-1-7340733-1-7

Library of Congress Control Number: 2020902261

1. Christ 2. Generation Z 3. Millennial 4. Communion 5. Communication
6. Truth 7. Experience 8. Story

I Fox, Andrew K.   II Experiencing the Body and Blood of Christ

Experiencing the Body and Blood of Christ may be purchased at special quantity discounts for book clubs, colleges, universities, or educational purposes for churches, study groups, and nonprofits of any denomination. For more information or to have Dr. Fox speak at your event: andrew@drandrewfox.com or (512) 897 7886

Editor: Cheryl K. Chambers
Cover and Interior Layout and Design: Lynne Hopwood
Publishing Consultant: Mel Cohen inspiredauthorspress@gmail.com

Contact Andrew for Reprints of specific chapters or the entire book and Rights, or Licensing Agreements

Publisher: Oxford Publishing
Website: www.drandrewfox.com

Printed in the United States of America

DEDICATION

To Renee, my wife and best friend.

ACKNOWLEDGEMENTS

Having the time, resources, and the heart to undertake writing this book was made possible by a lifetime of people contributing to my own experience and understanding of God. To all those people, in different countries, with different perspectives, and from different cultures, I am deeply grateful:

To Renee, for her patient endurance, loving kindness, gentleness, sacrifice, encouragement, and support revealed in her own experience of God as a woman of noble character. Renee, I am profoundly indebted to you, and I am proud to call you my wife. You are, and always will be, my best friend. To my three children, Daniel, Zachary, and Olivia, for allowing their dad to take time out to study, travel, and write during some of your most vulnerable years of transitioning towards adulthood. The stories that our family relationships tell throughout life are far more important to explaining experiences than any study can produce.

To my parents, Malcolm and Margaret Fox, for adopting me and nurturing the Christian faith in me until I could say for myself, "Your God and my God, your Father, and my Father" (John 20:17). To Diane, a remarkable and enduring lady who gave birth to me. To the parents of my wife, Brian, and Jose Downward, for nurturing the same Christian faith in her until 1993 when we vowed, "I do" and "I will" in a new experience of God as husband and wife.

From Nottingham to Bournemouth in Great Britain, I am grateful to those who influenced me giving me the opportunity to develop in my own experience of God. From Washington to Texas in the United States of America, I am equally grateful. I am thankful for those who have come into my life – some momentarily, while others remain - teaching me the disciplines of reading, study, writing, and personal preparation.

To the students, faculty, priests, and campus ministry of St. Edward's University in Austin, Texas, for investing the time needed to investigate an experience of the body and blood of Christ. You have collectively deepened my own experience of God as I have seen Him at work in your own lives far beyond tradition.

To all these people, and many more, I am deeply grateful.

PREFACE

It was a typical Sunday morning in the small English town of Tiverton in Devon. I was twenty-seven. My small congregation gathered to worship and celebrate Communion. From hymns, prayers, and sermon, the order of service was predictable. **Then the unpredictable happened.** As I officiated over the bread and wine of Communion, a lady in the congregation encountered Christ. And, it was no ordinary lady. To keep her anonymous, I will call her "Isabel."

Isabel had been horribly abused by a man whose actions led to a long-term prison sentence. It left Isabel emotionally and socially deprived of any meaningful interaction with others. Her life was nothing short of being surrounded by a dark cloud. No eye contact, no conversation, and certainly no physical contact. She was the last to arrive on a Sunday and the first to leave at the closing hymn. **But this week was different.**

When Isabel received the bread and wine, it was as though a new day had suddenly dawned. I remember because her behavior was unfamiliar. She looked at me; not a stare, but a look of delight as though she was about to laugh. Like a long-lost relative she hugged me, and in that embrace were volumes of unspoken words. She hugged other people in the congregation as well. From that day on, she was first to arrive and last to leave. Isabel began volunteering to work with different programs in the church. **Something had happened.**

Pentecostals might say she had been filled with the Holy Spirit; Methodists that God set her free; Catholics that she had an epiphany; Presbyterians may say the Scriptures had become a light to her feet and lamp to her path; Evangelicals that she had encountered the joy of the Lord; and, others may say she had an awakening. I say she experienced Christ while receiving the bread and wine of Communion. **Over the past thirty years I have witnessed similar experiences.**

This book is based on two documented facts. First, since Christ said, "This is my body...this is my blood" (Matt. 26:26-28),[1] people have experienced Him while celebrating Communion. These experiences cannot be predicted or guaranteed, but they can be anticipated. Therefore, such experiences can be called **lived experiences** at some point during Communion. Second, Communion has been preserved with its local and universal characteristics. A significant universal characteristic is that celebrating Communion means the retelling of the story of redemption. A significant local characteristic is how an individual's story enters the redemptive story becoming part of the retelling. I believe this is what happened with Isabel, and in that moment of liminality she encountered Christ, the Redeemer.

In this book I will explore **how Communion serves to communicate biblical truth** by retelling the redemptive story, specifically in postmodern/post-Christian environments where people gather and are connected by their participation in Communion as a Christian celebration.

My interest in writing about Communion is not isolated to Isabel. It comes from thirty years of pastoral ministry in Great Britain and the United States. During that time, I have observed people encounter Christ. Admittedly, I do not know what is happening in a participant's life. However, there have been random, unpredictable, and unsolicited experiences like Isabel. Furthermore, it seems to me these experiences are increasing, especially among Millennials and Generation Z who currently have this postmodern/post-Christian worldview. I make this observation after participating in Communion while visiting twenty-nine countries outside the United States. **I found a common trend** through observation and inquiry among participants over these years: people are attracted to the celebration of the Communion, but not necessarily to the biblical truth it espouses.

I have been the Pastor of three churches in two countries. I have also taught classes on theology through the lens of culture and communication in several universities as faculty, adjunct, and

---

[1] All Scripture quotations, unless otherwise noted, are from the New International Version.

guest lecturer. Pastoring and teaching have allowed me to observe and inquire how people explain a variety of personal encounters with Christ. Each encounter is unquestionably real in the sense that it was not fabricated. From time to time it may be embellished, but a keen observer would detect this. It was the disconnection with biblical truth that Communion espouses that intrigued me. It appeared that Christ was not hindered in revealing Himself by a lack of knowledge, understanding, or even commitment to the Christian faith. **Did Christ have a different rite of passage to celebrate Communion than His Church?** I am careful to admit – but confident to write – this does seem to be the case.

From these inquiries and observations, I began to wonder if the spirituality represented in the current western cultural era of Postmodernity was connected in an experience of Christ at Communion. Not only was Christ unhindered, but He also appears to perfectly communicate Himself to a postmodern culture of deconstruction.[2] It was my curiosity about this connection of current culture and spirituality represented in Millennials and Generation Z that motivated me to write this book.

By exploring the connection to Christ through Communion, I wanted to know how Communion as a Christian celebration functioned as a vehicle for communicating biblical truth by retelling the redemptive story specifically among Millennials and Generation Z with a postmodern/post-Christian worldview. In what ways did Communion function in retelling the story? **Why was there a disconnection between a lived experience of Christ during Communion and biblical truth the celebration espouses?** Answering these questions would provide me and other ministry practitioners with a deeper and more nuanced understanding of how Communion, as a celebration, can effectively function to tell and retell the redemptive story.

Why is this important? So many mainstream church denominations and non-denominations have reduced Communion to a monthly, quarterly, and even annual celebration. If people do encounter Christ during Communion, why reduce the opportu-

---

[2] A phrase that Jacque Derrida uses to describe postmodernism. I shall address this in a later chapter four.

nity? I recently heard one general explanation that can be verified throughout church history. Prior to the Protestant Reformation, Communion was a central feature of Christian worship. After the Reformation, sermonizing became central. During the late twentieth century, the music team became central to Christian worship. Now, Communion is on the peripheral edge. While this explanation has broad brushstrokes, it does chart the celebration of Communion from central to peripheral with many mainstream church denominations.

Christ said that we were to eat the bread and drink the wine in remembrance of Him. It is not difficult to acknowledge that we can easily forget the universal characteristics of the redemptive story in favor of a local self-centered application when Communion is an infrequent celebration. **Do we remember correctly by minimizing the practice of Communion?** Does this reduction feed into the disconnection between Communion participants and biblical truth the celebration espouses?

The logic and design of this book took shape as I began to think of the major areas implicated in trying to understand how Communion as a Christian celebration functions to communicate biblical truth by retelling redemptive story. This included the experience and explanations of 425 participants, an assessment of those experiences, the community of those participating in Communion, and an examination of the biblical text and Communion in church history.

For example, though Communion was first named such by early Christians in the second century, it was first introduced by Christ prior to His crucifixion. Since that introduction, Communion has endured throughout church history to the present day. Undoubtedly, many church developments that included the interpretation of Scripture, sacerdotal power, and varying uses of liturgy impacted the ways participants experienced Christ throughout history. **What direction did biblical interpretation take throughout church history about Communion, and why?** How did sacerdotal power develop, and for whose advantage? How was liturgy used and understood in written and spoken form? More importantly, how did biblical interpretation, sacerdotal power, and the use of liturgy impact an understanding of the redemptive story throughout church history?

I wanted to know the ways participants in Communion experienced Christ as documented in church history. What I found was quite provoking. Investigating church history along the lines of church developments, interpretation of Scripture, and the varying use of liturgy provided the historical background for an understanding of participants in Communion with a postmodern/post-Christian worldview. What I found was equally provoking.

Despite these discoveries, I observed a growing phenomenon among those who were attracted to Communion. Christ was being encountered, as described by participants, in ways that challenge the current ecclesial language about Communion. As such, I am convinced that the redemptive story, retold through the celebration of Communion, compliments a postmodern/post-Christian worldview. Consequently, there is no better time to readdress the function and practice of Communion as a vehicle to communicate biblical truth through retelling the redemptive story to Millennials and Generation Z.

CONTENTS

LIST OF FIGURES

FORWARD

You may well ask why a professional evangelist has been asked to write a foreword to a scholarly book on how the practice of Communion transmits biblical truth to 'Late Millennials and Generation Z.'

It is a good question, so let me give you two reasons. The first is that Andrew graciously claims it was my message many years ago in Nottingham that was 'the tipping point' that brought him to faith. Well, I am glad the Holy Spirit spoke through me and am delighted how Andrew has gone from young convert to respected Christian academic.

The second, is that this is the sort of fascinating book that comes about when intelligent, well-read academics address serious issues. The problem Andrew approaches is well-known and urgent: the church is not making the impact that it must make with those to whom those labels of 'Late Millennials' and 'Generation Z' can be attached. Those of us in the holy business of evangelism are supposed to be fishers of people but individuals from these groups are proving to be elusive fish to catch. So, for example, we evangelists find ourselves somewhat perplexed that, having spent years rehearsing the logical argument for the truth of Christianity, that particular bait attracts little interest from many of our younger hearers.

In response to this question of how the church is to connect with the children of post-modernism, Andrew has made a fascinating and stimulating proposal. Is it possible, he suggests, that the church's act of Communion (however we call it) can actually be an entry point to the road of faith? Can the physical sharing of the bread and the wine, with all that it means, touch those who are resistant to the spoken word?

Now, as Andrew admits, this is challenging for two reasons. First, the church has always seen evangelism as preaching – in some way or another – propositional truth: proclaiming verbally some collection of beliefs in Christ and his death on the cross that 'outsiders' must in some way agree to be true, in order for them to enter into the faith. But it is not hard to see the problem in proposing truth to a post-truth generation.

Second, although almost all Christians agree that Communion is essential to the Christian life, exactly what that act or ceremony means is a subject that is shunned rather than sought. The reasons are well known. Sadly, despite the use of the word *communion* with its implications of unity, what we have had is an ordinance that has instead fueled division. What exactly happens with the bread and the wine and how it is to be interpreted helped split the church apart at the Reformation and has subsequently fueled divisions within the Protestant churches. The inevitable result of this has been an acceptance that this is an area over which we do not simply agree to differ, but we agree not to discuss. Gently, wisely, but provocatively, this book opens up the whole issue of Communion in the context of evangelism and its conclusion can be summed up in two words: *communion communicates.*

One advantage of climbing mountains is it allows you the possibility of seeing things from a very different perspective. There is a sense in which this is a mountain of a book and there are certainly points within it where the path is steep. Yet there are welcome returns: there are many places where you can catch your breath and, as you do, enjoy splendid views on culture and theology.

The challenge that the church faces today is very great. Tomorrow's church will be made of converts from those who are today in their teens, 20s and 30s and, if they are not made, then there will be no church. We must reach out to those around us. God-given biblical truth has been put in our possession and, somehow, we have to transmit it to the confused and value-free world of our younger contemporaries. But between us and them lies a great gap that must be bridged. It is a gap that this stimulating book, faithful to both the Word and to our world, may point the way to bridging.

Reverend Canon J. John
Evangelist
Canonjjohn.com

INTRODUCTION

Since the revival of Marvel Comic characters, everyone has **a favorite hero.**

Philosophy has its heroes. In the West, the big three are Socrates (470-399BC), Plato (428-348BC), and Aristotle (384-322BC). The East has its philosophical heroes in Buddha (563-483BC), Confucius (551-479BC), and Lao-Tzu (601-531BC). Both triads of philosophers had one thing in common: they believed in the power of the human mind to think, explain, predict, and understand life. Through logic and reason, enlightenment and harmony, these six men gave us their remarkable minds.
Christ gave us His eternal body and blood.

Perhaps the heroes of philosophy were trying to save us from our ignorance by providing new and exciting knowledge. Despite their profound knowledge none of them disclosed a clear reason why we needed to be saved from ignorance. There are so many things I still do not know, but am I worse off for not knowing them? What is clear about Christ is that He came to save us from sin and death through His body and blood celebrated through participation in Communion. Furthermore, Scripture explains this universal redeeming story that also prevents ignorance. I can say that I am better off knowing and experiencing the redemptive story. Philosophers from the West and East believed they were presenting truth as they perceived it.
Christ said He was the Truth.

As Greeks, Philosophers Plato, Socrates, and Aristotle believed in many gods. Buddha taught that he was not a god, only a man. Confucius and Lao-Tzu did not believe there were any gods; rather, the universe was a type of power. Perhaps the word god can be replaced with the word *celebrity* today. Either way, our present culture has made our six philosophers somewhat celebrity. Another fact that all six men had in common was that they predated Christ, the Son of God. Even so, they were not ignorant of the writings of Jewish prophets who wrote about God and His Messiah, not His celebrity.

Christ said that seeing Him was to see God.

Buddha wanted people to follow his teachings, but not him as a person. Confucius and Lao-Tzu more or less said the same thing. Though Aristotle followed Plato, and Plato followed Socrates, only Aristotle wrote down his own teachings. Well, Christ did not write down his teachings either. However, we have the teachings of Christ because Matthew, Mark, Luke, and John did write them down while eyewitnesses were still alive. In those teachings we read, "Come to me" (Matt. 11:28), "Come, follow me" (Matt. 4:19), and "Anyone who loves me will obey my teaching" (Jn. 14:23). So, not only did Christ want us to follow Him but also His teaching that became a written record. One of His most enduring and universally recognized teachings occurred shortly before he was crucified.

Christ said, "This is my body...this is my blood" (Matt. 26:26-28).

Scripture records that Christ gave this teaching to the disciples during the last days of His life while eagerly participating in the Jewish celebration of Passover. By personifying the Passover bread and wine, Christ did two significant things. First, He empowered His disciples to celebrate His death, resurrection, ascension, and return by simply doing what He did with the bread and wine as recorded in His own words, "do this [bread and wine] in remembrance of me" (Lk. 22:19).

Second, He personified Passover and future heavenly celebration, called the Wedding Supper of the Lamb, by promising to "not drink from this fruit of the vine from now on until that day when I drink it new with you in my Father's kingdom" (Matt. 26:29). By looking back historically at the Passover and forward eschatologically to the Wedding Supper of the Lamb from the perspective of Communion, the teaching of Christ is set in a cosmic story of drama, poetry, and prose. So, the redemptive story serves as a metanarrative seen in the successive table celebrations of Passover, Communion, and the Wedding Supper of the Lamb. Since the Wedding Supper of the Lamb is attended by "every nation, tribe, people, and language" (Rev. 7:9), by default the redemptive story is cross-cultural and intercultural at the same time. If the Wedding Supper of the Lamb does not belong to any particular culture, does Communion really belong to church denominations, or is it something churches get to celebrate? It is not difficult to comprehend the drama, poetry, and prose of the redemptive story touching every nation, tribe, people, and language.

What began as a simple act of experiencing the empowerment and promise of Christ has been interpreted and applied differently throughout successive phases of church history. And, each phase is punctuated with questionable practices from the sublime to the ridiculous. Despite these varying interpretations, Communion has been remarkably preserved. Fr. Alfred McBride (2006) notes how Pope John Paul II testified to its preservation and its applied diversity:

> "I have been able to celebrate Holy Mass in chapels built along mountain paths, on lake shores, and seacoasts; I have celebrated it on altars built in stadiums and city squares. This varied scenario of celebrations of the Eucharist [Communion] has given me a powerful experience of its universal and, so to speak, its cosmic character. Yes, cosmic! Because even when it is celebrated on the humble altar of a country church, the Eucharist [Communion] is always in some way celebrated on the altar of the world. It unites heaven and earth. It embraces and permeates all creation."

When Christ introduced Communion, He asked that participants remember Him whenever they eat the bread and drink the wine. However, **Christ did not predetermine what a participant ought to experience as he or she remembered Him.** Simple, right? As such, it can be assumed an experience of Christ would be much like a fingerprint. It is personalized from a common feature. This fact alone makes an experience during Communion highly subjective to the participant. I found what people perceived in their experiences when they participated in Communion sincerely genuine, and nothing to snub or arrogantly dismiss. However genuine those encounters were, I also found that participants could not explain their experiences in light of the biblical text. Such a discovery came from appropriate qualitative methods so I could understand what people perceived in their experiences as they celebrated Communion.

Though an experience during Communion is subjective to the participant, there are aspects of the celebration that ought to happen as prescribed by Christ's words and actions when He first introduced Communion. These words and actions comprise a ceremonial celebration—more so, a Christian ceremonial celebration. Do not be put off by the word ceremony. I am using it as a type of middle ground between ritual and blasé. I found a number of ways in which the lived experiences of Millennials and Generation Z could be understood within this Christian celebration. This specifically helped me in understanding how the redemptive story can connect people like Millennials and Generation Z with a postmodern/post-Christian worldview to biblical truth that Communion espouses.

Again, I noticed a common trend: participants were sincerely attracted to Communion. This trend compelled me to ask what was going on in the gathering at Communion to create such an interest. Were there more encounters with Christ like Isabel? I hypothesized that people were finding meaning for what they believed and valued, where active participation in Communion served as a significant factor. This activity, through which participants appeared to find meaning, was the environment for understanding a postmodern/post-Christian worldview. I began to comprehend the characteristics of spirituality and religious beliefs and behaviors of the people who participate in Communion, and the curiosity of those who observed. What I found helped me discover how spirituality and religious beliefs and behaviors were influenced by the gathering at Communion, and not necessarily by traditional teaching methods.

While I observed that people were attracted to Communion, again, they were not necessarily attracted to biblical truth Communion espouses embedded in the redemptive story. I think it goes without saying, though I am saying it, that Christ is not a Marvel Comic character. Nevertheless, from the perspective of Communion, the biblical text does express how God was experienced in biblical times. What I found in the text helped me compare both experiences: biblical times and our current time. Discovering how God was experienced in the biblical text gave me points of comparison with the experience of current participants and, ultimately, for understanding how the redemptive story can be retold that makes sense to Millennials and Generation Z.

So, the whole **purpose of writing this book was to understand how Communion can function to communicate biblical truth towards developing a theoretical model to retelling the redemptive story to Millennials and Generation Z with a postmodern/post-Christian worldvie**w. Understanding what people perceive to be their experience was absolutely essential towards developing a theoretical communication model. Equally essential was identifying an age group that best represented a postmodern/post-Christian worldview. Through appropriate qualitative methods, I found the best representative sample group between eighteen and twenty-three. This is where Millennials and Generation Z come into play. More specifically, late Millennials and the beginning of Generation Z.

The current literature on Millennials and Generation Z showed me the most documented sample group between eighteen and twenty-three were students enrolled in higher education. So, higher education was the context. Also, the literature showed me the phrase *"none"* is a derivative of late Millennials and Generation Z, much like the *United Kingdom* is a derivative of Great Britain. So, for my purposes, the best representation of a postmodern/post-Christian worldview were Millennials and Generation Z – or "nones" - who attended college. The overarching question that the Barna Group and the Impact 360 Institute asked in their research with Millennials and Generation Z sums up this age group: **"How do you talk about truth in a way that**

'feels' true?" (2019, 74) With this provoking and subjective question in mind, the purpose of this book was reinforced.

For the sake of clarity, I will briefly outline the literature that gave me insights. First, Michael Lipka (2015) highlights the absence of biblical truth in spirituality among undergraduate students. He points out that 36% of those between the ages of eighteen and twenty-four abandon an affiliation with organized religion calling themselves "nones" by rejecting biblical truth. "Nones" identify as atheists and agnostics, claiming that their religion is nothing in particular while still remaining spiritual. Some are leaving their childhood religion to become unaffiliated, or "nones," while 67% who were raised without a religious affiliation are remaining religious "nones," which is a higher retention rate than most other major religious groups. The increasing population of "nones" typically **do not become more religiously affiliated as they get older**. And yet, "nones" are continually attracted to religious ceremonies like Communion because it seems to engage their spirituality.

A year after Lipka's research was published, Elizabeth Drescher (2016, 40) threw some light on the connection of "nones" to Communion: progressive Protestant churches were moving to an open Communion table for participants who are not baptized or have a Christian background. Now, for many mainstream church denominations an open table is tantamount to liberalism. However, the attraction was to a community with shared beliefs and values. In the same year, Corey Seemiller and Meghan Grace (2016, 43-44) found that students with a religious affiliation would move into the category of "spiritual" or "none" during college. Nothing new there because they still believed in God, but not **the way religion was being organized around conservative political views.** In many ways, students opt out of a religious affiliation in order to reconcile their faith with social values, not political views. If you think that worshipful postures during patriotic songs is an oxymoron, this is precisely how Millennials and Generation Z perceive the religious-political world around them. As a result, similar to Lipka, Seemiller and Grace (2016, 44) found the category of "no religion" the third largest religious group in the world. What this means is that students' representative of Generation Z will outgrow organized religion as the younger siblings of late Millennials.

Three years after Drescher, the research of Tim Clydesdale and Kathleen Garces-Foley (2019, 143) added a more nuanced definition to twenty-something "nones": though "nones" do not identify as religious, they do have religious beliefs and practices. Clydesdale and Garces-Foley believe that a clear definition of "nones" is about as clear as a definition for Postmodernism: complex and difficult. For example, "nones" now represent conservative and liberal values, secularism and supernaturalism, atheists, agnostics, theists, and deists (2019, 143). **Will the real Millennial and Generation Z stand up?**

Undoubtedly, "nones" cannot be described in a single set of characteristics. They are complex and multi-categorized. However, attraction to Communion as a religious ceremony is a common characteristic among the majority of "nones." As such, a postmodern/post-Christian worldview appears to be compatible with the cultural characteristics of "nones."

So, Christianity has its single hero. He gave us His body and blood. He asked us to follow Him and His teaching. His incarnate Jewish name was Jesus. His title is Christ. Cross-culturally and interculturally **He is known as Jesus Christ.** Late Millennials and Generation Z are encountering Him.

Overview

I want to give you, the reader, a brief overview of the six sections that comprise the logic and design of this book. If you are investing your valuable time into reading this, I want you to know in advance the flow of my arguments, discussions, and observations before arriving at a conclusion. Each section can be read as a stand-alone piece or, better still, read as a whole. The first section is certainly the longest as it tells us how we got to a postmodern/post-Christian worldview today from a small upstairs room where Christ said, "This is my body…this is my blood" (Matt. 26:26-28).

Section One

The first section in this book deals with participants and observers in Communion who experienced Christ described in church history. It creates a historical background from the upstairs room where Christ introduced Communion through the present day. I use three lenses to investigate church history like looking through a particular pair of glasses that relate to the complexities of late Millennials and Generation Z with a post-modern/post-Christian worldview: (1) how significant church developments granted or denied access to the Communion bread and wine; (2) how biblical passages were used to describe Communion; and (3) how liturgy was used to retell the redemptive story of God.

The historical context is not only important to define what participants perceived as their experience when they celebrated Communion, but also the way their experience can be understood within the celebration. There are similarities and differences that can help us today. For example, the historical context shows how Communion evolved with regard to who could, or could not, receive the bread and wine and how the redemptive story was retold right up to the present day. What this means is that a lived experience during Communion today has a rich history shedding a bright light and long shadow on how participants came to celebrate Communion in the way they currently do. The bright light and falling shadow are cast by comparing the arguments of priests, bishops, professors, academics, lecturers, pastors, revivalists, and other church leaders. Would it surprise you if I said that Communion was not original, but the adaption of Passover as a preexisting ceremony? And, as you will come to see, Passover itself was an adaption of preexisting Mesopotamian practices.

This is important towards developing a theoretical model of how Communion functions by retelling the redemptive story in a way that informs a lived experience through biblical truth without detaching from its historical context. Different ideas about the orientation of spirituality and religious beliefs and behaviors are seen throughout history. To that end, I deliberately avoid commencing this book with a postmodern/post-Christian worldview and then imposing it onto church history. Rather, I want the reader to see how we got here today by allowing it to emerge.

Section Two

Building on this rich history, the second section involves the discoveries of Communion experiences from students enrolled in higher education through the method of interpretative phenomenological analysis (IPA). **Section two addresses what it is that students experienced when they participated in Communion; not what they should or ought to experience, but what is actually experienced.** The theory of IPA is a qualitative method committed to examining how people make sense of their lived experiences in detail, and recognizing the meaning associated with those experiences identified by the experiencer. IPA explores an experience through the students' explanations, in their own words. The method brackets, or suspends, predetermined language, allowing the students to define their own explanation. In short, they were unhindered by the language of "isms" and "ologies" often associated with religious philosophy, sociology, or anthropology, to name a few. In short, IPA begins with the substance and works towards the form, whereas traditional interpretation begins with the form and works backwards to the substance.

I demonstrate how bracketing works by comparing seven theological explanations of an experience during Communion that have predetermined language. Knowing what students experience as they participate in Communion, in their own words, was important to uncovering authentic discoveries, moving towards a theoretical model of how Communion serves to communicate biblical truth by retelling the redemptive story. In this second section, I disclose two discoveries that surprisingly had no historical or biblical context. First, I found that students had to sense or feel something in a lived experience in order to form meaning. Second, Communion did, indeed, serve as a vehicle of communication to retell the redemptive story. By bracketing predetermined language, both discoveries also show that the mental faculty of imagination was highly engaged and necessary for the students to explain their lived experience.

Section Three

While IPA includes a descriptive account of the way an experience happened during Communion in its own terms, it does not go far enough to analyze the context in which it occurred—namely, within a Christian ceremony around a table of bread and wine. **The third section deals with the way a lived experience can be understood within this ceremonial context.** Whereas IPA suspends all predetermined language, analyzing the context introduces the assessment of how words and actions are used during Communion. Bearing in mind I examine Communion as a Christian celebration, assessing performative words and actions distinguishes baptisms, ordinations, funerals, weddings, dedications, christenings, and memorials from Communion.

I also used four systems that acted like lenses to assess the perceived experiences of the students. Again, like wearing specific glasses, it will help you see what is going on in their lived experience during Communion. From assessing how a lived experience can be understood, a third discovery emerged, moving towards a better understanding of Communion as a communication vehicle for theory development. What the students believed approaching Communion actually shaped what they got out of the ceremony. Once again, I found that imagination was a necessary mental faculty highly employed in the students' approach to Communion.

Section Four

Writing the fourth section involved drawing on qualitative methods and data used to write sections two and three. Having journeyed through the history of successive cultural eras, I describe the characteristics of spirituality and religious beliefs and behaviors of students who currently participate in Communion. I show their experience of spirituality and religion; how others influenced the way they describe their experience of spirituality and religion; the way Communion facilitates the expression of an experience of spirituality and religion; and how the students describe God.

So, having discovered what students experience as they participate in Communion in section two and how that lived experience can be understood within a Christian ceremony in section three, section four contextualizes the *what* and *how* in a description of spirituality and religious beliefs and practices of late Millennials and Generation Z who participated in Communion. I made two important discoveries that paint a picture of what a postmodern/post-Christian worldview looks like. First, four characteristics moved in a repetitive circular fashion; and second, this movement began with self. Simply put, the picture that I paint of a postmodern/post-Christian worldview challenges sacerdotal power, or the power and authority of the person officiating the Communion ceremony.

Section Five

Because my interest concerns how Communion functions to communicate biblical truth by retelling the redemptive story in a postmodern/post-Christian environment, knowledge of the biblical text is necessary. How else can a ministry practitioner relate their lived experiences with the redemptive story unless he or she knows the biblical text? Coming full-circle to the historical investigation in section one, the fifth section interprets the biblical text centered around the words of Christ, "This is my body...this is my blood" (Matt. 26:26-28). As a side, I would have thoroughly enjoyed listening to church leaders debate these words during the Protestant Reformation, but I would have left the room when they literally started to throw punches.

From the perspective of Communion, I look back historically to Passover and forward eschatologically to the Wedding Supper of the Lamb showing how God was experienced as expressed to participants in the bread and wine in the text of Scripture. I show that there is a contrast between how God is expressed in the biblical text and how each student experiences God today. Showing this contrast focuses the two final things I discovered. First, God can be depicted in different ways in the biblical text; and second, God can be experienced at each table celebration in a set of beliefs grounded in biblical truth connecting the past and future to the present with the participant and observer in mind. Consequently, a lived experience informed by the biblical text makes sense as Christian theology.

I take the experiences of God in all three table celebrations and assess them through the four systems from section three. From this assessment, I bring out commonalities and differences. The way each system assesses how God is experienced in the biblical text from the perspective of Communion in the Passover and Wedding Supper of the Lamb is summarized with discussion on what the findings mean towards theory development of how Communion functions to communicate biblical truth by retelling the redemptive story informed by the biblical text.

Section Six

The final section brings together all seven discoveries that emerge throughout this book, developing a theoretical model of how Communion, as a Christian ceremony, can function to retell the redemptive story in a postmodern community populated by late Millennials and Generation Z who participate or observe in Communion while holding sub-orthodox biblical views. In short, what I am asking in section six is simply, "So what?" and, "Why does this matter?"

Assumptions

Transubstantiation, divine mystery, transelementation, re-ordination, and *consubstantiation* metaphysically deal with the bread and wine of Communion. This book is not concerned with a metaphysical interpretation. The substance of the book is concerned with the individual experiences of people as they participate in Communion. The theological research is limited to the three biblical events that could be called a *ceremonial table of cel-*

ebration: Passover, Communion, and the Wedding of the Lamb. I utilize both Old and New Testaments. The centrality of these events is the Communion table. Therefore, I look back historically to the Passover table and forward eschatologically to the Wedding of the Lamb table.

I make the assumption that God has revealed Himself to humankind throughout history and is active in that same history, present, and future. God reveals Himself to individuals and to a community of peoples. He does that within theological frames we create, and those we have yet to discover and acknowledge. Communion is a way God reveals Himself to participants and observers. Also, I assume a better understanding of how Communion serves as a vehicle towards a theoretical model of communication that retells the redemptive story building a homiletical bridge between a lived experience and biblical truth that Communion espouses. Documented accounts in church history do show that participants and observers have experienced Christ when Communion was being served. What I am questioning is how the celebration at the Communion table itself informs those experiences today with sound orthodoxy.

Appreciation

In advance, thank you for investing your time in reading through this book. It is my hope that others will take the research further and discover how weddings, funerals, ordinations, memorials, dedications, christenings, and baptisms can function to retell the story of redemption.

SECTION ONE

EXPERIENCING CHRIST THROUGH COMMUNION IN CHURCH HISTORY

The first section involves how participants in Communion have experienced Christ as described in church history. **But whose church history?** If you are Roman Catholic, I assume you would comb through historical documents guided by Vatican II (1962-65) or the Medellin Conference (1968). However, if you are Anglican, I equally assume you would look for precursors to the Thirty-Nine Articles (1571), or the Book of Common Prayer (1549-1662). If Lutheran, I assume you may look for Lutheranism before Luther (1483-1546). What if you are Methodist? Do you rummage through church history using the lens of John Wesley's expulsion from the Anglicanism (1766)? Perhaps you are Episcopalian, Pentecostal, Evangelical, or non-denominational? Perhaps you have faith in God, or something, but reject the church? Through what lens do you read church history like wearing a particular pair of glasses?

If we are to understand an experience of Christ through Communion in church history, we must acknowledge there is more than one Christian tradition, therefore, more than one history. So, throughout this section, I compare the arguments of priests, bishops, professors, academics, lecturers, pastors, revivalists, and other church leaders that surround Communion. I like the statement that Gary Macy makes, "Before the reformation, Christians were simply Christians –eastern and western Christians sometimes, but mostly simply Christians" (2005, 9-10). I like it because Macy is Catholic and, yet, he does not impose his Catholicism into church history. Undoubtedly for non-Catholics, it is easy to use the Protestant Reformation (1517) as a gigantic lens for church history. I will try and adopt Macy's approach.

In order to prevent any ambiguity, I define an experience of Christ during Communion in two ways. First, as the empowerment of Christ to actively participate in receiving the bread and wine, repeating what He did in obedience to His command, "do this [bread and wine] in remembrance of me" (Lk. 22:19). Second, in hearing Christ's promissory words of hope and anticipation that He would "not drink from this fruit of the vine from now on until that day when I drink it new with you in my Father's kingdom" (Matt. 26:29). Therefore, **an experience of Christ in church history concerns the empowering actions and promissory words of Communion.** In short, empowerment and hope.

The historical context provides the parameters and background to a postmodern understanding, not a particular church denomination. What today's participants experience has a rich history that sheds light and a long shadow on how we have come to celebrate Communion. My investigation begins after the first Communion and extends to the present day. The phases of Western church history are divided into four eras: Classical Age (100-600); Middle Ages (601-1500); Modernity (1501-1965); and Postmodernity (1966-2017). At the end of each era, there is a section summary.

I make three generalizations that explain how each era is determined: (1) eras as common periods of time; (2) amplified issues that surround Communion; and (3) church history. An explanation of the timing of each era is determined by two factors: (1) what was actually written about Communion; and (2) widely accepted dates that define each era. Three lenses in each era are used to examine the following: (1) church developments that granted or denied access to Communion; (2) differences in how biblical passages were used to explain Communion; and (3) how liturgy was used to retell the redemptive story during Communion. The three lenses were chosen because they explain the context for how participants historically came to celebrate Communion in the way that we do today. This is important towards understanding how Communion functions to communicate biblical truth by retelling the redemptive story because it shows how participants viewed the celebration as an expression of spirituality throughout church history.

Three Generalizations

First, the eras represent common periods of time. Within each of these eras, a number of smaller phases are determined. For example, in the era labeled **Classical**, there is the Ante-Nicene period (100-325) followed by the Post-Nicene period beginning in 325. The same idea applies to each era. The eras are labeled **Middle Ages, Modernity,** and **Postmodernity,** with smaller phases within each one. These four commonly held eras do not simplify what is being discussed, but it does provide a way to more readily discuss historical movements without drifting away from Macy's statement that there were "just Christians" (2005, 9-10).

Second, issues that surrounded Communion were already being thought of, written about, debated, and discussed prior to and after each era. At no point did any issue simply appear in a designated era and, just as quickly, disappear from church history. In each era, discussion focuses on issues about Communion that were written about, debated, and discussed pertinent to the focus of this section: experiencing Christ through Communion in Church history.

Similar to the second generalization, each common period of time did not begin precisely on the designated date. For example, it would be inaccurate to suggest that the Protestant Reformation in the era of Modernity began when Martin Luther posted his 95 theses on the church door in the German town of Wittenberg precisely on October 31, 1517. Rather, each era is guided by what was written about Communion.

Timing Factors

In the Classical era, the **Church Fathers** had something significant to say about Communion embedded in a greater discourse. What determined the time extended to 600 was the generally accepted beginnings of the Early Medieval era, or, the Middle Ages. The research of Ian Levy, Gary Macy, and Kristen Van Ausdell (2012) was particularly helpful in understanding the greater discourse. Also, the work of Alexander Roberts, James Donaldson, and Cleveland Coxe (1999) provided a useful source in their editorial work of **Ante-Nicene documents** to clarify dates and details.

While I determined the timing of the Middle Ages from 601-1500 by widely accepted dates, focus is given to the **Fourth Lateran Council of 1215** as the most attended gathering of church leaders for that period of time. I am sure you can imagine what happens when a large gathering of church leaders gathers together in conference. It makes argument between Republicans and Democrats today decidedly tame. Focus on the importance of the Fourth Lateran Council is central to the era as part of the historical summary. Philip Schaff (1999) provided a useful collection of sources in his editorial work of the Nicene and **Post-Nicene Fathers** to understand what happened before and after the heated debate at Fourth Lateran Council.

Modernity is divided into three smaller phases: early Modernity in the reforms of **Martin Luther, Huldrych Zwingli,** and **John Calvin** (1500-1564); mid-Modernity in **Puritanism** and the **Great Awakening** (1730-1900); and late Modernity in **Pentecostalism** (1900-1965). The work of Lee Palmer Wandel (2005, 1), was helpful in discussing the year 1500 as the beginning of Modernity for these three phases. Focus is particularly given to what was happening in Europe and America.

While Brian McBride (2015, 26) suggests that dating where Modernity ended is somewhat arbitrary, he points out that 1966 is a "strong candidate for the Year Zero of postmodernism." I shall expand his thoughts on dating Postmodernity this way in chapter four; but for now, it is not a far stretch to say that the end of Modernity and the beginning of Postmodernity is a matter of opinion. For my purposes, the timing of Modernity is 1500-1965.

CHAPTER 1

CLASSICAL AGE 100-600

One of the most important observations in the Classical Age is a lack of material that specializes on the celebration of Communion. For example, it was not until the eleventh century that detailed material began to emerge that was written specifically on the function of Communion. However, in the absence of specific material, we can explore a variety of issues about the bread and wine of Communion embedded in a greater context of church history than the celebration itself.

> One of the most important observations in the Classical Age is a lack of material that specializes on the celebration of Communion.

Church Developments That Granted or Denied Access to Communion

One of the oldest non-canonical documents is the *Didache* (or The Teaching of the Apostles), written in the early first century. One could say that it was the first Christian education book. The *Didache* excluded those who were not baptized in water from participating in Communion. "But let no one eat or drink of your Eucharist [Communion], unless they have been baptized into the name of the Lord" (*Did.* 9.5; Roberts, Donaldson and Coxe 1999a,

380). Using this document, early Christian apologist **Justin Martyr** defended the practice of Communion against accusations by addressing **Emperor Antoninus Pius** in 150 in his *First Apology*. In his defense of Communion, Justin clearly articulates inclusion and exclusion to the celebration. "And this food is called the Eucharist [Communion], of which no one is allowed to partake, but the man who believes that the things which we teach are true, and who has been washed with the washing that is for the remission of sins, and unto regeneration, and who is so living as Christ has enjoined" (*1 Apol.* 66; 1999a, 185).

Identical to the *Didache*, Justin believed a participant in Communion should be baptized in water before receiving the bread and wine.[3] Religious pluralism may have been a key issue for Justin's insistence on water baptism. Worshipers in Mithraism imitated Communion, so a differentiation had to be made. To further justify a distinction between Mithraism and Christianity, Justin (1 Apol. 66; Roberts, Donaldson, and Coxe 1999b, 185) also insisted in his *First Apology* that Christ "gave it [the bread and wine] to them [Christians] alone."

In 180, **Irenaeus** wrote in *Against Heresies* about the universal accessibility and inclusive nature of Communion, teaching the bread and wine was an offering to all people throughout the world. Between 198 and 203 **Clement of Alexandria** wrote in Patchwork that a participant must personally examine him or herself before receiving the bread and wine. Quoting Paul's first letter to the Corinthians (6:4, 10-11) Clement (Str. 1.1; Roberts, Donaldson and Coxe 1999c, 300) writes, "One's own conscience is best for choosing accurately or shunning." However, between 207 and 208 in *The Crown*, similar to Justin, **Tertullian** insisted Communion participants should be baptized in water before being permitted to receive the bread and wine.

Despite his exclusive tone, in 197, Tertullian had previously insisted on an open invitation to celebrate Communion in his

---

[3] Aaron Milavec (203, 23) notes that Justin's literary source for excluding non-baptized participants was the *Didache* in *The Didache: Text, Translation, Analysis, and Commentary*. Collegeville, MN: Michael Glazier.

Apology. In his view, men and women, rich and poor, young and old alike were always welcome. In 200, one of the most important theologians in his day, **Hippolytus,** alludes to an inclusive daily practice in his *Refutation of all Heresies.* In a letter to Pope Cornelius,[4] written between 251 and 253, **Cyprian** (*Laps.* 54.2; Roberts, Donaldson, and Coxe 1999e, 337) notes Communion must "not to be granted by us to the dying, but the living." Cyprian qualifies "the dying" as non-Christian and "the living" as Christian. Furthermore, he adds a note of exclusion writing, "the Eucharist [Communion] is appointed for this very purpose" (*Laps.* 54.2; Roberts, Donaldson, and Coxe 1999e, 337). Hence, Cyprian was an advocate of excluding non-Christians from Communion.

By 313, **Emperor Constantine** had announced the "Edict of Milan." As a result, accusations against the church diminished as Christianity was officially sanctioned by Constantine. Relieved of persecution, the church relocated from private to public residences of worship. House churches are described by Robert Gehring (2009, 18-19) as private and domestic homes architecturally unaltered or adapted to fit the needs of a group. Either way, it was private and domestic. The house church gradually relocated to renovated and permanent places of worship, some of which were built by Constantine in the architectural style of a basilica. Along with that relocation, the name *ekklesia* (assembly), traditionally held as an identifier for a Christian gathering, gradually was used to identify buildings where Christians gathered. As a result, house churches slowly ceased to exist. In contrast, Communion developed within its new residence much like upgrading furniture with a new home.

Accompanying the grandeur of the new church buildings was a grandiose Communion. The celebration took the ceremonial forms of an elaborate procession metered by chanted litanies, incense, bells, and genuflections that included kissing sacred objects. Those who served in the church wore clothing similar to that

---

[4] Though the letter is written by Cyprian to Pope Cornelius, it has been widely recognized as a letter from the entire African synod (Roberts, Donaldson and Coxe 1999e, 336 vol. 5).

of a **Roman Senator**. Elaborate patens and chalices replaced domestic wicker baskets, plates, and cups of the house church for the bread and wine. Edward Foley (2009, 120) makes an interesting observation that, "the vessels for worship begin to acquire their own sacrality." In addition, "The altar cloth emerged as a further means to honor the altar itself" (Wandel 2005, 28). Prosperity and official sanction by the state elaborately dressed up Communion along with its ministers.

Between 413 and 426, **Augustine** (Civ. 19.19; Schaff 1999a, 397) wrote in *The City of God*, "The office of the Bishop requires work rather than dignity...and so no man can be a good Bishop if he loves his title but not his task." Augustine points out two concerns: one, how dressed up church ministers had become, and two, a negative motive for wanting to become a church minister. Regarding this negative motive, more people sought their way out of municipal obligations by entering the ministry of the church. Becoming a minister had financial benefits as a career. In addition, ecclesiastical courts were given judicial power by the state. Like Foley, Susan J. White (2006, 79) also makes an interesting observation that with societal and judicial influence the church grew in numbers but declined in spiritual sincerity. William De Arteaga (2015, 11) states more or less the same thing, that numerical growth and power was probably more important to the church than spiritual sincerity. However, officially sanctioning Christianity, extending municipal exemption to its dressed-up ministers, and granting judicial power in addition to ecclesial power, played a considerable role in spiritual insincerity. Some would say this is an alarming description of church gatherings today.

During the **First Council of Nicaea** in 325, the formulation of **Canon 11 and 13** specifically addressed inclusion and exclusion to Communion. Both demonstrate the use of ecclesial power. For instance, Canon 11 reads, "As many as were communicants, if they heartily repent, shall pass three years among the hearers;[5] for seven years they shall be prostrators; and for two years they shall communicate with the people in prayers, but without obla-

---

[5] Classifications of exclusion are defined in the following paragraphs.

tion" (Can. ap. Schaff and Wace 1999b, 24). This particular Canon derived its existence from the **Great Persecution** in 303, where some Christians abandoned their faith, but wanted to return back to the church. According to Canon 11, the consequence to abandoning faith, and then wanting to return, was exclusion from the Communion bread and wine for up to twelve years. Consequently, individuals who abandoned their faith must have had a compelling desire to celebrate Communion knowing that access to the bread and wine would be considerably delayed.

Canon 13 derives its existence from a much different reason than the Great Persecution. If a participant could not attend the church because he or she was near death, he or she could receive the bread and wine of Communion. "But, if anyone should be restored to health again who has received the communion when his life was despaired of, let him remain among those who communicate in prayers only" (*Can ap.* Schaff and Wace 1999b, 29). Canon 13 includes participants if they are dying but excludes them if they recover. Charles Hefele (2007, 419-420) points out that although a dying participant is included in Communion by taking the bread and wine to his or her bedside, he or she lapses in participation in a church gathering. One must remember that *ekklesia* (assembly) was now understood as the physical place where Christians gathered, and not the gathering of Christians. Consequently, Canon 13 excludes the recovered participant until he or she has the permission of the Bishop.

Canon 11 and 13 created two classes of Communion participants: **communicants and penitents.** George H. Dryer (2005, 239-252) describes penitents as four groups: mourners, hearers, kneelers, and bystanders. The **mourners** could not enter the place of worship but were allowed to stand in a reserved area outside the church building. "They could neither hear the reading of the Scriptures nor the preaching; still less could they join in the prayers and sacred mysteries" (2005, 283). In contrast, the **hearers** stood in the lobby where they could hear everything the mourners could not. Even so, they could only hear and not participate. The **kneelers** were permitted to posture themselves near the pulpit and were recognized as part of the congregation, albeit an erring part, and were dismissed before Communion was celebrated. **Bystanders** occupied the final station of penitents. They were allowed to communicate with Communion participants in prayer and stay in the service during the celebration, but they were excluded from participation in the bread and wine. Again, individuals who abandoned their faith must have had a compelling desire to celebrate Communion knowing that access to the bread and wine would be considerably delayed.

During the fourth century **Donatists**[6] called congregants and priests, who turned away from Christianity during the Great Persecution, traitors. Under Constantine, penance provided a way for congregants and priests to return back to the church. However, the Donatists rejected this idea claiming both congregants and priests were unfit for being members of the church. Consequently, the Donatists also rejected the idea of a traitor serving or receiving Communion. Such were the views of the Donatists that if a traitor priest did serve the bread and wine, they believed it caused spiritual pollution and corruption in the whole congregation. If congregants and priests could return to Christianity under Constantine, after their penitentiary period was completed, they would experience the empowering actions and promissory words of Christ again. However, the position Donatists took on traitors who wanted to return ensured that former congregants and priests would never experience the empowering actions and promissory words of Christ again. The Donatists were undoubtedly a vindictive group of people that lacked compassion.

Summary Thought

Throughout the Classical Age, the church had developed from meeting in private and domestic residences to permanent places of worship as Christianity officially became a sanctioned religion. Accordingly, Communion developed with it. Several of the early church fathers taught that water baptism gave a participant access to the bread and wine. While there could have been individuals who did

---

[6] Primarily within the Roman province of North Africa.

not experience the empowering actions of Communion in a private and domestic residence, because they were not baptized, they would at least hear the promissory words. When the First Council of Nicaea introduced gradations of exclusion, the ability to hear those promissory words was removed for penitents categorized as mourners. Though the penitents classified as hearers, kneelers, and bystanders could hear the promissory words, they could not experience the empowering actions of Communion for themselves. The Donatists went to greater measures by making it impossible for traitors to ever experience the empowering actions or promissory words again.

Differences in How Biblical Passages Were Used to Explain Communion

A historical view of the **Passover** is seen in how the **Early Church Fathers** used biblical passages[7] to explain Communion. Up until the end of the fourth century, Jewish and Gentile Christians were in dispute over the relevance of the Passover. The dispute involved an interpretation of an Old Testament passage, "This is a day you are to commemorate; for the generations to come you shall celebrate it as a festival to the Lord—a lasting ordinance" (Exod. 12:14). Christians who insisted on celebrating the Passover were known as **Quartodecimans**[8] (meaning 'fourteeners' in Latin).

Between 175-185, **Irenaeus** (*Haer.* 3; Roberts, Donaldson, and Coxe 1999, 569b) wrote in *Fragments from the Lost Writings*, "inasmuch as these things had been always observed by John the disciple of our Lord, and by other apostles with whom he [Polycarp] had been conversant." Also, in 180, Irenaeus (*Haer.* 3.3.4;

---

[7] All biblical passages noted are the same passages the Early Church Fathers used in their respective works.

[8] There is no known record in church history that identifies who introduced the term *Quartodeciman*. However, scholars acknowledge its etymology from the Latin Vulgate, "On the fourteenth day [*quarta decima*] of the first month the Lord's Passover is to be held" (Num. 28:16) (Tennent 2013, 3).

Roberts, Donaldson, and Coxe 1999b, 416) writes in *Against Heresies,* "But Polycarp...always taught the things which he had learned from the apostles, and which the Church has handed down, and which alone are true." **Eusebius** (*Hist.* eccl. 5.24.2; Schaff 1999c, 242) quotes **Polycarp** in his **Epistle to Victor**, "We observe the exact day; neither adding, nor taking away." In the same Epistle, Polycarp names Melito, who "kept the Passover on the fourteenth day of the month, in accordance with the Gospel [John], without ever deviating from it, but keeping to the rule of faith" (*Hist. eccl.* 5.24.6; Schaff and Wace 1999, 242c). Evidentially, Polycarp was not only a student of John, but also a practitioner of Quartodecimanism.

In the mid-second century, Melito wrote the *Homily on the Passover*. After analyzing Melito's sermon, Gerard Rouwhorst (1997, 165) observed that he used typological language to explain the relationship of the Jewish exodus from Egypt in Exodus 12 and the liberation of Christ's resurrection. Melito begins the sermon by pointing out the precise date of the fourteenth day of the first month and its continued observance for Christians. Not only was Melito a practitioner of Quartodecimanism, but, like Polycarp, he used John's gospel to explain his beliefs. Quartodecimanism came into conflict with Christians who rejected the idea of celebrating the Passover. At the **First Council of Nicaea** in 325, the Passover was officially rejected as a celebration for Christians in favor of an Easter celebration.

Eusebius (*Hist. eccl.* 5.23.2; Schaff and Wace 1999c, 241) records the decision made at the Council in *Church History,* "All, with one consent, through mutual correspondence drew up an ecclesiastical decree, that the mystery of the resurrection of the Lord should be celebrated on no other but the Lord's day [Sunday]." Eusebius (*Hist. eccl.* 5.23.2; Schaff and Wace 1999c, 242) adds, "a great many others, who uttered the same opinion and judgment, and cast the same vote. And that which has been given above was their unanimous decision." Consequently, the First Council of Nicaea sent a letter to all the churches that practiced Quartodecimanism. "All our brethren...who formerly followed the custom of the Jews [Passover] are henceforth to celebrate the said most sacred feast of **Easter** at the same time with the Romans and yourselves and all those who have observed Easter from the beginning" (2.32; 1999b, 54).

Easter and Quartodecimanism were similar in practice from the perspective of Communion. "The fact that they [Quartodecimans] started from a typological explanation of the Exodus story implied that they celebrated both the death and the resurrection" (Rouwhorst 1997, 165). Communion bread and wine represented the body of blood of Christ in Easter and Quartodeciman celebrations. Both recognized that Christ was resurrected and that He would return.

Summary Thought

Participants in both celebrations would experience the empowering actions and promissory words of Communion, whether it was called Easter or the Passover. The difference came down to an interpretation of Exodus 12:14. However, Rouwhorst (1997, 157) writes, "After the middle of the fourth century the number of Christians who stuck to the old custom of celebrating the Passover on the Jewish date, constituted a very marginal minority."

Retelling the Redemptive Story through Liturgy

Celebrating Communion was tantamount to obeying Christ's command to do what He did. Liturgical church history is divided on whether Christ introduced new liturgy or adopted liturgy from the **Jewish Passover.** In order to retell the exodus story during the Passover, liturgy was essential (Exod. 12:26-27).

Jewish liturgy began with the *Kiddush* (blessing) and ended with the *Birkat Hamazon* (thanksgiving). Between both, unitary actions and words **typologically retold salvific history.** However, salvific history in the Passover is primarily restricted to Jews.[9] Interestingly, typological salvific history is the connection between the Passover and the first Communion. Mark Throntveit (1997, 271) writes, "Jesus interpreted his death as a new Exodus in which the people of God were liberated from all that enslaves them and

---

[9] Exodus 12:48 included non-Jews.

freed to serve God in holy living." While there appears to be a liturgical connection between the Passover and the first Communion, Did Christ adopt the rich liturgy of the Old Testament table celebration as a means of retelling this liberation in Communion?

From the synoptic gospels, **nine new liturgical actions** can be applied to the first Communion. On one hand, Enrico Mazza (1999, 21) writes, "(1) he took bread, (2) gave thanks, (3) broke the bread, (4) gave it, (5) while saying, (6) he took the cup, (7) gave thanks, (8) gave it, (9) while saying." On the other hand, Gregory Dix (2005, 48) writes, "Our Lord (1) took bread; (2) 'gave thanks' over it; (3) broke it; (4) distributed it, saying certain words. Later he (5) took a cup; (6) 'gave thanks' over that; (7) handed it to his disciples, saying certain words." Unlike Mazza, Dix believes these seven liturgical actions are **rooted in the Passover liturgy**. Furthermore, he believes they can be modified into **four liturgical actions**, "(1) The offertory, (2) The prayer, (3) The fraction, (4) The communion" (Dix 2005, 48-50). However, it could be argued that Dix's four liturgical actions as oversimplified. The liturgy of the first Communion can be set in a **broader context of the Passover** and other conventional meal patterns of the culture—something that Dix does not do or even recognize.

Despite the differences between Mazza and Dix, it is not difficult to see how the Passover liturgy possibly transmigrated to liturgy used in Communion. The Jewish blessing (*Kiddush*) and thanksgiving (*Birkat Hamazon*) are certainly present. Furthermore, the celebration transmigrates a typological retelling of the Jewish exodus story in the Passover to a new exodus in Communion. If elements of the Passover liturgy are, indeed, found in the first Communion, what factors helped the development of liturgy? There is a particular non-canonical document that records liturgy used during Communion written by a pilgrim named **Egeria** (1919).[10]

Itinerarium Egeriae (Travels of Egeria) was written around 380, shedding light on liturgy used for Communion for retelling

---

[10] Also known as Etheria; probably a wealthy lady or an influential nun (Halsall 2015).

the redemptive story. Churches that Egeria visited show how widespread a liturgical retelling of the redemptive story had become.[11] Similar to private and domestic church, or house church, Egeria (1919, 3) notes in her journal that Christian gatherings were "not great in size" but "great in grace." Those churches were composed of bishops, holy men, monks, and members of the community. In some cases, only holy men and monks resided there, with occasional traveling bishops.

There were exceptions to small churches. For example, she refers to "the great church, built by Constantine, which is situated in Golgotha behind the Cross" (1919, 29). The greatness Egeria points out is the basilica architecture, elaborate Communion vessels, and the décor. Egeria implicitly refers to similar churches throughout Constantinople, in addition to other locations. Interestingly, the bread and wine of Communion was readily made available to her, supporting the idea that she was an influential nun. It also tells us that the early church was not misogynist as some think it was.

Unlike Mazza and Dix, Egeria observed **four liturgical actions**: prayer, blessing, song, and reading of Scripture. She notes how the four liturgical actions were customary in each church, with only slight variations[12] at Sinai, Horeb, churches in Egypt, in the Jordan Valley, at the City of Melchizedek, Aenon, Edessa, at Rachel's Well, and the churches in Jerusalem. Again, the list of churches shows how widespread liturgy had become in celebrating Communion.

What makes the four liturgical actions intriguing is their **unitary and typological** retelling of the redemptive story rooted in the Passover story. For example, blessing generally mirrored

---

[11] Rodney Stark (1996, 6) estimates that Christianity in the Roman Empire had grown by 40% per decade from the year 40 to the conversion of Constantine. From this calculation, Stark calculates there were 33,882,008 Christians by 350, an equivalent of 56.7% of the population. Stark's account sheds light on how widespread a liturgical retelling of the redemptive story could have become.

[12] Egeria observed a variation of songs and passages of Scripture that were read.

Moses' words and actions over Israel.[13] Songs were mostly from the Psalms that exemplified God's saving power. This was specifically seen in the church at Sinai, Horeb, the Valley of Jordan, the church in the City of Melchizedek, and an unnamed church. In Jerusalem, Easter was celebrated on the Lord's Day.[14] She writes, "On the Lord's Day after the first cockcrow the bishop reads in the Anastasis [pulpit] the account of the Lord's Resurrection from the Gospel, as on all Lord's Days throughout the whole year" (1919, 47). Interestingly, Egeria also notes how widespread the decision of the **First Council of Nicaea** had become in celebrating Easter and not the Passover.

> By the end of the Classical era, gradations of exclusion had been introduced to celebrating Communion.

Summary Thought

Whether Christ adapted the Passover liturgy or introduced new liturgy remains unclear. Nevertheless, an interpretation of the first Communion produced a variance of liturgical actions. Those actions were unitary in form and typological in their liturgical retelling of the redemptive story, specifically seen in Egeria's travels. If Egeria experienced the empowering actions and promissory words of Communion as a traveler, it can be assumed the experience occurred for other Christians who resided in the same locations she visited.

CONCLUDING THOUGHT

By the end of the Classical era, gradations of exclusion had been introduced to celebrating Communion. These preventative measures do not appear to have any basis in the first Communion where Christ took the Passover bread and wine and personified

---

[13] Affirming God's covenant with lifted hands or the laying on of hands.

[14] Her observation sheds further light on the diminishing practice of Quartodecimanism (Rouwhorst 1997, 157).

it. As such, the promissory words and empowering actions of Christ were not always readily available to participants who wanted to celebrate Communion. The only significant dispute about the interpretation of Scripture is whether the Passover should be continued for non-Jews or not. Another interpretive dilemma presented itself in liturgy. Whether Christ adapted the Passover liturgy or not, there was a variance of liturgical words and actions that were unitary in form and typological in retelling the redemptive story. Those words and actions enabled participants to experience Christ during Communion.

CHAPTER 2

MIDDLE AGES 601-1500

The Middle Ages saw the Christianization of most of Europe. People were born into Christianity much like Muslims are born into the Islamic faith. Central to the Christian life was the celebration of Communion. Underlying this centrality was the developing belief that Christ was present in the bread and wine. The Middle Ages represent a period of time where things became very interesting. In some cases, people literally fought over the relationship of Christ and the bread and wine. This explores the controversial phenomenon.

Church Developments That Granted or Denied Access to Communion

Patrick Geary (2010, 430) explains the largest ecclesial gathering in the Middle Ages was at the **Fourth Lateran Council in 1215**, attended by 800 priests, 400 bishops, and representatives of all the princes in Europe. The Council represents significant sacerdotal and soteriological developments in the Middle Ages. Four specific developments involved ordained ministers of the church and congregants. First, regarding who could serve the Communion bread and wine, the formulation of Canon 1 states, "And this sacrament no one can effect except the priest who has been duly ordained" (Geary 2010, 431). Prior to Canon 1, deacons could serve the Communion. However, that privilege was officially given only to the priests by the Council.

Second, the effect **Canon 1** talks about is found in **Canon 21**, "Whose body and blood are truly contained in the sacrament of the altar under the forms of bread and wine; the bread being changed (*transsubstantiatio*) by divine power into the body, and the wine into the blood" (Geary 2010, 431). It was believed only the priest, ordained by the church, had power to effect transubstantiation, hence, the exclusion of deacons. This is what sacerdotal power implies.

Third, with the exclusive privilege of serving Communion came increased responsibility for the ordained priest. The formulation of **Canon 20** states, "But if he to whom such guardianship pertains should leave them [bread and wine] unprotected, let him be suspended from office for a period of three months" (Geary 2010, 431). Exclusive privilege and responsibility for the bread and wine came with exceeding consequences.

Fourth, Canon 21 also addresses required access to Communion for congregants, "All the faithful of both sexes shall after they have reached the age of discretion faithfully confess all their sins at least once a year...receiving reverently at least at Easter the sacrament of the Eucharist [Communion]...otherwise they shall be cut off from the Church (excommunicated) during life and deprived of Christian burial in death" (Geary 2010, 431). Though access to Communion was limited to at least once a year, it was also necessary to participate in that limited capacity or face permanent denial. This is what **soteriological** developments imply.

While the Fourth Lateran Council clearly marks developments in the formulation of three specific ecclesial laws, the precise steps that led to them in the Middle Ages are unclear.[15] "Long before Lateran IV, the Host and the wine had acquired quite different devotional lives" (Wandel 2005, 37). For example, from ap-

---

[15] Darwell Stone (2014, 193) writes, "In the West the history from the ninth century to the fifteenth century is continually broken by controversy." I discuss this controversy in the next section in how biblical passages were used to explain Communion.

proximately the year dated 1160, canon lawyers, theologians, and liturgists debated when Christ became present in the bread and wine of Communion. The result of those debates certainly contributed to the belief of transubstantiation affirmed at the Fourth Lateran Council. Again, long before the Council, belief that Christ was present in the bread and wine was already widespread.

For example, there was a deep desire from congregants to see the Communion bread. However, congregants were obstructed from seeing the bread by various partitions until the priest elevated it high enough for congregants to see. "We have accounts of Christians cutting holes in walls [patricians] to be able to view the Host, so great was the desire simply to see the Host" (Wandel 2005, 38-39). Robert Donaldson (1999, 569) suggests it is not easy to determine when the bread was first elevated prior to the Fourth Lateran Council. However, Medieval scholar Thomas Izbricki (2015, 8) points out that elevating the bread was not officially established until **Pope Honorius III** in 1217, two years after the Fourth Lateran Council. According to Fr. Benedict J. Groeschel and James Monti (1997, 211-212), others suggest it was first practiced in Paris shortly before or after the episcopate of *Eudes de Sully* between 1196 and 1208, prior to the Council. Either way, the Council made it official.

Not only is it difficult to be clear about the precise steps that led to the four developments in Communion at the Fourth Lateran Council, it is also difficult to mark precisely when congregants were excluded from specifically receiving the wine. Jewish author Joe Lantz (2007, 117) suggests it was a gradual process, mostly for hygienic reasons and overly indulging in drinking from the common cup. Practically, withdrawing the wine from congregants prevented any of it from being spilled. According to the eighteenth-century ecclesiastical historian, Joseph Bingham (2010, 353), spilling the wine was thought to be *theologically* tantamount to spilling the blood of Christ. Whether the reasons for withdrawing the wine were theological and/ or practical, a conundrum was created. Jaroslav Pelikan (1985,

123-124) writes, "When communion under both species [bread and wine] had been the usage of the church, reception under only one was wrong; now the church prescribed one species, the original practice was wrong." The church changed the interpretation of the words of Christ so only the priest could receive both bread and wine. For example, when Christ said, "Drink from it, all of you" (Matt. 26:27), the "all of you" was interpreted as "all of you priests."

> The Fourth Lateran Council marks the significant sacerdotal privilege, power, and responsibility of the priest and the soteriological implications for the congregants.

Summary Thought

The Fourth Lateran Council marks the significant sacerdotal privilege, power, and responsibility of the priest and the soteriological implications for the congregants. Without an ordained priest, Communion would not occur. Without Communion, an experience of the empowering actions and promissory words would be void in a church service. Also, congregants were required to receive the Communion bread (not wine) from a priest at least once a year at Easter.

Differences in How Biblical Passages Were Used to Explain Communion

In the ninth century, a fierce argument between the Carolingian theologians, **Paschasius Radbertus** and **Ratramnus** involved the literal or figurative transformation of the bread and wine during the Communion celebration.[16] The argument undoubtedly contributed to the steps that led to the formulation of Canon 21 (transubstantiation) at the Fourth Lateran Council. Respectively, the Benadictine monk **Lanfranc**, and French theo-

---

[16] I further discuss their argument in the following section that deals with the use of liturgy to retell the redemptive story.

logian **Berengarius**, took up the argument of Radbertus and Ratramnus[17] using biblical passages to support their views.[18]

About 1047, Berengarius attracted significant attention through his teaching on Communion. At the same time, Lanfranc attacked the views of Ratramnus in support of Radbertus' views. Fr. James T. O'Connor (2005, 98) notes that in the defense of Radbertus, Berengarius wrote a letter to Lanfranc that was read at the Council of Rome in 1050. The letter supported the views of Ratramnus. Essentially, Berengarius favored a figurative view of the bread and wine in Communion, not the literal view of transubstantiation. Subsequently, the figurative views of Berengarius were rejected by the **Council of Rome**, resulting in his excommunication.

However, Berengarius was given an opportunity to appeal his excommunication at the **Council of Vercelli** that same year. He did not formally appeal and, as a result, his condemnation was affirmed at the **Council of Paris** in 1051. In 1054 at the **Council of Tours**, Berengarius reversed his opinion, aligning himself with the literal view of transformation of the bread and wine. However, shortly after the Council of 1054, Berengarius reversed his opinion again, resorting back to a figurative view seen in *On the Sacred Book of the Supper* (Advent 2015). He justified his second reversal claiming he was forced to change at the Council of Tours. The second reversal of Berengarius is the basis for Lanfranc's *On the Body and Blood of the Lord*.

Lanfranc accused Berengarius of leading congregants into eternal punishment through an incorrect exposition of Scripture regarding Communion. He writes, "You frequently say that you draw from Sacred Scripture...little considering the words of the Lord as he [Christ] threatens anyone who scandalizes one of his little one's (Matt. 18:6)" (Lanfranc 2009, 30). Lanfranc concludes

---

[17] I examine the Lanfranc's *On the Body and Blood of the Lord* translated by Fr. Mark Vaillancourt (2009), and Berengarius's *On the Sacred Book of the Supper.* "There is no complete edition of the works of Berenarius. Only one volume has been published by Visher in Berlin (1834)" (Advent 2015). Therefore, I cite Berengarius's views found in Lanfranc's work (Lanfranc 2009).

[18] All biblical passages noted are the same passages that Lanfranc and Berenagrius used in their respective works.

that Berengarius not only sins against his brothers in Christ, but against Christ Himself (1 Cor. 8:12). However, Berengarius insisted "that in every way it [body and blood] is still bread and wine that remains on the altar" (Lanfranc 2009, 40). In support of his view, Berengarius draws on a passage from Ephesians 2:20:

> "For just as when someone says: 'Christ is the chief cornerstone, he is not removing Christ, nor is he establishing absolutely [what] Christ is: so it is that, in a similar fashion, when someone says: 'The bread on the altar is only a sacrament,' or: 'The bread of the altar is only the true body of Christ,' he does not deny that it is bread on the altar, and he confirms the fact that it is indeed bread and wine on the table of the Lord." (Lanfranc 2009, 42)

In response, Lanfranc draws attention to creation where dirt is changed into a living person (Gen. 3:19). In his view, the passage in **Genesis** proves any substance could be changed into something else by God. He writes, "when the divine page [Scripture] calls the body of the Lord 'bread,' this is done in a sacred and mystical way...it is the body of the Son of God who is the bread of angels, and 'upon whom,' just as the prince of the apostles says, 'the angels desire to look'" (Lanfranc 2009, 42). Unlike Berengarius, Lanfranc denied the Communion bread is simply the substance of bread seen on the altar.

Berengarius continues his argument by presenting two realities: one visible and the other invisible. "The reality, that is, the body of Christ, if it were before our eyes, would be visible, but since it has been raised up into heaven (1 Pet. 3:22) it cannot be called down from heaven until the time of the restitution of all things (Phil. 3:21)" (Lanfranc 2009, 51). Berengarius' use of Peter's first epistle establishes the visible reality of Christ in heaven and the invisible representation in the bread and wine. However, Berengarius' meaning of invisibility differed from Lanfranc's meaning.

According to Lanfranc, Christ's two realities are visibly present in heaven and in the bread and wine. He argues that the people

An experience of the empowering actions and promissory words of Communion would have been determined by whether congregants were taught the view of Berengarius or Lanfranc.

used reason when they heard Christ say, "Very truly I tell you, unless you eat the flesh of the Son of Man and drink his blood, you have no life in you" (John 6:53) (Lanfranc 2009, 53). In Lanfranc's view, accepting the bread and wine as the flesh and blood required simple faith. Therefore, the man of faith would not argue, scrutinize, or reason how the bread and wine are changed into flesh and blood. He could accept the bread and wine are changed, much like a child who does not question God. Making reference to Matthew 21:16, Lanfranc (2009, 61) writes, "Christ perfects the praise of those who take upon themselves the simplicity of a child."

Summary Thought

After examining both views, Berengarius believed the Communion bread and wine were figuratively transformed into the body and blood of Christ after the words of consecration, whereas Lanfranc believed they were literally transformed. An experience of the empowering actions and promissory words of Communion would have been determined by whether congregants were taught the view of Berengarius or Lanfranc.

Retelling the Redemptive Story through Liturgy

The argument of **Berengarius** and **Lanfranc** reflected a liturgical shift that sheds more light on the steps that led to the formulation of **Canon 1, 20,** and **21** at the **Fourth Lateran Council** in 1215. The figurative and literal view of the bread and wine emerged in liturgy used during Communion as an **allegorical representation** or as **sacramental realism** in order to retell the redemptive story. From the ninth to the thirteenth century, a number of authors wrote substantial commentaries on liturgy.

About 820, the Frankish liturgist **Amalarius** wrote *Ecclesiastical Offices* where he describes the liturgical dramatization of the redemptive story using **allegorical representation**. For example, the entrance of a priest into the Communion celebration represented the incarnate entrance of Christ into the world. The conclusion of Communion represented the ascension of Christ into heaven. Between a dramatized entrance and conclusion, further dramatization is seen in allegorical representations of the altar and vessels and the posturing of the priest.

The altar allegorically represented five different things in the retelling of the redemptive story. At the beginning of Communion, it represented Jerusalem, where the gospel was first preached, as the Book of the Gospels was placed on it. The priest represented God the Father when standing to the right of the altar. At a later point in Communion, the altar becomes the upper room where Christ celebrated with His disciples, the cross where Christ was crucified, and the tomb where Christ was buried. In addition to the altar itself, the Communion vessels also took on an allegorical representation. Water mixed with wine represented unity of participants with Christ. The towel Christ used to wash His disciples' feet is represented in a napkin covering the bread and wine. Also, at a later point in the Communion, the napkin represented the burial clothes of Christ. Finally, various elevations of the bread and wine represented Christ lifted up on the cross and taken down from it.

In many ways, Amalarius used liturgy as "a kind of sacred drama that has for its function to represent our redemption by Christ and the events that make it up" (Mazza 1999, 168). Vital to a dramatization, Amalarius frequently uses the Latin verb ostendere (to show), emphasizing the visibility of Communion to the congregants. In his view, a liturgical dramatization should teach and help participants remember the redemptive story. If this was the case, an experience of the empowering actions and promissory words during Communion necessitates the visibility of the bread and wine. However, between Amalarius and the **Fourth Lateran Council**, the visibility of Communion became obscured from congregants.

Though Amalarius favored allegorical representation, his view falls short of the redemptive story described by Christopher

Wright (2006, 64) as God's singular mission to reveal Himself in creation, fall, redemption, and future hope. By emphasizing os-tendere (to show), the liturgy of Amalarius lacks an ontological dimension for the literal presence of Christ between the entrance and conclusion of the Communion celebration. Several promi-nent authors favored sacramental realism addressing the **onto-logical dimension** lacking in the liturgy of Amalarius.

Celia Chezelle writes about three theologians who provided an ontological explanation for sacramental realism used in Com-munion liturgy to retell the redemptive story, of which, two we already know - **Paschasius Radbertus** and **Ratramnus**. The third is somewhat of a mystery even to church historians. His name is **John Scotus Eriugena**. Scholars are divided on whether Eriugena was a real person or a pseudonym of Ratramnus. I will side with those who believe Eriugena was an Irish theologian and philos-opher as a separate person based on the details of his view that slightly differs from Ratramnus.

Between 831 and 833, Radbertus wrote On the *Body and Blood of the Lord* addressing the nature of Communion bread and wine. Radbertus explained the difference between what the eye could see and what faith could see in a liturgical retelling of the redemptive story (Chezelle 2012, 235). Radbertus maintained the bread and wine contained the historical body and blood of Christ, albeit unseen by the human eye. In his view, the literal body and blood were veiled from the participant by the substance of bread and wine so communicants would not be horrified by it. Conse-quently, the empowering actions and promissory words of Com-munion not only retold the redemptive story, they also taught what the eye can see in bread and wine and what faith can see in the literal body and blood of Christ.

In 843, Ratramnus offered a different ontological explana-tion of bread and wine in a response to Radbertus with the same title *On the Body and Blood of the Lord*. Ratramnus explained the natural perception of the congregant would always see bread and wine, not the flesh and blood of Christ. Ratramnus maintained that the historical presence of Christ, not His literal body and blood, were spiritually present in the bread and wine. In his view, the body of Christ had ascended into heaven so it could not be present in the bread. Although Christ was present in the bread and wine, it was "one that did not belong to the physical world" (Mazza 1999, 186). Similar to Radbertus, Ratramnus believed retelling the redemptive story through Communion was something that also taught congregants what to believe. However, for Ratramnus an ontological explanation located the literal body of Christ beyond human sight, but not beyond human perception in the bread and wine of Communion.

Eriugena appears to have partially agreed with the ontological explanation of Ratramnus. Yet, Eriugena's complete treatise on Communion is lost. Nevertheless, Dermot Moran (2004, 172) notes that observations can be made from Eriugena's *Commentary on the Gospel of John* written between 885 and 889. In this commentary, Eriugena insisted on the spiritual presence of Christ in the bread and wine at the exclusion of His physical presence. This is what makes Eriugena partially agree with Ratramnus. It is partial because there is no change in the bread and wine from natural to spiritual. By insisting on the spiritual presence of Christ at an undisclosed point in the Communion celebration, Eriugena's ontological explanation is vague.

> Metered from the Fourth Lateran Council were measures of sacerdotal power and a penitentiary system to exclude participants from the empowering actions and/or promissory words of Christ.

Summary Thought

Amalarius lays a foundation for a liturgical retelling of the redemptive story favoring allegorical representation. However, Amalarius lacks an ontological explanation of the presence of Christ. Building on his liturgical work, three authors ontologically explain what is lacking, favoring sacramental realism: Radbertus believed faith could see the literal body and blood of Christ in the bread and wine; Ratramnus and Eriugena believed Christ was spiritually present during Communion while literally present in heaven. Common to Amalarius, Radbertus, and Ratramnus, was the use of liturgy to teach participants by retelling the redemptive story.

CONCLUDING THOUGHT

By the end of the Middle Ages, celebrating Communion had significantly developed from the scene painted by the gospel writers where Christ personified the Passover bread and wine. Metered from the Fourth Lateran Council were measures of sacerdotal power and a penitentiary system to exclude participants from the empowering actions and/or promissory words of Christ. The interpretative intellect of Berengarius and Lanfranc fought over the consecration effects of the bread and wine. Amalarius made allegorical representation the agenda for Communion liturgy. Lacking in ontological explanations, Radbertus, Ratramnus, and Eriugena intellectually fought over the bread and wine much like Berengarius and Lanfranc. Nevertheless, people were still attracted to the celebration of Communion and its retelling of the redemptive story.

CHAPTER 3

MODERNITY 1501-1965

Church developments during the **Protestant Reformation** were complex and not limited to a single reform. Macy (2005, 135) writes, "There was not one but many separate reforms—almost, it sometimes seems, as many as there were reformers." For this reason, my investigation is limited in early Modernity to the reforms of **Luther, Zwingli**, and **Calvin**; in mid-Modernity to **Puritanism** and the **Great Awakening**; and late Modernity to **Pentecostalism**.[19]

Church Developments That Granted or Denied Access to Communion

With differing opinions on the presence of Christ in the Communion bread and wine, Luther, Zwingli, and Calvin all agreed on a significant issue: both the bread and wine should be offered to congregants, not just the bread (Wandel 2005, 79). For example, Kilian McDonnell (2015, 72) points out that in 1520, Luther specifically demanded the **Bishop of Meissen** should allow congregants to receive the bread and wine of Communion. Though his demand was denied, Luther's belief that congregants should receive both bread and wine is seen.

---

[19] Vinson Synan (1997), notes two focal points that place the beginnings of American Pentecostalism in late Modernity: 1901 (1997, 111) and 1906 (1997, 85).

In Zurich, under the direction of Zwingli in 1522, congregants were given bread and wine as part of Zwingli's rapid reforms. In doing so, his reform agreed with Luther. Finally, in 1542, the theological faculty from the **University of Paris** drew up twenty-five articles of belief. Calvin (2002, 86-87) notes that article seven limited congregants to the Communion bread. In response to the seventh article, Calvin argued that Christ gave all believers His body and blood in the bread and wine, "Hence, nothing remains for us but to obey his command" (Calvin 2002, 87). All three examples show that Luther, Zwingli, and Calvin agreed on the issue of offering the bread and wine of Communion to congregants.

Their ideas were populated through the vehicle of **Johannes Gutenberg's** printing press. The ability to read was not the pressing issue. What mattered was the relationship between the reader and the text. The relationship allowed congregants to question Medieval practices that surrounded Communion for themselves. Also, the relationship of reader and the text was not limited to a singular class of people. "In the first decades of the sixteenth century, theologians and pastors, carpenters, shoemakers, domestic servants, and peasants labeled the Mass, in its complexity and density, a human innovation...rejecting entirely the Mass in that term, human innovation—no longer connected in any way to the meal Jesus had shared with His disciples" (Wandel 2013, 5). Rejecting the Mass as a human innovation may have been the result of a desire to celebrate Communion in a simple way that Christ celebrated with His own disciples.

The insights of Glen Segger (2014, 97-99) show that throughout the 1640s and 1650s, access to Communion divided the Puritans. In 1643, the **Westminster Assembly** approved the authority of a minister to suspend congregants from participating in Communion for a variety of reasons. A number of ministers suspended entire congregations for up to a year. Decrying the neglect of Communion, **William Baxter** explained the extent of suspending congregants, "The far greater part of many parishes forbear the Communion of the Church in the Lord's Supper, and have done many years together" (2008, 120). In 1645, Puritan **William Prynne** challenged suspending congregants from Communion.

Prynne argued that Communion was a "converting ordinance" (Segger 2008, 121). Another prominent Puritan who agreed with Prynne was John Humfrey. For example, in 1652, Humfrey believed the bread and wine could bring about a conversion experience in *An Humble Vindication of a Free Admission*. Emerging from the division among Puritans was an experience of the empowering actions and promissory words of Communion in the form of conversion.

Following Prynne and Humfrey, Paul McDowell (2012, 34) writes about a **Half-Way Communion** developed by **Solomon Stoddard** in 1672. Stoddard's development is described as the means for a participant to receive the bread and wine, prior to becoming a member of the church through baptism. By default, church members received "full communion" (McDowell 2012, 17). The **Judd Manuscripts** contain a record from Stoddard's wife describing her husband's Christian conversion while celebrating Communion. Her testimony sheds light on why Stoddard may have developed a Half-Way Communion:

> "He [Stoddard] caught such a full and glorious view of Christ and his great love for men as shown in his redemptive work, that he was almost overpowered with emotion, and with difficulty went forward with the communion service. By reason of this peculiar experience of his, he was led to think, that the place the soul was likely to receive spiritual light and understanding was at the Lord's Table—that there, in a special manner Christ would present to reveal himself in all his fullness of love to the souls of men." (McDowell 2012, 34)

In light of his own experience, Stoddard believed a Half-Way Communion was an open invitation to the possibility of Christian conversion. Therefore, accompanying an experience during Communion was the possibility of conversion.

It also appears that the founder of Methodism, **John Wesley**, held to a similar inclusive view as Stoddard. Having investigated the idea of a "**conversion ordinance**," Lorna Lock-Nah Khoo (2005, 52) found that Wesley believed Communion could be a means of spiritual conviction that led to Christian conversion. For example, in 1739 Wesley noted in his journal that a woman was converted while receiving the bread and wine. However, Henry Rack (2002, 405) throws caution at Wesley's converting ordinance because it was "so unusual and has so little precedent." In Rack's view, Wesley should have referred to a "**confirming ordinance**" not a converting ordinance. Though "Luther and Calvin admitted Communion might sometimes, exceptionally act to bring remission of sins," Christian tradition has little to say about a converting Communion (2002, 405).

Scholars of church history consider the early 1700s to the late 1800s as a period of **Great Awakening in America**. The period can also be characterized by two opposing factions according to Thomas Kidd (2007, xiv) in "new lights" and the "old lights." Essentially, new lights were **revivalists** and old lights were **anti-revivalists**. Also, Jessie Haas (2012, 30) explains that each "light" had a different view of inclusion at the Communion table. On one hand, new lights favored a dramatic conversion experience with visible signs of spiritual rebirth in order to be included. On the other hand, old lights favored gradual conversion followed by obedience to the established clergymen.

Differing views to inclusion at the Communion table are seen in the accusations of the congregationalist minister **Charles Chauncy**, a prominent old light, against revivalist **George Whitefield**, a prominent new light. Chauncy's accusations reflect the emphasis of obedience to established clergymen as the means for inclusion. Quoting Chauncy, Frank Magill (1963, 589) writes, "But for ministers to make a business of going out of their own way into other men's parishes, unask'd, or at the desire of only some disaffected people—and this in known opposition to the settled pastors." Not only does Chauncy accuse Whitefield of not being an established or settled clergyman, he questions the sincerity of the audience's response. Douglas Sloan (1973, 242) also cites Chauncy writing, "I am clearly in the sentiment that the great stress that has been laid upon such terrors as have evidently been produced by the mechanical influence of awful words and frightful gestures has been a great disservice to the interest of religion."

Because revivalists like Whitefield were considered unsettled clergymen who favored dramatic conversion, Eldon Hay (2012, 22) concludes anti-revivalists "rejected the practice of inter-communion or open communion." In contrast to this rejection, revivalist Jonathan Edwards writes that all pastors, "should act as fellow-helpers in their great work. It should be seen that they are animated and engaged and exert themselves with one heart and soul, and with united strength to promote the present glorious revival of religion; and to that end should often meet together and act in concert" (Center for National Humanities 2009, 3). Promoting the revival of religion is later seen in Pentecostalism.

In the early part of the twentieth century, Pentecostalism[20] adopted a more inclusive than exclusive approach to Communion with few binding rules for receiving the bread and wine.[21] However, Gordon T. Smith (2010, 122) points out the bread and wine was "reserved for only those who have made a conscious decision of faith." How that decision was understood is not clear in Smith's work. Nevertheless, Smith does point out that children were typically excluded, and a warning against casual observance was usually given by the minster, quoting Paul's first letter to the Corinthian church (11:27-32).

Taking a different approach to Smith, Keith Whitt and French Arrington (2012, 250) analyzed Communion practices of church leaders in contemporary Pentecostalism concluding, "The Table of the Lord can be a place where the Spirit reveals sin and brings the guilty to repentance." Whitt and Arrington imply that Pente-

---

[20] Though Pentecostalism may be considered anti-modern or postmodern, I discuss the movement because it falls within the parameters of the designated eras.

[21] *The New International Dictionary of Pentecostal and Charismatic Movements* (Burgess, McGee, and Alexander 1988, 653-654) makes no reference to a closed table. At the same time, it makes no reference to an open table. However, in the context of sacrament, a recipient with no faith is explicitly mentioned showing that they are welcome to the table.

An experience of the empowering actions and promissory words during Communion are accompanied with an expectation and openness towards the Holy Spirit in Pentecostalism.

costalism does have an inclusive view of Communion with an expectation for conviction of sin to take place in the believer, and the possibility of conversion for the unbeliever similar to Stoddard and Wesley. Johnathan Alvarado (2013, 180-181) contends the prayer of invocation in Pentecostalism is the point of possible conversion where the Holy Spirit interacts with the participant during Communion. However, he does not attribute everything Pentecostalism offers in Communion as coopted traditions from church history:

> "This unrestricted openness to God distinguishes Pentecostals from the other Christian traditions in a very practical way. Rather than restricting the interest of the Spirit to only one conceptual outworking with which the Church is theologically acclimated, Pentecostals pray with reckless abandon for the Spirit to function as the Spirit desires on the people and the [Communion] elements, always maintaining openness and receptivity to the surprises of God." (Alvarado 2013, 188)

Summary Thought

Whereas the Great Awakening was divided on the issue of inclusion, it appears that Pentecostalism, historical and contemporary, has an inclusive approach to celebrating Communion (believer and unbeliever), where Christ is made available to the participant in the bread and wine through the Holy Spirit. An experience of the empowering actions and promissory words during Communion are accompanied with an expectation and openness towards the Holy Spirit in Pentecostalism.

Differences in How Biblical Passages Were Used to Explain Communion

Similar to the Early Church Fathers in the Classical Age, biblical passages[22] in the sermons, treatise, commentaries, and lectures of Modernity connect the **Passover to Communion**. In addition, the literary works in Modernity connect the **Wedding Supper of the Lamb** and Communion.

In 1540, **Luther** published his sermon "Exhortation to Walk as Christians," where he historically explains the Passover (Exod. 12) as a prefiguration of Communion (Luther 2000, 181-193). "The old has given place to something wholly new. A different and better Passover sacrifice succeeds that of the Jews...in other words, we receive remission of sins and comfort and strength through this our Passover, Christ" (2000, 191). Quoting Paul (1 Cor. 5:7), Luther explains the apostle was pointing out the true character and purpose of the Passover in order to reveal the kingdom of Christ. In doing this, Luther assumed a Passover of any kind was no longer necessary, beyond a historical remembrance during Communion.

An example of this is seen in his sermon "Parable of the King Who Made a Marriage Feast for His Son" (Matt. 22:1-14), first printed in 1523 (Luther 2000, 229). **Luther eschatologically** explains the Wedding Supper of the Lamb in the parabolic light of the banquet through Communion. However, he personifies the **Papacy** as the figurehead who perverts an invitation to the banquet, preventing participants with fear, avarice, and destruction. For Luther, Communion was an eschatological warning against papal perversions. Consequently, historical and eschatological explanations from the perspective of the Communion table are negatively colored with his disdain for the papal system.

---

[22] All biblical passages noted are the same passages found in the respective works cited.

In 1527, **Zwingli** published his treatise *Refutation of the Tricks of the Catabaptists* [Anabaptists]. He explained Communion in relation to baptism (Col. 2:12) under a new covenant. From this relationship, Zwingli **historically explains the Passover** (Exod. 12) in relation to circumcision under the old covenant (Gen. 17). As circumcision was necessary for the Passover, baptism was equally necessary for participation in Communion. However, rather than nullifying the old covenant like Luther, Zwingli (1972, 237) points out Paul's spiritualization of the old in the new (1 Cor. 5:7; Col. 2:11), "So far upon one and the same testament, church and people of God." Zwingli uses biblical passages to historically explain the Passover from the perspective of Communion, in concert as a single narrative.

In *Refutation*, Zwingli draws attention to the parabolic story of the ten virgins (Matt. 15:1-13). Similar to his reforming peers, Zwingli (1972, 132-133) inserts the papal system into the passage characterized in the foolish virgins, "proceeding from an evil demon and the Roman pontiff." Consequently, for Zwingli, it appears the foolish would not feast at the Wedding Supper of the Lamb. However, Larissa Taylor (2001, 67) writes, "Zwingli deemed any sermon useless if it did not call people to repentance of their sins." If this is the case, Zwingli demonstrates the far reaches of repentance by extending it to the foolish virgins in the papal system. Unlike Luther, **Zwingli eschatologically explains Communion** as a point of repentance for access to the Wedding Supper of the Lamb.

In his *Commentaries*, **Calvin** (2003a, 221) **historically explains the Passover** (Exod. 12) as "a type of Christ, who by His death propitiated His Father, so that we should not perish with the rest of the world." In Calvin's view, Christ is historically set before the Israelites in the Passover as the true and heavenly Exemplar realized in Communion. Calvin also typifies the sprinkled blood of the paschal lamb with the blood of Christ (1 Pet. 1:2). As the Israelites applied the blood of the paschal lamb to their homes, so the Christian should apply the blood of Christ to theirs through participation in Communion. In doing so, protection and profit would follow "only if its conspicuous sign existed among them" (2003a, 221).

Again, in his *Commentaries*, Calvin eschatologically explains the parable of ten virgins (Matt. 25:1-13, 170). Objecting to Jerome's "childish speculation" to praise virginity, Calvin (2003b, 170) states, "By this term is meant the future condition of the church." In his view, parabolic use of virgins suggested two relative nuances: first, the original audience would identify with a customary tradition that virgins accompany the bridegroom; and second, the same audience would comprehend a perpetual readiness. "It is not enough to have been once ready and prepared for the discharge of duty, if we do not preserve to the end" (2003b, 171). For Calvin, preservation meant continued participation in Communion. Although implicit, Calvin **eschatologically talks about the Wedding Supper** of the Lamb as a state of preparedness through participation in Communion.

Commenting on Whitefield's sermon "The True Way of Beholding the Lamb of God," James Paterson Gledstone (2008, 228-229) writes that **Whitefield historically explains the Passover** (Exod. 12) as a foreshadowing of Christ. Whitefield himself states (2008, 229), "So Christ, our Passover...was burned and roasted in the fire of His Father's wrath before He actually expired on the cross." In 1742 at the Cambuslang Revival, Whitefield's sermons frequently used Old Testament passages to shed light on Communion. For example, referencing 2 Chronicles 35, he described large conversions to Christ "like the Passover in Josiah's time" (2008, 119). In another sermon, Whitefield (2008, 192) **eschatologically explained the Wedding Supper of the Lamb** implicitly in the narrative of the first miracle of Christ referencing John 2:10, "Thou hast kept the good win [wine] until now."

In the early 1800s, prominent revivalist **James McGready** preached several notable sermons on this topic. McGready (2010, 350) talks about the Passover in his sermon "Saving Sight" as a precursor for the triumph of Christ on the cross celebrated in Communion. McGready also notes the Passover was the precise timing of God for all nations to see Christ (John 12:21) celebrated in Communion. It is not difficult to agree with Kimberly Long (2011, 69) that McGready's sermons on Communion had a common theme: "Proclaim the gospel to unbelievers...who may be aroused by the Spirit, experience conversion, and come for the first time to the Lord's Table." In one sermon, "Nature and Tendency of Unbelief," McGready (2010, 326) connects the openness of Communion eschatologically with the openness of heaven where "the marriage supper of the Lamb is prepared." By connecting Communion to the Wedding Supper of the Lamb, he explains the parabolic banquet (Matt. 22 1-14), "tell them to come for all things are now ready" (2010, 327). What becomes apparent in the sermons of Whitefield and McGready is the **lack of an explicit historical and eschatological** perspective from Communion.

Hunger for God and the motif of eating and drinking metaphors were common in the language of early Pentecostalism. For example, Chris Green (2012, 88) writes that participants in Communion drink "new wine" while being "fed" by God. Between 1906 and1908, writers who contributed to *The Apostolic Faith Newspaper* drew attention to biblical passages that connect Communion historically to the Passover and eschatologically to the Wedding Supper of the Lamb. For instance, the Passover illuminates the salvation experience of the Christian, typifying a complete redemption (Apostolic Faith 1907, 2). An eschatological view of Communion "is the Lamb's wedding feast (described in Rev. 19:7-10) that more than any other single biblical figure determines early Pentecostals' understanding of the eating/drinking motif" (Green 2012, 88).

The nuptial language of bride and groom in Revelation 19:7-10 anticipates the return of Christ celebrated in Communion. However, a Pentecostal approach towards the bread and wine of Communion errors on doctrinal shallowness in favor of Zwingli's teaching rather than Luther or Calvin. Keith Warrington (2008, 165) writes, "For most Pentecostals, it [Communion] is fundamentally a celebration of a past event though in recognition that it is destined to redundancy in heaven (1 Cor. 11:26)" (2008, 165). A Pentecostal celebration does connect **Communion to Passover and the Wedding Supper of the Lamb** retrospectively, remembering Christ, and realizing a new celebration in heaven.

Summary Thought

In early modernity, the differences in how biblical passages were used to explain Communion were subtle. From the perspective of Communion, Luther viewed the Passover as a redundant celebration beyond its historical remembrance, whereas Zwingli spiritualized it. Calvin viewed the Passover as the celebration where Christ was prefigured as the heavenly Exemplar. Again, from the perspective of Communion, Luther viewed the Wedding Supper of the Lamb as a point of warning for the papal system, Zwingli as a reason to repent, and Calvin as a point of preparedness. In mid-modernity, the historical and eschatological aspects of Communion are explained with vagueness. Biblical passages are largely used to explain the urgency of conversion. In late Modernity, Pentecostalism used a feasting motif to connect Communion to the Passover and the Wedding Supper of the Lamb.

Retelling the Redemptive Story through Liturgy

At the close of the Middle Ages, Roman Catholic liturgy had essentially become a singular pattern for celebrating Communion in the West. With that pattern, sacramental realism had become more popular than allegorical representation in liturgy used during Communion. However, the **Protestant Reformation** also impacted liturgical reform.

In 1520, **Luther** published *On the Babylonian Captivity of the Church* outlining three issues that he felt hindered the participant in Communion: exclusion from the wine, transubstantiation, and repeating the sacrifice of Christ. All three issues impacted how the redemptive story was retold through liturgy. Regarding the wine and transubstantiation,[23] Quoting Luther, Paul F. Bradshaw and Maxwell E. Johnson (2012, 238-239) write, "The sacrament [bread and wine] does not belong to the priests but to all men…it is not

---

[23] Though Luther favored consubstantiation (Mazza 1999, 237), Calvin considered the concept equivalent to Catholic transubstantiation (Mazza 1999, 242) as it relates to a liturgical retelling

> the real agents of worship were not the priests, the Latin language, or the bread and wine, but the community of participants

necessary in the sacrament that the bread and wine be transubstantiated...both remain there at the same time." Regarding the issue of repeated sacrifice, Luther writes, "We firmly hold that the mass is the promise or testament of Christ" (2012, 270).

For Luther, the words of Christ, "This is my body...this is my blood" (Matt. 26:26-28) were liturgical, announcing the promise of continued salvation available for the participant while receiving the bread and wine. To that end, he believed a participant must focus on what liturgy used in celebrating Communion reveals, not the bread and wine. Consequently, experiencing the empowering actions and promissory words of Communion were essential for a participant to understand a reformed liturgical retelling of the redemptive story.

Luther also wrote two liturgies for Communion in **Latin** and German, reducing the seven sacraments of Rome Catholicism[24] to two sacraments.[25] By writing in his own German language, Luther demonstrated the real agents of worship were not the priests, the Latin language, or the bread and wine, but the community of participants. In 1577, at the **Formula of Concord**, article ten summarizes Luther's focus on the community of participants:

> "Ceremonies neither commanded nor forbidden
> in God's Word but instituted alone for the sake of
> propriety and good order, are not even a part of the
> service of God. The Church of every time and place
> has the power to change such ceremonies, as may
> be useful and edifying...No church should condemn
> another because one has less or more external

---

[24] Armstrong (1999, 96-98) outlines the seven sacraments: baptism, confirmation, Communion, penance, anointing of the sick, holy orders, and marriage.

[25] Luther's two sacraments were baptism and Communion (Bradshaw and Johnson 2012, 236).

ceremonies not commanded by God than the other, if otherwise there is agreement among them in doctrine and in right use of the Holy Sacraments." (Bradshaw and Johnson 2012, 255)

Luther's liturgical reforms retell the redemptive story by directing the community of participants to focus on the saving power of God in the words of Christ.

In 1526, **Zwingli** wrote "On the Lord's Supper" commenting on the words of Christ (Matt. 26:26-28). Quoting Zwingli, J. F. White (2010, 201) writes, "And this he signified by the words: 'This is (that is, represents) my body,' just as a wife may say: 'This is my late husband,' when she shows her husband's ring." For Zwingli, a representation of Christ in the bread and wine demonstrated the separation of matter and spirit in terms of who, and what, brings about salvation. In short, it was Christ, not the bread and wine, which saved. Like Luther, experiencing the empowering actions and promissory words of Communion was essential for the participant to understand his liturgical reforms.

Again, like Luther, Zwingli wrote two liturgies, also in **Latin** and **German**. Regarding the latter, "Almost all traditional liturgical texts and ceremonies have disappeared in favor of a radical simplicity, with communion itself being brought to and received by the congregation in their places" (Bradshaw and Johnson 2012, 262). Zwingli goes further than Luther in his liturgical reforms by placing a greater emphasis on serving the community of participants. Instead of coming forward to receive Communion, the bread and wine was taken to where congregants were seated. Surprisingly, Zwingli was quite content in limiting a liturgical retelling of the redemptive story to **Christmas, Easter, Pentecost,** and the feast of **Saint Felix**.

The middle ground between Luther and Zwingli is occupied by the liturgical reforms of **Calvin**. Some have labeled that middle ground **pneumatological instrumentation** based on Calvin's 1541 publication *Short Treatise on the Holy Supper of Our Lord and Only Saviour Jesus Christ*. Calvin's *Treatise* does something different than the liturgical reforms of Luther and Zwingli. His

(2012, 264) retelling of the redemptive story places participants in the historical church "as the visible embodiment of God's will to save." Therefore, pneumatological instrumentation is seen in a God-to-us liturgical focus, affirmed by the work of the Holy Spirit.

His *Treatise* also addresses the active work of the Holy Spirit in the participant when he or she receives the bread and wine. If the participant has no faith, what they receive is just bread and wine, and not the body and blood of Christ. However, in 1559, Calvin offered a cautionary note regarding the liturgical reforms of Luther and Zwingli in *Institutes of the Christian Religion*. His caution addresses their theories of the bread and wine and the work of the Holy Spirit, "Let us remember how far the secret power of the Holy Spirit towers above all our senses and how foolish it is to wish to measure his immeasurableness by our measure" (Calvin 2006, 1370). The work of the Holy Spirit is seen in his emphasis on the spiritual presence of Christ in the bread and wine. Calvin (2006, 1363) believed the bread nourished, invigorated, and enlivened the soul, as the wine refreshed, strengthened, and gladdened the soul referring to both as "spiritual things."

In all probability, **George Whitefield** was the instigator for downplaying the role of liturgy in the act of worshiping God during the **Great Awakening** in the 1740s. D. G. Hart (1996, 17) notes, "Whitefield's audiences may have sung praise, he may have led them in prayer and confession of sin, and he might even have begun with an invocation, but the chief reason why people came to hear him was to hear his message, not to worship God."[26] In spite of Whitefield's passion for an open Communion table, if Hart is correct, a non-liturgical Communion was replaced by an opportunity to meet with Christ in the form of an altar call. For instance, Melanie Ross (2014, 6) writes that worship in the Great Awakening tended to "soften up" the audience prior to a "fervent sermon" followed by an altar call where bread and wine were received. This process effectively marginalized a liturgical Communion. If this was the case, a liturgical retelling of the redemptive story was not a common practice during the Great Awakening.

---

[26] Hart's emphasis is that worshipping God must include liturgy.

The history of **Pentecostalism** shows that the words "sacrament" and "liturgy" were typically avoided. J. C. Holsinger (2015) underscores the fact that, "Pentecostals more accurately have ordinances and ceremonies." However, Holsinger is quick to point out Pentecostal ceremonies have the same goal as liturgies in continuity, performance, and education. In many ways, Western society has become more personalized and rationalized, destroying the purpose of continuity in society. If this is the case, a retelling of the redemptive story would be anchored in personal, not **salvific, history**.

Shortly after Pentecostalism began the **Liturgical Movement** that had already begun. In 1914 the Liturgical Movement challenged Western individual rationalism, represented by Protestant and Roman Catholic churches. Pentecostalism may have found a new freedom of personal expression, but the Liturgical Movement found a refreshed expression of ancient church history. Freedom of personal expression and ancient church history can complement each other.

For example, though Pentecostals have no written liturgy, a complementary pattern at the Communion table can be seen in reflection, thanksgiving, open worship, focus on the death of Christ, and proclamation. Such a pattern underscores the Pentecostal motivation to evangelize the world whether the liturgy is expressed from the ancient or contemporary style. A contemporary Pentecostal expression is what Green (2016, 110) calls "extemporaneous and improvisational rather than pre-scripted or formalized."

For Pentecostals, it is not a question of whether worship during Communion is liturgical or not, rather how that liturgy is used. The observations that Green (2016, 109-111) made in Pentecostal[27] liturgy from 1911 and 1981 show a progressive use of liturgy. In the former, a pastor calls for the deacons to come forward and kneel with the whole congregation in preparation for the bread and wine of Communion. An adapted prayer from the 1622 **Book of Common Prayer** is given by the pastor. The pastor receives the

---

[27] International Pentecostal Holiness Church.

> By the end of Modernity, celebrating Communion had become the centerpiece of debate, argument, fall-outs, rebellion, and ultimately a reformation.

bread and wine with the deacons repeating specific words about the death of Christ. The same is done with the wine before serving the congregation. To conclude, the pastor remains kneeling with the congregation leading them in the **Lord's Prayer**.

In 1981, the celebration of Communion moved from once a week to once a month. The pastor stands by the Communion table and reads from 1 Corinthians 11:23-27 offering a simple prayer. The deacons served the bread and wine and were instructed to distribute among the congregation. Once everyone has received the bread and wine, the pastor gives simple instruction on what the elements mean before they are received by the congregation. Finally, a prayer of benediction is offered by the pastor. By comparing the examples given by Green (2016, 109-11), Pentecostals are not against the use of liturgy, but they demonstrate a freedom to change in order to express their worship at the Communion table.

Summary Thought

In early Modernity, the Protestant Reformation was accompanied by liturgical reform. Luther's reforms seem to focus on what liturgy reveals, whereas Zwingli's reforms seem to focus on what is revealed in the congregants. Between both liturgical views, Calvin's reforms seem to focus on what the Holy Spirit reveals. In mid-Modernity, the role of liturgy played a lesser role in retelling the redemptive story in favor of an altar call. By late Modernity, liturgical renewal to retell the redemptive story had begun.

CONCLUDING THOUGHT

By the end of Modernity, celebrating Communion had become the centerpiece of debate, argument, fall-outs, rebellion, and ultimately a reformation. While church leaders during the Great Awakening struggled with the matter of inclusion, Pentecostalism had less of an issue with it. There was a distinct openness to the work of the Holy Spirit, not only in the bread and wine, but in the hearts of participants and observers. Biblical interpretation had three specific viewpoints: Luther occupied the right with prejudice, Zwingli the left with equal prejudice, and Calvin in the middle. Though the Passover and the Wedding Supper of the Lamb were biblically understood as the historical and eschatological dimensions of Communion, the end of Modernity saw a vagueness in their connections. Even so, the openness of Communion gathered pace resulting in a new understanding conversion during the celebration. Retelling the redemptive story through liturgy seemed to find a second breath.

CHAPTER 4

POSTMODERNITY 1966-PRESENT

In the introduction to this book, I sketched generalizations that determined each period of time. Also, I sketched two factors that shed further light on the dates in each period of time. In this chapter, I will begin by expanding from generalizations to specifics regarding the cultural era of Postmodernity towards a definition. Then, I will begin to unpack a response through the three lenses.

Dating Postmodernity

Notable eras of time in the West are typically defined by their cultural components represented in philosophy, science, and a variety of art forms. By making the Greco-Roman era a starting point - a period I call the **Classic** era - a succession of cultural eras is typically recognized as Romanesque, Gothic, Nominalism, Humanism, Renaissance, Protestant Reformation, Mannerism, Baroque, Rococo, Neoclassical, Age of Enlightenment, Realism, Art Nouveau, Modernity, and Postmodernity. For the sake of clarity and to prevent sheer boredom on behalf of the reader, I move from **Modernity** to **Postmodernity**.

Determining when Postmodernity began is probably a matter of process than precision. So, dating the beginning of Postmodernity may be somewhat arbitrary and a matter of opinion. Moving back through cultural eras, we can ask: **When did Modernity end?**

Precise dates are difficult for one dominant reason. Each era is defined by its cultural components that tend to emerge in an unsynchronized way from pre-existing cultural components. With this in mind, dating cultural eras can be approximated by asking a dominant question: When did multiple changes in the cultural components occur in rapid succession that appeared connected by a common ideology breaking away from a previous ideology? For example, Anthony Giddens and Christopher Pearson (1998, 94-117) suggest Modernity broke away from the ideology of intellectual reason, individualism, skepticism, humanism and science in the Age of Enlightenment. Likewise, Postmodernity has broken, or continues to break away, from the ideology represented in Modernity.

Using this process, Brian McHale (2015, 64) believes it is highly probable that the beginning of Postmodernity can be located between **1954** and **1975.** For example, some of the cultural changes that occurred in rapid succession in **1958** are noted by the founder of **Fluxus**, Dick Higgins (1978, 101).[28] He identified a cultural change in artists, composers, designers and poets who began to rapidly shift from cognitive questions to post-cognitive questions. The ideology changed from knowledge and interpretation to being and doing.

Sally Banes (1993, 174-175) draws attention to the rapid cultural change in **1963**. She recognized a social intersection of pop-stars, dancers, artists, poets and performers converging in Greenwich Village in New York City. Like a cultural ground-zero this convergence detonated the ideology of avant-garde by minimizing conventional ideology. Others, like Gunther Hellmann (2006) and Mark Kurlansky (2005) observed the rapid cultural changes that occurred in **1967** and **1968** respectively. The changes were so ferocious, they became known as the revolutionary years.

Postmodern ideology became topical expressions in journalistic phrases: *Summer of Love, Detroit and the National Guard,*

---

[28] Fluxus was an international, interdisciplinary community of artists, composers, designers and poets during the 1960s and 1970s who engaged in experimental art performances which emphasized the artistic process over the finished product.

Swinging London, Youth Culture, Protests, Parades, the musical domination of Sergeant Pepper's Lonely Heart by the Beatles, Spring Prague, and the first television interracial kiss between Captain James T. Kirk and Uhura during the third season of *Star Trek,* just to name a few. Once more, conventional ideology was overridden by avant-garde experimentation in being and doing. Similar to the revolutionary years, Andreas Killen (2006) notes that 1973 was a year where rapid cultural change occurred in politics. *Roe v. Wade* and the *Watergate Scandal* gave expression to liberal politics enhanced by George Lucas' *American Graffiti,* and so much more.

In addition to philosophy, science, and a variety of art forms, Charles Jencks (2011) identified **1972** as the year where architecture rapidly changed. The Twin Towers were opened becoming part of the New York City skyline. In Munich Germany, the *Olympiastadion* (Olympic Stadium) was considered revolutionary in design. The ideology portrayed in the Berlin Stadium that hosted the 1936 Olympic Games was no longer important. Back in the United States, the *Pruitt-Igoe* housing project in St. Louis was abruptly demolished. It was an architectural statement that fifty block buildings would no longer define urban America. All three examples, and many more, firmly closed the door on the architectural ideology of Modernity.

These examples are simply the tip of a very large cultural iceberg where multiple changes in rapid succession were connected by a common avant-garde ideology breaking away from ideological forms of Modernity.

Considering the examples given between 1954 and 1975, Frederic Jameson (1991) and Marianne DeKoven (2004), both point to a general consensus among scholars of cultural studies that Postmodernity emerged out of the 1960's. As such, the **1960's** was a particular decade that became representative of cumulative cultural changes prior to and following the 60's. However, caution is needed. Events that occur in any society are not necessarily synced to an understanding of culture. There is overlap like art imitating history and history imitating art.

The overlap is precisely why McHale (2015, 28) makes the bold statement that 1966 is a "strong candidate for the Year Zero of Postmodernism." He argues that 1966 was the specific year that best represents the cultural changes that occurred in the 1960's as a representative decade. So, 1966 is a symbolic year of Postmodernism. Even so, McHale does not state the ideology of the 1960's, or specifically 1966, which connected cultural changes in a new era of Postmodernity.

> If dating the beginning of Postmodernity may be somewhat arbitrary and a matter of opinion, giving definition to Postmodernity can also be a difficult task.

Summary Thought

If locating the end of Modernity and the beginning of Postmodernity is a matter of process than precision, putting a date to it really is arbitrary and a matter of opinion. For the sake of clarity, I tend to agree with McHale about 1966. If discretion and opinion are used to date Postmodernity, identifying its theme(s) must use the same approach. A more precise accounting of Postmodernity will certainly be accomplished by looking back to today from the future. For now, the theme(s) that connects cultural changes can help towards defining Postmodernity.

If dating the beginning of Postmodernity may be somewhat arbitrary and a matter of opinion, giving definition to Postmodernity can also be a difficult task.

Framing Postmodernity

Two approaches are necessary. First, as postmodern philosophical thinkers, the ideas of **Jacques Derrida** (2016) and **Michel Foucault** (1980) are helpful towards framing a definition to Postmodernity. Second, as ministry practitioners and students of Postmodernity, the descriptions of Earl Creps (2002), Stanley Grenz (1996), and Howard Young (2005) paint the picture of Postmodernity within the frame.

The idea of deconstructionism was first introduced by Jacque Derrida in 1967. Basically, **deconstructionism** attempts to understand the underlying assumptions hidden within written text that form the basis for truth. Therefore, the idea concerns literary criticism by challenging the assumed meaning in the text (Derrida 2016, 15). Derrida points out that when human beings try to define and understand reality it leads to dominating textual forms of truth. In order to define and understand truth, it must be experienced (2016, 21).

Furthermore, any experience of truth concerns the local and particular characteristics of culture disconnected from meaning understood in the past (Derrida 2016, 250). This is what makes the cultural era of Postmodernity fascinating. Can an experience of Christ during Communion be a precise experience disconnected from the eternal dimension of Christ? Deconstructionism challenges all forms of textual truth by contrasting meaning that is assumed (2016, 346). Consequently, meaning is never concretely present in the text but subject to the experiential interpretation of the reader. So, does the text of Scripture still mean what it meant? According to Derrida, an experience of Christ during Communion can mean multiple things.

The ideas of Michel Foucault (1980, 108-132) concern the relationship of **power and truth** and how they are used to control people in societal institutions. He defines truth "as a system of ordered procedures for the production, regulation, distribution, circulation and operation of statements" (1980, 133). "Truth is linked in a circular relation with systems of power which produce and sustain it, and to the effects of power which it induces, and which extend it" (1980, 133). He illustrates this linked relationship of power and truth in the act of war, and what follows after war.

The role of power is to "re-inscribe it [truth] in social institutions, economic inequalities, in language, in the bodies themselves in each and every one of us" (Foucault 1980, 90). Whoever won the war has power to re-inscribe truth in the people who were defeated. Re-inscribing involves creating, teaching, and compounding truth over time until it becomes the acceptable way of doing things (1980, 93).[29] If there is power in truth, the one who creates truth is the one in power (1980, 51-52). However, Foucault also points out that creating truth corresponded with the need to build architectural forms to display power that include the church.

Summary Thought

Considering Derrida and Foucault, Postmodernity is framed by a subjective experience in order to interpret truth at the cost of how others have interpreted truth in the past, and how truth is inscribed and re-inscribed through power, whether it is healthy or abusive. In all probability, re-inscribed truth occurs when a church organization has reached a particular size or number of attendees. I shall come to this shortly. Within this definitional frame, a picture of Postmodernity can be painted.

Defining Postmodernity

Earl Creps (2002, 57), gives seven character traits of postmoderns: (1) centrality of community; (2) primacy of experience; (3) subjectivity of truth; (4) complexity of human perception; (5) unreality of absolutes; (6) enormity of the spiritual; and (7) plurality of worldviews. Viewed together, these character traits show that postmoderns have a need to individually discover truth within a community, and what they discover is highly subjective to the individual within the community. Because postmoderns are **highly pragmatic** and spiritual in their quest to discover truth, they tend to be open to any number of messages from their peers (2002, 58).

However, if that truth appears to advocate a monolithic or exclusive view of truth, postmoderns also tend to respond with **skepticism** and **suspicion**. Nevertheless, "The audience wants (and needs) to experience God in the discovery of truth and in the outworking of that truth in the world" (Creps 2002, 59). What stands out towards giving definition to Postmodernity is no apparent dis-

---

[29] One example of that Foucault (1980, 57-58) gives are the social institutions of the nineteenth and twentieth century as a result of Marxism.

tinction between knowing truth and living truth. It appears that truth has to be experienced by an individual within a community.

Similar to Creps, Stanley Grenz (1996, 8) talks about postmoderns operating with a community-based understanding of truth. However, arriving at any understanding of truth not only involves community, it also involves **individualism**. Regarding the truth of the Bible, Grenz (1996, 6) notes that postmoderns tend to believe truth is not inherent in the text but emerges as the individual enters into dialogue with the text within community. This approach fits the theory of Derrida. Furthermore, because truth is dependent on the interpretation of the one who enters into dialogue with the text, there are as many truths as there are interpreters. This implies that a plurality of truths can exist alongside each other. Truth is highly interpretable by the individual within community. It looks the same as the observations Creps made, with the added emphasis of the interpreter.

According to Howard Young (2005, 34), postmoderns tend to posit the idea that truth can be achieved through the perception of the individual. Like Creps and Grenz, Young highlights the tendency that truth is entirely experiential and individual within a community. Interestingly, Young (2005, 35) points out that postmoderns evaluate community based on **common values** within the group. If this is the case, truth evaluated as monolithic and exclusive is not something postmoderns are going to hear because it is not valued. As a result, the values held by postmoderns both define the individual and the community, and provide truth for both (Young 2005, 35). The individual and the community are both necessary in order to discover truth.

> knowing and living truth that is highly interpreted by the individual in a community of shared values resistant against re-inscribing that truth by monolithic structures.

Considering the observations of Creps, Grenz, and Young as ministry practitioners and students of Postmodernity as it relates to this book, and the frame of Derrida and Foucault which they think within, a definition for Postmodernity does begin to emerge: knowing and living truth that is highly interpreted by the individual in a community of shared values resistant against re-inscribing that truth by monolithic structures.

However, even with a definition for Postmodernity, a narrower focus is needed for the three lenses used in previous eras. Exploring the mainstream denominations that have emerged throughout church history is not only exhausting, I fear it would miss the point: communicating the redemptive story through celebrating Communion. If the monolithic organization is something that postmoderns naturally resist, what follows fits that narrower lens. I shall narrow "church" down to "multi-site church." Though multi-site churches are not strictly postmodern, they flow out of the current era as a significant presence in Postmodernity emphasizing Communion experimentation as a means to experience truth.

Summary Thought

Postmoderns tend to individually discover truth within a community, and what they discover is highly subjective to the individual within the community. There can be as many truths as there are interpreters of truth implying a plurality of truths can exist alongside each other. Postmoderns also evaluate a community based on the values they observe.

Multi-Site Churches as a Postmodern Focus

Senior lecturer Sam Hey (2013, 9) summarizes a consensus among church leaders that the early twentieth century marked the beginning of the American **mega-church**. The research of Greg Ligon and Warren Bird (2009, 91-92) show that American **multi-site** churches[30] had evolved from the mega-church. Both types of churches are not the only church developments in the

---

[30] Surratt, Ligon, and Bird (2009, 91-92) note that a case can be made that multi-site church began in the New Testament era. However, they also note multi-site has become a particular focus among congregants across the United States in the twenty-first century.

twentieth and twenty-first centuries. However, Ed Stetzer (2014) points out that both represent a postmodern culture, particularly the multi-site church. Smaller church sites are less **monolithic**. What follows will focus on the multi-site church as representative of Postmodernity much like 1966 is representative of when the cultural era began.

The discoveries in the research of Geoff Suratt, with Ligon and Bird (2009, 7) show that multi-site churches are strategic and less monolithic than the mega-church. According to a recent cross-denominational survey of multisite churches compiled by Bird, a multi-site church is strategic because it greatly involves the laity in the functioning of a church service.[31]

> "These churches also experience very high levels of lay participation. Multi-site [multi-site] churches touch five million people weekly through congregations of all sizes. Their number includes many of North America's largest, most visible, and most influential churches: 89% of multi-site [multi-site] churches are over 500 in current attendance, 72% are over 1,000, 20% are over 5,000, and 8% are over 10,000." (Bird 2014, 2)

In the following discussion, Communion is explored in the context of twenty-first century multi-site churches. Five multi-site churches were selected that represent postmodern culture in America. Austin Stone Community Church based in Austin, Texas; Celebration Church based in Austin Metro, Texas; Life.Church based in Edmond, Oklahoma; National Community Church based in Washington D. C.; and Northpoint Community Church based in Alpharetta, Georgia. Much like the sermons, lectures, publications, and treatise of church leaders in earlier periods of history, I explore the material of multi-site church leaders.

---

[31] The report claims over five million attend a multi-site church in the United States. "89% of multi-site churches are over 500 in current attendance, 72% are over 1,000, 20% are over 5,000, and 8% are over 10,000 (Bird 2014, 2).

Church Developments That Granted or Denied Access to Communion

Overall, 88% of churches who changed from being a monolithic mega-church to a strategic multi-site experienced increased and widespread lay participation (Bird 2014, 11). An example of lay participation in a multi-site situation is seen in the Small Group Curriculum of Austin Stone Community Church. "You don't need to be a pastor or a priest to lead communion. If you feel uncertain on how to properly lead communion, just use the outline given in Week Six to help you facilitate this time with your people" (Austin Stone Community Church 2016, iii). The curriculum in Week Six encourages the laity to include all those who are present in a small group to celebrate Communion (2016, 33).

If multi-site churches intentionally involve the laity, one would assume Communion is frequently celebrated. Interestingly, multi-site churches are divided on when and how often Communion ought to be celebrated. Some are moving towards a weekly celebration in a Sunday service (McConnell and Stetzer 2009, 101). Others are moving in the opposite direction. I was curious to know what the five multi-site churches had to say about Communion.

Austin Stone Community Church celebrate Communion once every three months on a Sunday by including all who are present. Still, others like **Celebration Church** in Austin Metro offer Communion once a month in a Wednesday evening service to whoever wants to receive it:

"A unique time of communion in the presence of
God when the elements of bread and grape juice (the
Body and Blood of the Lord Jesus Christ) are taken
in remembrance of Jesus' sacrifice on the Cross."
(Celebration 2019a)

Similarly, **North Point Community Church**, the fastest growing multi-site in Metro Atlanta,[32] does the same:

"We greatly value the practice of sharing Communion, but we do not include it in our weekly services. Our Sunday services are structured to provide a safe environment for the unchurched to hear the life-changing truth that Jesus Christ loves them and died for their sins. We are a non-denominational church and our mission is to lead people into a growing relationship with Christ. Several times during the year we offer the Lord's Table at Nights of Worship and the person leading decides the scripture and introduction to use. These are services of worship music and prayer. We also encourage our small groups to share communion whenever they desire. No one is excluded." (Burns 2016).[33]

Life.Church has Communion readily available in their church services for whoever wants to participate the bread and wine:

First, is it possible to take communion at home? Yes, it is. Actually, when Jesus first modeled the spiritual tradition of communion, He did it in someone's home. If you're a Jesus follower, you can take communion just about anywhere. Did you grow up in a church that offered communion as part of the service every week? Or maybe once a month? If you're attending Life. Church, you've probably noticed that communion is always available along the side or rear walls. We hope you'll take the opportunity to participate in communion as God leads you during our worship time together (Life.Church, 2019).

---

[32] *Outreach Magazine* (2014) rated North Point Community Church as the fastest growing multi-site church in North America.

[33] Burns (2016), a personal email from JoAnn Burns from Ministry Services.

Also, the **National Community Church states:**

> "We all need a place to go back to: the home you grew up in, a favorite vacation spot, the place where you got engaged. Spiritually speaking, communion is a pilgrimage back to the foot of the cross. It's the place we go back to. It's the place where we are reminded that Jesus loves us enough to die for us." (National Community Church, 2019)

Laity involvement and intentional inclusion do not necessarily translate into continuity or frequency of celebrating Communion in multi-site churches. They range from celebrating weekly, monthly, or quarterly on a Sunday or Wednesday. However, a common theme in multi-site churches is an open invitation to celebrate Communion to those who are present in the church service or small group. Also, the issue of sacerdotal power appears to be a none-issue for multi-site churches.

a common theme in multi-site churches is an open invitation to celebrate Communion to those who are present in the church service or small group.

A recent addition to an inclusive invitation in the twenty-first century is an online Communion. According to Bird (2014, 20), only 28% of multi-site churches have an online celebration, with only 10% more planning to launch one, and 62% affirming they had no plans to launch one. He does not give a reason for a lack of interest in an online Communion. However, online participation presents two overarching questions. First, in what way does an individual include and serve him or herself while online? Second, in what way does an individual without an immediate physical community experience truth? Questions like these are more than likely going to find a concrete answer in the future. For the present, multi-site churches have a definite inclusive approach to celebrating Communion involving the laity.

Summary Thought

Monolithic mega-churches have moved toward multi-site churches. With this move a greater involvement is seen among the laity in serving Communion. If Modernity introduced an open Communion table, Postmodernity celebrates that openness. It is not surprising that the characteristics of inclusion, involvement, and openness could be the means of attraction for postmoderns. I shall enlarge on this later. For now, it would be accurate to say that experiencing the empowering actions and promissory words of Christ during Communion is made readily available, understood in simplistic ways, and largely left for the participant to figure out for themselves.

Differences in How Biblical Passages Were Used to Explain Communion

According to Grenz (1996, 12), Postmodernity marks the end of a single, **universal worldview** with renewed respect for difference and a celebration of the local and particular at the expense of the universal. The observation of Grenz, even in the 1990's, perfectly fits the worldview of postmoderns today. Considering this worldview, how do leaders of multi-site churches use biblical passages to explain Communion?

Pastor Joe Champion from **Celebration Church** states their beliefs about Communion from Matthew 26:26-29 (Celebration Church 2019a). Contrary to the observations of Grenz, Champion focuses on the local and particular, but not at the expense of the universal. From the archived sermons, Champion has been noted to say the bread and wine are for the individual believer.

However, he further describes Communion not as a point of excluding the unbeliever, but as a point of clear meaning for the believer, and for all believers throughout church history. Including the unbeliever appears similar to Calvin's middle ground between **Luther** and **Zwingli**. Champion's approach is also similar to the converting ordinance of **Stoddard** and **Wesley**, and the Half-Way communion of Stoddard. The sermons that Champion preached between January 2018 and September 2019 were largely topical, with a strong application to the individual believer anchored in a historical and eschatological universal worldview (Celebration Church 2016b).

Pastor Craig Groeschel from **Life.Church** explains Communion from Matthew 26, Luke 22, Mark 14, and 1 Corinthians 11 as something more than a time of remembering the death and resurrection of Christ. In his view, the church in every locality should also remember how dependent Christians are upon Christ, sharing in a deep anticipation of His return (Life.Church 2019). From a clear statement of belief and biblical interpretation, Groeschel does not celebrate the local and particular at the cost of the universal (2019).

On the contrary, he celebrates the universal by explaining an eschatological Communion. The sermons that Groeschel preached between January 2018 and September 2019 emphasized both the community and the individual. One particular theme from 2014, *Come to Worship*, implicitly connects Communion historically to the Passover and eschatologically to the Wedding Supper of the Lamb in four sermons (Life.Church, 2019). In an almost liturgical fashion, he titles each of the four sermons as the use of hands, heart, knees, and giving. Again, Groeschel contextualizes his outline in the community and individual.

Pastor Andy from **North Point Church** explains the Passover (Exod. 12) as a celebration, commemoration, and specific time of remembrance.[34] In Stanley's view, a three-fold explanation also reveals the intentionality of Christ to introduce Communion specifically at the Passover. Paraphrasing the words of Christ, Stanley (2010, 50-51) writes, "You've been eating the Passover meal since childhood, but from now on, when you eat it, this is my body." There are no current or archived sermons available on the North Point website that address the Communion.[35]

---

[34] His explanation is found in a collaborative publication edited by Craig Groeshel (2010, 47).

[35] Up to September 2019.

If the claims of *Outreach Magazine* (2014) are true, North Point Church is the fastest growing multi-site in North America at the time of writing this book. Explaining and celebrating Communion is not part of their strategy. The top three sermon categories for Stanley's sermons between January 2018 and September 2019 were spiritual growth, character, and influence (faith and purpose tied equally with character and influence) (Northpoint Community Church, 2019a). Similar to the observations of Grenz (1996, 12), the emphasis of each sermon celebrated the local and particular at some cost of the universal.

From **National Community Church**, Pastor Mark Batterson (2011, 180) explains Communion (Matt. 26:26-29) as a means of moving forward by looking back to the cross. He cautions that participants should not receive the bread and wine without thinking for themselves (Batterson 2009, 59). According to Mark Batterson and his son Parker Batterson (2015), it is essential for a participant to remember key exchanges that took place on the cross. For example, Paul's second letter to the Corinthian Christians, where Christ became sin with the participant's sin, that the participant might become the righteousness of God (2 Cor. 5:21).

> multi-site leaders tend to drop the historical and eschatological explanations of Communion

However, a historical and eschatological explanation of Communion is lacking. The theme of local and particular is seen in the sermons Batterson (National Community Church, 2019b) preached at National Community Church between January 2018 and September 2019. Highlighting individualism and lacking in historical and eschatological perspectives celebrates the local and particular at some cost of the universal as Grenz observed twenty-three years earlier.

Summary Thought

The four multi-site leaders mentioned do not follow the pattern of Grenz in light of the sermons they preached. However, Grenz's description of postmodernism did not completely fit the sermons of Champion and Groeschel. Nevertheless, Groeschel reduces the universal to community. Similar to the sermons in the Great Awakening, the sermons of multi-site leaders tend to drop the historical and eschatological explanations of Communion or, as Grenz (1996, 12) would put it, "the universal perspective." If this is the case, an experience of the empowering actions and promissory words of Christ during Communion tend to focus on the local and particular at the general cost of the universal.

Retelling the Redemptive Story through Liturgy

In an interview with *Ministry Today*, Pentecostal scholar Simon Chan shares his views with Sean Fowlds on liturgy in the twenty-first century. Fowlds (2015) editorializes, "Chan's writings have garnered international appeal, as he draws from sources as diverse as Puritan pastors and Asian mystics." Although liturgy may be associated with external worship, "liturgical worship will form worshipers more fully because it embodies a more holistic gospel...we become more truly the church by celebrating both Word and sacrament, whereas most non-liturgical churches tend to focus only on the Word" (2015).

From Chan's observation of Christian worship, Fowlds notes that worship may have been impoverished of any historical context regarding belief and prayer. Chan remarks, "This is why they [young church leaders] are going back into church history, especially early Christian history. They firmly believe that the early church fathers have something very important to teach us" (Fowlds 2015). Exploring liturgical church history also explores the theology of the Church Fathers.

In concert with Holsinger's caution on rational personalization, Fowlds writes that Chan also cautions that without a **theological foundation to liturgy**, a liturgical patchwork-quilt is highly probable. The image of a patchwork-quilt is explained as a craving for novelty in place of integrity. Chan (Fowlds 2015) adds what novelty looks like: "It is our pragmatic concern over making worship meaningful to non-Christians that has undermined the integrity of contemporary worship." It seems that Chan believes real liturgical worship is naturally evangelistic. Also, Spirit-led worship does not mean unplanned spontaneity as "a liturgically planned service not only can be Spirit-led, it is in fact better led by the Spirit" (2015).

Regarding a planned and Spirit-led church service, Bird's (2014, 24) report on multi-site church planting states, "The future is certain to be full of experimentation." Part of that experimentation is the development of semi-liturgical churches. Throughout the report, worship is referred to as an abstract act. For instance, "worship attendance," "worship service," "worship gathering," "worship leader," "worship arts," and "worship music" are used throughout (2014, 2-37). Bird admittedly delivers a report, not a biblical treatise like a Protestant Reformer. However, within his report Bird (2014, 24) states, "The weekly worship experience is probably the single most important factor in launching a new campus[36] successfully." One participant in the report summarized the emphasis on a worship experience as "semi-liturgical" (2014, 24). If this is the case, Bird's report shows that a worship experience is important but not necessarily as liturgical as Chan describes.

Regarding the five multi-site churches, liturgy was not explicit. For example, Groeschel strongly encourages people to pray, teaching them how to pray.

> "This four-week series focuses on Paul's prayers for
> the early church and the 'so that' statements he used
> in his writing. Each week, we learn to pray so that
> Christ may dwell in our hearts, we'll understand every
> good thing in Christ, we'll have one mind and voice to
> glorify God, and we can discern what is best."
> (Life.Church, 2019b)

Retelling the story of redemption does take place in his teaching, but not explicitly as liturgy during Communion. Stanley has a sim-

---

[36] A multi-site church campus includes borrowed buildings (Bird 2014, 12).

ilar approach, as does Champion. The same can be said for Batterson, not only from his sermon archives, but from his book *The Circle Maker* (2014). However, Austin Stone Community Church amplify the thoughts of Chan regarding liturgy (2019b).

Summary Thought

A liturgical retelling of the redemptive story is growing in interest, especially among multi-site churches according to Chan. His widespread observations are not typical as the five multi-site churches above do not always align in practice with his thoughts. Though Chan recognizes a liturgical retelling must connect to church history, he also recognizes that theological integrity must take priority over novelty, something that semi-liturgical worship may not recognize. Hopefully, an experience of the empowering actions and promissory words of Christ during Communion would contain a rich heritage dating back to the Church Fathers.

CONCLUDING THOUGHT

While dating Postmodernity can be arbitrary, it can be framed as a subjective experience in order to interpret truth by individually re-inscribing it. A picture of Postmodernity is painted within this frame. It is painted by many interpreters of truth depicting many subjective truths. The ability to have multiple truths in the same picture is based on shared values.

This framed picture appears to give people who attend multi-site churches a greater involvement in serving Communion. Postmodernity celebrates an open Communion table justified by inclusion, involvement, and openness. It is not surprising that the substance of sermons in multi-site churches are focused on the local and particular at the general cost of the universal, or historical and eschatological.

There is greater interest in Postmodernity of using liturgy to retell the redemptive story but not necessarily among multi-site churches. A liturgical retelling must connect to church history while maintaining theological integrity over novelty. For now, it would be accurate to say that experiencing the empowering actions and promissory words of Christ during Communion is made readily available, understood in simplistic ways, and largely left for the participant to figure out for themselves.

SECTION SUMMARY

The historical context of Communion provides the background to a postmodern understanding of the celebration. What participants experience during Communion today does, indeed, have a rich history to it that sheds light on how they came to celebrate in the way they currently do.

Scripture records the empowering actions and promissory words of Christ during the last day of His life when He introduced Communion. Since that time, the celebration has been remarkably preserved throughout where participants have experienced those actions and words. Viewing church history through the lenses of church developments, interpretation of biblical passages, and liturgy as separate entities can paint three distinct pictures. However, an investigation can also be understood when all three entities are approached together throughout different phases of church history.

Such an approach is important towards understanding how celebrating Communion can effectively communicate biblical truth through retelling the redemptive story, in that, all three lenses contribute towards a lived experience of postmodern participants. Looking back over the four eras, an **intertwining pattern seems to emerge**. With no particular starting point, how biblical passages were used to explain Communion tended to determine how liturgy was used to retell the redemptive story in a culturally changing environment which also framed who could, and who could not, participate in the bread and wine.

This intertwining pattern tended to repeat itself throughout different eras of church history. For example, a changing environment from private to public residences of worship came a clearer interpretation of biblical passages that made Communion distinct from any other religious celebrations. From this distinction came more elaborate developments in celebrating Communion. The intertwining continues in the Middle Ages seen in how **Ratramnus, Radbertus, Eriugena, Berengarius,** and **Lanfranc** interpreted biblical passages in order to develop liturgy which determined who could, and who could not, participate.

Admittedly, in the Classical era only those who had been baptized could receive the bread and wine, but in the Middle Ages exclusion went much further in the intertwining pattern. From a more elaborate celebration, penitentiary measures were imposed on congregants, as biblical passages were fiercely argued over to determine who could and could not retell the redemptive story by participating in Communion. Not only were participants under the sternness of canon law, but the priests found themselves equally under it. What this meant was the bread and wine appeared to be more valuable than the people for whom Christ died.

The **Protestant Reformation** in Modernity seems to repeat the intertwining pattern of church developments, understanding biblical passages, and liturgical retelling of the redemptive story. This was particularly seen in the anti-papal theme in the works of **Luther** and **Zwingli**.

Issues of inclusion, biblical passages, and liturgy to a lesser degree are seen in the revivalist and anti-revivalist themes of new lights and old lights during the **Great Awakening.**

In Postmodernity, re-focusing on Communion revealed the element of experimentation in order to retell the redemptive story. Thus, Communion in multi-site churches is currently celebrated on Sundays, Wednesdays, or any day when a small group meets. It is celebrated in private and domestic homes, in online settings, in borrowed buildings, in purposely built places of worship, and officiated with the help of laity. Postmodernity, the current phase of church history, intertwines all the preceding eras of church history with two exceptions: participants are not excluded from the bread and wine, and prayer seems to replace liturgy, but not completely.

Gradations of exclusion are found throughout church history. This is an important observation in that the idea of excluding people from a position of **sacerdotal power** is not characteristic of a postmodern community that celebrated Communion. Also, throughout the four eras of church history, leaders of the church, theologians, lecturers, professors, academics, and revivalists interpreted biblical passages in a number of ways. This is another important observation in that biblical interpretation that described Communion was determined for participants and not with them or by them. Deciding for people challenges the postmodern characteristic of knowing truth and its equality with experiencing truth. What if an experience of Christ was different than an interpretation of Scripture? Interstation of Scripture must involve the participant.

However, because multi-site church is **full of experimentation**, the possibility of including congregants in biblical interpretation is increased. Regarding the use of liturgy, it was common throughout church history that the story of redemption was retold. Specifically, when Luther and Zwingli wrote liturgies in their own language, they demonstrated the real agents of worship were not found in sacerdotal power, the Latin language, or the mysteries that surrounded the bread and wine, but in the community of participants. Once again, this is an important observation: how the redemptive story is retold must come from cultural orientation that makes sense to participants.

The cultural orientation I am interested in is postmodernity. Viewed together as an intertwining pattern, these discoveries in the current era of Postmodernity indicate the realities of postmodern spirituality by which the meaning and function of Communion is approached. The current era, then, creates a significant time in church history where Communion can function to communicate biblical truth, not just on Sunday as the traditional day for corporate worship, but on any day, and at any time, and inviting anyone. The current era recognizes a variety of locations for worship during Communion that may have only been considered viable in the early part of the Classical era. Also, the current era welcomes the help of laity in their involvement to officiate the bread and wine similar to Pentecostalism and other mainstream church denominations and non-denominations.

The current era of Postmodernity lends itself to what Bird (2014, 24) refers to as "full of experimentation" in the development of new church campuses. The same experimentation could not be exclusively said for previous eras. Though Pope John Paul II did not use the term Postmodernity, his observations of a varied Communion highlight the significance of the current era where the celebration can function to communicate biblical truth through retelling the redemptive story. Even so, some may disagree with the idea of experimentation regarding Communion, such as: the day it is celebrated, the location of the celebration, and the involvement of laity.

So, by exploring Communion through my three lenses in church history, I can say four things in light of the current era of Postmodernity that seem to intertwine (see Figure 4.1).

First, Church history provides the background for the realities of postmodern spirituality and explains how current participants came to celebrate Communion in the way that they do. Second, excluding people from Communion is not characteristic of Postmodernity in the twenty-first century. Third, including participants in biblical interpretation is attractive to a postmodern community because it is full of experimentation. Fourth, liturgy must come from the community of participants using cultural elements that make sense to the community.

Having laid the historical foundation for Communion, in the next section I will address what it is that students at St. Edward's University experienced during Communion. However, the qualitative method I used does not allow me to define an experience as the empowering actions and promissory words of Christ. Rather, experiences are explored through the students' explanations, understood in the students' own words.

This is precisely what the era of Postmodernity lends itself to—experimentation. All predetermined language and definitions are bracketed, or suspended, allowing the student to define their own experience. Knowing what students experience as they participate in Communion is important to uncovering key discoveries towards understanding how biblical truth is communicated to postmoderns through Communion during by retelling the redemptive story.

Figure 4.1. Realities of Postmodern Spirituality

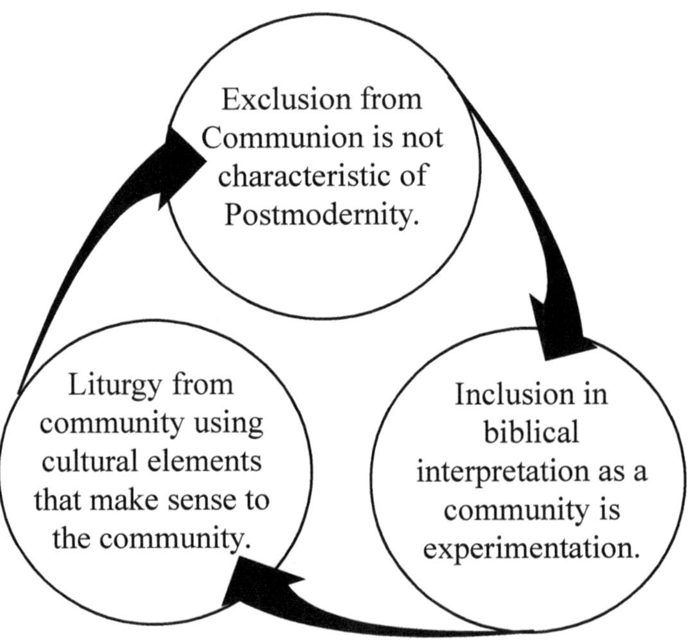

SECTION TWO

FIGURING OUT A LIVED EXPERIENCE

In this section, I will deal with what the students at **St. Edward's University** (SEU) perceived to be their experience during Communion. If you feel suspicious about this endeavor, I would not blame you. I was skeptical about perusing this undertaking myself until I began digging deeper into a recent qualitative method called **interpretative phenomenological analysts** (IPA). Do not let the lengthy academic phrases put you off. So, what does it mean?

Jonathan Smith, Paul Flowers, and Michael Larkin (2009, 3) have a simple definition of IPA: a method committed to examining how people make sense of their experiences. The method is informed by the theoretical principles of **phenomenology, hermeneutics,** and **ideography**. As such, IPA is concerned with two categories: describing a participant's lived experience in detail, and identifying the meaning associated with that experience (Smith et al 2013, 12). I hope that makes more sense.

Before describing the students' experiences, I will examine seven theological explanations about a lived experience during Communion and measure each description against the three theoretical theories of IPA. After describing the student's experiences, I will explore the commonalities and differences between the students and their experiences. Finally, I will show three initial discoveries that emerged towards understanding how biblical truth is communicated to postmoderns during Communion by retelling the redemptive story.

First, and for the sake of clarity, I will briefly explore the theoretical principles of IPA, so it really does make sense to you.

CHAPTER 5

APPROACHING A METHOD

The purpose of this chapter it to explain the basic theoretical principles involved in IPA: **phenomenology, hermeneutics, and ideography**. After a brief explanation, I describe two methods for assessing the validity and reliability of IPA. What I avoid is go into the details of my methodological design. I want you to grasp the basic function of IPA and how relative the method is in qualitative research. IPA was first used in the field of psychology but expanded to the fields of **anthropology, sociology,** and medicine. My focus is with anthropological and sociological aspects.

Phenomenological Principle: The Thing Itself

Phenomenology is a philosophical approach to studying experiences. This approach allowed me to explore a student's lived experiences in the way they occurred and in his or her own terms (Smith et al 2013, 12). Rather than attempting to locate that experience in my own predefined or overly abstract bias, focus was given on what **Edmund Husserl** (2012, 79) refers to as **"the things themselves."** Husserl argued that we can quickly fit "the things" into a predetermined category. For example, I could quickly fit an experience of Christ into a pre-determined theological frame. To prevent that forced approach I took the necessary steps to avoid a bias attitude towards an experience in order to examine it. Quite often, we are caught up in activities in the world around us and end up taking for granted experiences within that world.

So, Husserl suggested we put aside a bias attitude and adopt a phenomenological one. This attitude "involves and requires a reflexive move, as we turn our gaze from, for example, objects in the world, and direct it inward, towards our perception of those objects" (Smith, et al 2013, 2). I found that "the things themselves" came in an experience of Christ while participating in Communion, especially the objects of bread and wine. IPA helped to lead me away from the distraction, misdirection of assumption and preconception, and back to the experience as a sequence of reductions. However, an experience is always "consciousness of something – seeing is seeing something, remembering is remembering something, judging is judging something" (2013, 13). An experience and the context in which it occurred are seemingly inseparable.

> An experience and the context in which it occurred are seemingly inseparable.

A contemporary of Husserl, **Martin Heidegger** (1962, 95), helps us **see, remember,** and **judge** without separating an experience from its context. He believed that experiences and their contexts could not be meaningfully separated. Nevertheless, an experience in the physical world had an overlap with how the experiencer perceived their experience. It is within this overlap that Heidegger believed a person could make sense of what they experienced, or what they see, remember, and judge. In short, his view paints the picture of a person embedded in their own experience.

Understanding an embedded experience is helped by **Maurice Merleau-Ponty** (1962). Though he was committed to understanding experiences in the world, Merleau-Ponty went further than Heidegger by exploring the primacy of our own embeddedness in the world. He believed all human beings viewed themselves differently than everything, and everyone (1962, ix). So, interpreting an experience would come from an individual's own **embeddedness.** This is where descriptive phrases like *white priv-*

ilege, gentrification, the one percent and *white trash* come from. Each experience shapes and re-shapes an individual as they interpret the world from their own embeddedness.

Adding another layer to the theoretical principle of phenomenology is **Jean-Paul Sartre** (1948). He coined the phrase "existence comes before essence" (1948, 26). The phrase describes a conceptual process. In his view, we are always **becoming ourselves** as self is not something we discover as a pre-existing reality, but rather like an ongoing project. In short, he was concerned with what we will become and not who we are now. Ironically, Sartre called this concept "nothingness" (1948, 42). As such, an experience adds to the ongoing project of becoming someone.

Figure 5.1. Basic Picture of Phenomenology as a Theoretical Principle of IPA

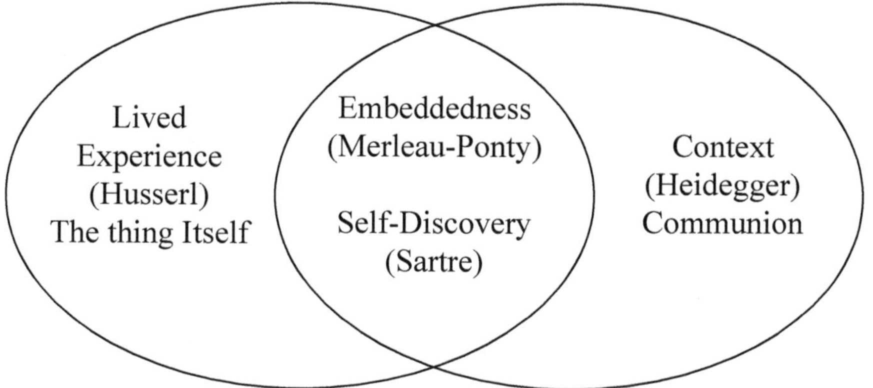

Summary Thought

Without trying to put all four philosophers in chronological order, they collectively paint a picture of what phenomenological studies involve. Husserl directs us to interpret an experience by focusing on the "thing itself," unhindered by preconceived ideas and language. Heidegger adds to this by not allowing us to separate the experiencer from the context of their experience. So, he focuses on the overlap between both. Merleau-Ponty amplifies Heidegger's idea by referring to the overlap embeddedness. Finally, Sartre takes all three ideas to show that experiences develop who we will become (see Figure 1.2). Now, to the second theoretical principle: hermeneutics.

Hermeneutical Principle: A Double Interpretation

Hermeneutics is the theory of interpretation. In its origin, hermeneutics was limited to interpreting the biblical text by asking specific questions: Who was the author? What were the intentions of the author? What were the author's influences? What did the author mean? Used in IPA, the questions change to accommodate a double hermeneutic allowing me to make sense of the student's experience, who tries to make sense of his/her encounter with Christ during Communion. This **double hermeneutic** "illustrates the dual role of the researcher as both like and unlike the participant" (Smith et al 2013, 35). On one hand, I am much like the students in our use of the skills of interpretation. On the other hand, I am unlike the students because it was the students' unique experience and not my own.

Friedrich Schleiermacher (1998, 8-9) helps us to comprehend the dual role of like and unlike a little more. He approached interpretation in terms of grammar used in written text and psychology in terms of the person writing. Viewed this way, Schleiermacher points out how someone writes and that what they write tends to reveal who the author is as a person. His approach to interpretation is intuitive to some degree because, "Every **understanding** is an utterance of **continued understanding**" (1998, 235).

So, unless I apply the theoretical principle of phenomenology to hermeneutics, I may miss what a student perceives as their experience by imposing my own bias. If the principle is applied, I can understand what a student describes explained in their own words, in their own way, with the meaning they associated with it. According to Schleiermacher, at some point the interpreter can know an author – and, in my case, a student's experience – better than they know themselves.

The idea of continued understanding is the focus of **Hans-Georg Gadamer** in his examination of historical and literary text (2013, xiv). He dialogues with the ideas of Husserl, Heidegger and Schleiermacher. So, it is necessary to keep one's gaze at the "thing itself" undistracted by the preconceived ideas of the interpreter. The gaze allows what Gadamer calls **"fore-conceptions"** or **"fore-projections"** to become replaced with conceptions and projections in the historical text (2013, 279). The gaze "breaks through what the interpreter imagines it to be" (2013, 282). As such, a lived experience can influence the interpreter and not the other way around.

It is not just a case of good listening, but intentional undistracted listening. An experience must tell the interpreter something he or she does not know at first glance. If a double hermeneutic is to take place, we cannot argue with the person attempting to interpret their own experience. Rather, we must know how to ask the right questions which involve a continued commitment towards openness (Gadamer 2013, 374-375). However, Gadamer is suspicious of Schleiermacher in that an interpreter cannot really know an author – experiencer – better than they know themselves simply because of the historical context (2013, 487). Rather than reliving the past, an interpreter can learn new things from an experience in light of the present day.

> There are always new things that can be learned from a lived experience in light of present understanding of the interpreter.

Summary Thought

Though hermeneutics is a huge subject, Schleiermacher and Gadamer paint a basic picture of a double hermeneutic where the interpreter is both like and unlike the person explaining their experience. There are always new things that can be learned from a lived experience in light of present understanding of the interpreter. If the old adage is true, that an old head cannot be put on young shoulders[37], the same applies to interpretation. The head of the interpreter must not replace the head of the experiencer (see Figure 5.2). Now, to the third theoretical principle: ideography.

Figure 5.2. Basic Picture of Hermeneutics as a Theoretical Principle of IPA

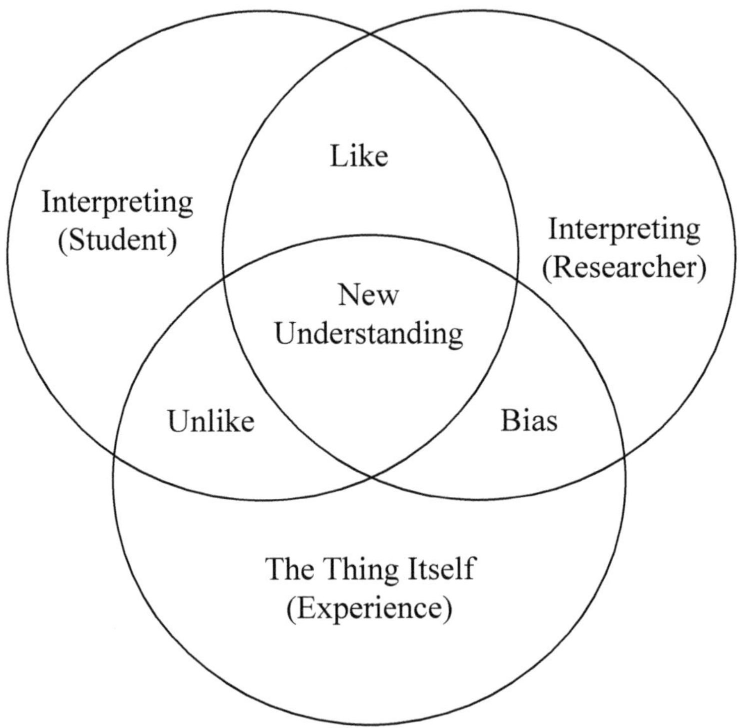

Ideographic Principle: Depth and Detail

Wilhelm Windelband (1921) introduced the terms *nomothetic* and *idiographic* into the realm of philosophical thought. The former dealt with general research laws and theories among groups, whereas the latter stresses the uniqueness of the individ-

---

[37] According to popular belief, the phrase come from an old Gaelic saying, or proverb.

ual. Idiographic studies are inductive and, as such, require fewer priori concepts because information emerges from each individual case. Ideography works as a theoretical concept for that precise reason - it deals with particulars.

So, the idiographic principle allowed me to determine how each student understood their own experience of Christ as individuals. It allowed me to be committed to the detail and depth of each student's experience rather than relying on generalizations. Nevertheless, a lived experience is not entirely focused on the individual. All experiences occur within a context. In my focus, a lived experience also has the property of Communion as a Christian celebration. No student can claim this enduring context as their own, only their experience within it.

Stephen N. Haynes and William Hayes O'Brien (2000, 110) point out that case studies can develop and implement research instruments that best fit the specific to the individuals. I had used a number of research instruments that included surveys. However, surveys provide generalizations and not definitive results. Individual cases can be grouped together for further analysis, but the individual case is vital towards that end.

Colin Robson (1993, 322) refers to this grouping as *analytic induction*. He claims that any hypothesis can be tested against each individual case. So, the hypothesis is revised to fit each case and not the other way around. It allows for reflection based in what comes to light in each case. By examining each case, good research should be able to arrive at a theoretical statement that fits all cases.

Summary Thought

Ideography paints an intricate picture specific to individual lived experiences. In many ways, it is not a painted picture at all. Rather, it is a high-definition photograph concentrating on the depth and details of an experience. Using ideography can result in isolated data unless it is combined with the theoretical principles of phenomenology and hermeneutics (see Figure 5.3).

Figure 5.3. Basic Picture of Ideography as a Theoretical Principle of IPA

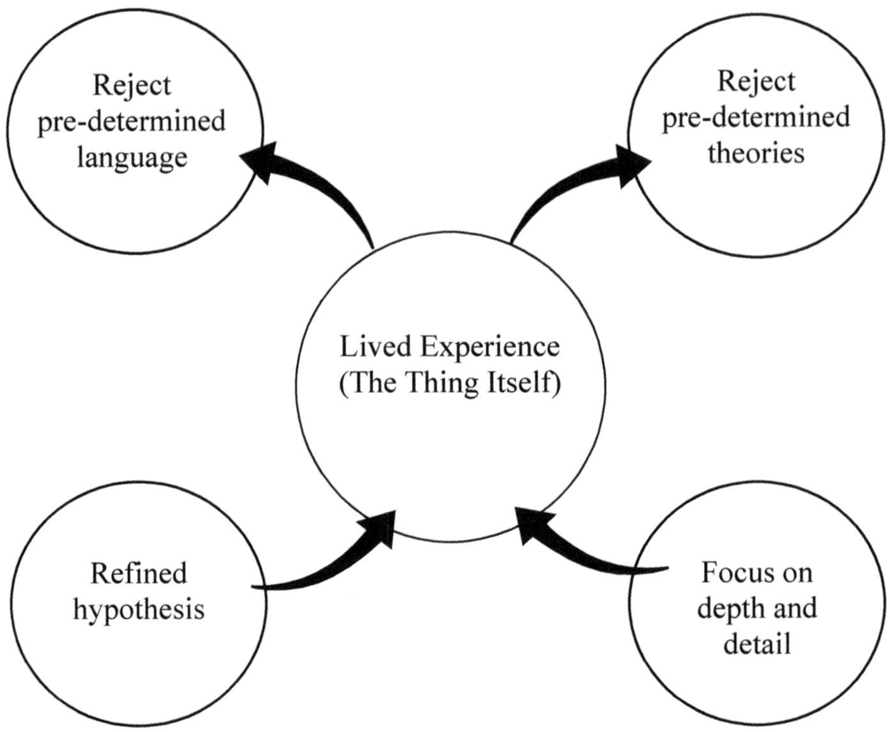

Sorting Out the Evidence

Due to the experiential nature of IPA and its relative newness, the existing literature did not limit me to a single method of working with data (Smith et al 2013, 79). However, an additional method was needed for assessing the validity and reliability of IPA. The best practices of Jonathan Smith (2011, 9-27) helped my assessment. Smith had reviewed 293 IPA studies between 1996 and 2008 in order to develop four best practices for assessing reliability and validity when working with IPA data. He concluded the research: (1) must clearly subscribe to the theoretical principles of IPA—phenomenological, hermeneutic and idiographic; (2) be sufficiently transparent so the reader can see what was done; (3) be coherent, plausible, and with an interesting analysis; and (4) must contain a sufficient sampling to show density of evidence for each theme. As far as I am concerned, research must always be **interesting.**

With these practices in mind, IPA was the best method for my own investigation consistent with the epistemological position I was pursuing: What do students at SEU perceive to be their experience when they participate in Communion? I assumed the data would tell me something about the student's experiences and how they made sense of each

> What do students at SEU perceive to be their experience when they participate in Communion?

one. The epistemological position was, therefore, a conceptual issue with a practical impact on my research. This became evident once the data was in front of me. There were many things that could have been inferred about what the students said, and the meaning associated with it.

However, in order to generate a **plausible** account of what the students experienced, the four principles described Lucy Yardley (2000, 215-228) were also applied. Those principles were: (1) sensitivity to context that continues through the analysis; (2) commitment and rigor, ensuring the student is comfortable and attending closely to what is being asked, while attention is closely given to what is being said in response; (3) transparency and coherence in the write-up of what is discovered; and (4) impact and importance on whether it tells the reader something interesting or useful. Again, as far as I am concerned, research must be interesting and **useful.**

If you initially felt suspicious that a lived experience could be discovered, and the meaning associated with it, I trust any suspicion has now turned into curiosity. In order to keep you interested, I will not bore you with the details of my methodological design because it would consume at least seventy pages. However, I will summarize by stating the design had: (1) two research instruments; (2) method for recruitment of students, tasks they performed, accomplishing tasks, and compensation; (3) staging interviews; (4) steps for data analysis; and, (5) established reliability and validity. For the sake of transparency, I assigned a gender relative pseudonym to each student named from the history of British monarchy. I had to get my **"Englishness"** in there somewhere without violating the rules for qualitative research!

Summary Thought

Assessing the validity and reliability of IPA must involve the three theoretical principles: be transparent so the reader can see what was done; be coherent, plausible, and with an interesting analysis; and contain a sufficient sampling to show density of evidence for each lived experience. In order to generate plausible data, sensitivity must be given to the context that continues through the analysis; commitment and rigor, comfortability to what is being asked, while attention is closely given to what is being said in response; transparency and coherence in the write-up of what is discovered; and impact and importance on whether it tells the reader something interesting or useful.

CONCLUDING THOUGHT

The method of IPA shows that attention must be given to **"the thing itself."** This attention could be referred to as the foreground. Because an experience cannot be separated from its context, the "thing itself" also has a background. Both foreground and background overlap with a certain **embeddedness**. One cannot exist without the other. It is within this embeddedness that a researcher is both like and unlike the person interpreting their own lived experience. This **double hermeneutic** shows there are differences and commonalities discovered in the overlap of embeddedness. Ideography reveals the **details** and **depth** of a lived experience within that overlap. Data must pass the test of three principles in order for it to be valid and reliable. That same data must pass the test of four more principles in order for it to be plausible. Because IPA suspends or brackets predetermined language, the next chapter compares seven theological explanations that have predetermined language.

CHAPTER 6

THEOLOGICAL EXPLANATIONS

My goal in this chapter is to demonstrate the necessity of suspending predetermined theological language and concepts in order to interpret a student's lived experience during Communion and the meaning they attach to it. To do that, I explore seven theological explanations of a lived experience during Communion. The exploration helps in moving towards a theoretical model of how Communion functions to communicate biblical truth through retelling the redemptive story. So, four authors offer seven theological explanations that relate to my problem: What is it that students at SEU experience when they participate in Communion?

Eschatological Experience: Tasting the Future

Evangelical theologian, Robert Webber offers four explanations in his *Ancient Future* publications. First, Webber (2008) believes **participants in Communion experience an eschatological foretaste of the Wedding Supper of the Lamb.** In his view, participants foretaste the culmination of the whole story of God in creation, incarnation, and re-creation. The story takes up residence in the participants as he or she eat the bread and drink the wine. So, Communion discloses God's story, pointing to its culmination. Admittedly, the whole redemptive story of God deals with the rescue of all creation, but to assume a participant can explain their lived experience in terms of eschatology is a false positive.

It is positive in the sense that Christ did say, "I tell you, I will not drink from this fruit of the vine from now on until that day when I drink it new with you in my Father's kingdom" (Matt. 26:29). It is false in the sense of assuming a participant knows Christ actually said this. If they did know, too much assumption is also made in knowing what Christ meant. Not only does an explanation of fore-tasting the Wedding Supper of the Lamb bypass **"the thing itself"** (Husserl 2012, 79), it brings attention to the **"fore-conceptions"** or **"fore-projections"** of eschatology without replacing them (Gadamer 2013, 279).

Another false positive is made by introducing the phrase eschatological into a lived experience regarding the time and place when the redemptive story finds its climax. Again, it is positive in the sense that Christ did say, "My Father's house has many rooms; if that were not so, would I have told you that I am going there to prepare a place for you? And if I go and prepare a place for you, I will come back and take you to be with me that you also may be where I am" (John 14:2-3). It is false in the sense that a student may have an experience that does not fit the idea of future or the end of things. Introducing eschatology can lead to **intellectual misdirection** while interpreting an experience and understanding what that experience means (Smith et al 2013, 35).

Sensational Experience: Feeling of Hope

Webber describes Maundy Thursday, Good Friday, and Saturday in the tradition of *The Great Triduum* specifically observed before Easter Sunday (2004). Though he refers to every Communion as "a little Easter" (2004, 139), the annual observance is his focus. "These three days are not to be taken lightly or to be fritted away in casual conversation, the search for pleasure, or the pursuit of business" (2004, 125). Webber suggests **participants experience the Holy Spirit revealing the truth of the resurrection to the human heart and senses through a retelling of the resurrection.** "Through sound and sight the church had passed from the stillness of death to the reverberations of life that had filled the sanctuary with praise" (Webber 2004, 139). This approach to the Communion table is attractive because it engages the heart and senses in the retelling of the redemptive story. It would not matter if a participant had previously experienced Communion at Easter or not (Sartre 1948, 26).

Maundy Thursday retells the introduction of Communion when Christ said, "This is my body…this is my blood" (Matt. 26:26-28). Good Friday retells either the Way of the Cross, the Three Hours Devotion, or the Veneration of the Cross. No matter which part is retold it is always a solemn time as participants will leave the service in silence. If there is a service on Saturday, Scripture is typically read, and prayers are gently offered. What follows on Sunday is where Webber refers to the sound and sight the church passing from the stillness of death to the reverberations of life that fill the church service with praise. By creating an annual retelling of the redemptive story, a sensational experience can be assumed. From Thursday through Sunday it can feel like death that culminates in expressive life on Sunday. If resurrection is the context on Sunday, it leaves an interpretation of a lived experience focused on "the thing itself" (Husserl 2012, 79). The challenge to a ministry practitioner is to allow for a sensational experience outside *The Great Triduum.*

Symbolic Experience: Thinking backwards and Forwards

Third, Webber (2003) points out the power of symbolic communication as participants interact with the Holy Spirit during Communion. In his view, not only are the bread and wine symbolic of the body and blood of Christ, they are also symbolic of the Christian memory of the past and the Christian anticipation of the future. In this way, **participants experience a fuller understanding of the symbolic meaning in the bread and wine.** "He [Christ] feeds us under the remembrance of his salvation" (2003, 114). The challenge for a ministry practitioner is to not over intellectualize the bread and wine of Communion.

For example, *transubstantiation* refers to the transformation of the Communion bread and wine into the body and blood of Christ after the prayer of consecration while the appearance of bread and wine remain. Also, *consubstantiation* refers to the co-existence of bread and wine with the body and blood of Christ, again after the prayer of consecration. Webber's unique word **"de-supernaturalization"** (Webber 2004, 134) refers to the logical and rational approach to the bread and wine without any expectation to become nourished on the body and blood of Christ. In many ways, the latter is only a memorial of remembrance. All three words cannot be considered **"fore-conceptions"** or **"fore-projections"** (Gadamer 2013, 279) because the bread and wine create the context for an experience (Heidegger 1962, 95). However, if a ministry practitioner makes the bread and wine "the thing itself" he or she is overintellectualizing a lived experience.

Historically, there is no evidence in the Didache or the works of **Justin Martyr,** who quoted it, to how God made his presence known among Communion participants in the early church. Martyr does not refer to transubstantiation, consubstantiation, or any other theory of how Christ is made present. "It is a simple statement – Jesus is here in a real presence nourishing us in the faith as we feed on the bread and wine" (Webber 2003, 114). If a participant believes Christ is present, a symbolic experience is general enough to accommodate a participant's explanation of their lived experience that Christ was present without predetermining the symbol. Again, Webber's observation is attractive as long as the presence of Christ is not **overintellectualized.**

Healing Experience: Making a Full Recovery

Pointing out that many young Christians are attending churches where Communion is celebrated every Sunday, Webber (1999) believes young **people experience sacramental healing**. When the bread and wine are received by faith, healing is made available. "For them, worship has broken through the lifeless nature of what, for some may have been an empty form and has opened them to the joy and healing that come from the gracious and active presence of Christ in the sacrament" (1999, 111).

A healing experience during Communion is not a guarantee, but the redemptive story does reveal that the sacrifice of Christ on the cross, his burial, and his resurrection open the way for someone to be healed. The guarantee is that Christ heals and saves. It sounds a little predictive and borders on predetermined language and concepts. It is easy to say that Christ heals all forms of sickness and disease (Matt. 4:23). It is just as easy to say that Christ saves us from sin and death (Eph. 2). To say these things assumes that a student understands the biblical text. What if a student was convicted by the Holy Spirit about reconciling a broken relationship that caused deep hurt? A lived experience is initially a painful one before it becomes a healing one.

I like what Webber had to say to his students who sought out his counsel when they felt pain or hurt: "Go to the Table of the Lord just as fast as you can, because it is there that God can and does touch his people in a healing way" (Webber 1999, 111). As a ministry practitioner, I would champion Webber's counsel to his students, but as a researcher I have to say that **"the thing itself"** is probably the pain and hurt (Husserl 2012, 79). Admittedly, a lived experience of pain and hurt is not an end in itself but determining an experience and its meaning is what the method of IPA strives for. For example, in my introduction I wrote about Isabel.

> What I am suggesting throughout this book is that people can experience Christ during Communion. It is this experience that amplifies biblical truth.

Though her pain was obvious to all in church, "the thing itself" was her healing. I am not suggesting that a ministry practitioner avoids communicating truth found in the death, burial, and resurrection of Christ. What I am suggesting throughout this book is that people can experience Christ during Communion. It is this experience that amplifies biblical truth.

Dramatized Experience: Act I, II, and III

Similar to Webber, Dominican Friar Timothy Radcliffe (2009) also offers an explanation of a lived experience. He believes **participants experience faith, hope, and love as three primary acts in the drama the redemptive story retold during Communion** (2009, 7). In act one, participants experience their faith renewed as they listen to Scriptures being read reaffirming Christian beliefs; in act two, hope is experienced as participants repeat the words of Christ (Matt. 26:26-28) remembering what He has done; and, in act three, when the Lord's Prayer is repeated, participants experience the love of God, preparing them to go into the world as living witnesses to Christ's resurrected life. According to Radcliff, all three acts are successive in the experience of the participant.

The fact that Radcliffe refers to celebrating Communion as a drama is attractive in the sense that the redemptive story is the retelling of all human experiences (2009, 7). Communion is also the context in which a lived experience occurs (Heidegger 1962, 95). However, labeling the three acts as faith, hope, and love is too predictive unless they become categories for the **depth** and **detail** of a lived experience (Windelband 1921). Radcliffe appears to do this. He frames Communion as a drama in which a participant may encounter Christ in any of their human experiences. He points out that an experience during Communion is emotional, because emotions are human (2009, 5). Left within this frame, the ideographic principle can reveal any human experience within the three dramatized acts of faith, hope, and love.

Due to the fact that Communion is a Christian celebration, and that Christ has provided all that we need for life (2 Peter 1:3), the context allows for the three positive experiences of faith, hope, and love. However, the three acts must not interfere with the theoretical principle of hermeneutics (Smith et al 2013, 35). If sorrow, depression, sadness, isolation, or desperation are experienced by the participant during Communion, surely the ideographic principle navigates these emotions to the positive category of faith, hope, or love? Anything else ignores the fact that a participant may be experiencing a negative human emotion.

Socialized Experience: Getting Along Together

Anglican vicar Julie Gittoes (2013, 45-46) identifies the social and political impact of "your kingdom come" (Matt. 6:10) in the experience of **participants during Communion and ethical behavior in relation to others**. Her explanation deals with the outcome of a lived experience as it relates to a participant's daily life accommodating what Schleiermacher identified in the hermeneutical principle. However, because Gittoes specifically frames that outcome as social and political, she will miss **"the thing itself"** (Hurssel 2012, 79).

Gittoes believes that prayer during the Communion provides a springboard for active mission in social and political fields. "Indeed, the Eucharist [Communion] cannot be fully understood without reference to its social significance" (Gittoes 2013, 46). Undoubtedly, the Kingdom of God is not a resemblance of any kingdom in this world, past, present, or future. So, an encounter with Christ will impact an individual's work in the social and political fields. However, making this primary claim limits a lived experience during Communion to this context: God's mission to the local community within a social and political field. Surely activity in God's mission is a **"fore-conception"** or **"fore-projection"** (Gadamer 2013, 279)?

What if a participant experiences Christ in a healing way, or a symbolic or sensational way as Webber suggests? In what way are these experiences directly connected with social or political significance? Webber's explanations do provide evidence to be a witness of Christ in the world which could be interpreted as God's mission field (Acts 1:8). Nevertheless, Gittoes does not allow for the depth and details of a lived experience (Windelband 1921), or the room for a participant to know more about **themselves** (Sartre 1948, 26).

Though Gittoes makes a good case for a relationship between an experience during Communion and the Kingdom of God as it relates to social and political issues, her case is also a classic example of imposing bias into what *should* be experienced. In many ways Gittoes is a throwback to the Middle Ages, albeit a gentle and harmless one. There is, however, a definite social aspect to the spirituality of postmoderns as we have seen in the first section of this book. That aspect emerges in community but not as a social issue.

Paradoxical Experience: Unlimited Limitation

Similar to Webber (2008, 146), professor of religion Laura Hartman (2008, 159) identifies an experience of eschatological hope or, as she precisely puts it, "God's fondest wish for the future." In Hartman's view, a **participant in Communion experiences the paradox of death to life, and limitation to abundance, as they receive the bread and wine.** A paradoxical experience envisions the future fulfillment that God intends for the whole world as resembling a feast (Hartman 2001, 160).

She recognizes that a paradoxical experience can occur resembling a feast during Communion if the participant has been fasting. This would require a measure of preparation and discipline in anticipation of a paradoxical experience: hunger to nourishment. Suggesting the paradox of fast and feast does not appear to disregard any of the theoretical principles in IPA because it is the context of Communion (Heidegger 1962, 95). Fasting before receiving the bread and wine of Communion prepares a participant for the possibility of a sensational experience (Webber 2004, 139). However, naming an experience as eschatological goes against the **hermeneutical** principle (Gadamer 2013, 279).

> The cultural/biblical method explains what ought to be experienced, not necessarily what was being experienced.

Hartman's explanation about the future is attractive, I would dare to say, especially in the present day. There are unprecedented peaceful (and violent) protests, novels, movies, TV shows, and scholarly articles that address the state of the world today. In many ways, all of these genres fit an apocalyptic context that places people in one of two groups: fix the world or belief in a better world to come. It is the latter that makes Hartman's explanation attractive.

Summary Thought

All four authors identify and interpret an experience during Communion and its meaning by examining cultural trends in the light of biblical text. The cultural/biblical method explains what ought to be experienced, not necessarily what was being experienced. Even Webber's explanation of the Holy Spirit revealing truth through sensation, and his explanation of sacramental healing, lacked a qualitative approach interacting with participants and their experiences. The authors assume too much in advance. Though all four explanations have a measure of openness to them, they assume what *ought* to be experienced at the cost of other lived experiences (see Figure 6.1).

Figure 6.1. Imposing What Ought to be Experienced

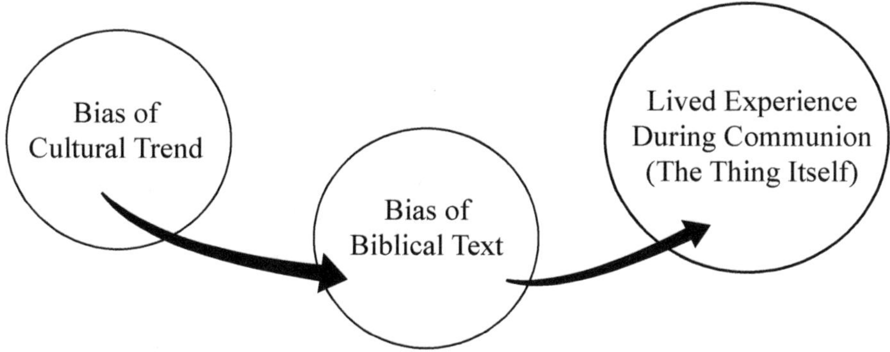

CONCLUDING THOUGHT

IPA differs from this cultural/biblical approach in that it is qualitative and not theological. IPA explores an experience through the participant's explanation and researcher's interpretation as a double hermeneutic; whereas a cultural/biblical approach explores a religious belief system about God, or ultimate reality, within culture. The qualitative method of IPA helped me discover what students at SEU experience when they participated in Communion and the meaning associated with it in their own words. IPA also gave me insights into how students think about their own pursuit of spirituality as participants in the celebration. In the next chapter, I show what the students *actually* experienced and the meaning *they* associated with it.

CHAPTER 7

EIGHT LIVED EXPERIENCES

Eight specific experiences were discovered: (1) presence, (2) ceremony, (3) belief, (4) community, (5) remembering, (6) family, (7) completeness, and (8) imagination. Each experience had a corresponding theme highlighting the meaning associated with a lived experience. In order to illustrate the meaning, I use verbatim extracts showing what immediately came to mind as each student began interpreting the detail and depth of their experiences. What follows are simple highlights from lengthy transcripts. So, bear in mind two important things as you read this chapter. First, you are only reading highlights. Second, each extract is cited precisely, so the reading does appear elementary as a necessary part of focusing on "the thing itself." I point out whether my questions and the student's answers were made in terms of narrative, structural, contrasting, evaluating, feeling, circular, comparative, probing, picturing, sensing, or reflective.

> "I believe that my God is female, nurturing, caring completely forgiving, no matter how wrong you can be she'll always be there for you; she's always the rock that you need" (Sophia).

Presence: Identifying God's Presence in Relation to Self

The first lived experience established a distinct sense of **Presence** identified as God by each student. In each case, the **students described how they felt** God's presence. For example, Sophia and Victoria both described Presence in terms of a female God. "I believe that my God is female, nurturing, caring completely forgiving, no matter how wrong you can be she'll always be there for you; she's always the rock that you need" (Sophia). "I picture him [God] as a woman, and this is like my mom or my aunt" (Victoria).

For Sophia and Victoria, God's presence aroused maternal feelings. For example, "I feel calm, more at ease" (Sophia) and "how warm my soul feels" (Victoria). In the case of Samuel, he described Presence in terms of an approachable father, "like I was sitting down with my dad, like right before my first communion." While Presence is approachable for Samuel, it is "really nerve wracking." I followed his evaluating response with a probing question, drawing out of Samuel a defensive rhetorical question: "Do you really want to go deep into it?" William described Presence as God in a circular response, "he [God] is only present when we call him." William went further than a descriptive and circular response using a combination of feeling and evaluating comments stating it was "warming to feel something."

Each student distinctly felt God's presence at different stages of Communion. This was not limited to a particular stage during the celebration. Sophia and Victoria connected the meaning of Presence with the maternal characteristics of a loving mother or aunt. For Samuel, the paternal characteristics of a disciplined father were tied with the meaning of Presence. William connected the meaning of Presence in an act of invocation with personal benefits outside any maternal or paternal feeling.

Ceremony: Personal Understanding of Ceremony

The second lived experience that emerged was a form of Ceremony. Each student was asked to tell me about his or her experience the first time they participated in Communion. All students gave a reflective response recalling their first Communion after receiving educational instruction from their Sunday school teachers - or parents, in the case of William. "It didn't have a purpose for me when I was little" (Sophia). "At first I was like, I don't get it" (Victoria). "I remember being very nervous the first time I ever had my first communion even though I did not really understand it all" (Samuel). "I didn't even think about what we are doing" (William). Despite the educational efforts of teachers or parents, each student **recalled a lack of understanding** Communion as Ceremony when they first participated in the bread and wine.

Each student was then asked to tell me about how they came to want to celebrate Communion. Sophia and William gave a contrasting answer to their first experience of Ceremony. "I actually believe in it, and I believe it's Jesus Christ, and I'm receiving" (Sophia). "I don't think I understood it until I became a believer myself and accepted Christ as being my savior when I was a teenager" (William). When celebrating Communion today, Sophia and William demonstrate a definite understanding, unlike the first time they received the bread and wine.

In both cases each student needed more than educational instruction to understand Communion as Ceremony. They needed a personal experience of Christ. For example, Sophia's current understanding is seen in her structured and sensitive comment, "leaving my spot, coming closer to the altar, coming closer to this holier place, and taking Jesus Christ." William's current understanding is also seen in his reflective and evaluative comment, "reflective time to really think if I haven't spoken to Christ and to open up directly to him."

After asking the same question, Victoria made a sensitive comment about her current understanding of Communion as Ceremony, "My expectation is to feel closer to God—Jesus—because, you know, I am partaking of Him with everyone, with everyone else, so it's like sharing a meal with everyone." From her comments, Victoria made a picturing remark, "You are kind of shy, and you understand that this expectation is like someone's hand you kiss." Again, Victoria needed more than educational instruction to understand Communion as Ceremony. She needed to feel the affectionate love of Christ in her experience, unlike the first time she received the bread and wine.

Samuel made no sensitive comments. In contrast, he made a structured comment demonstrating no further understanding of Communion as Ceremony since his first Communion, "It's just sort of one of those extra things that I do." Reinforcing his structured comment, Samuel made an evaluative statement, "There's not really a personal effect that it really does have on me." Consequently, it appears that Samuel may not have had an encounter with Christ like Sophia, William, or Victoria in order to understand Communion as Ceremony. Also, he does not indicate any current expectation of it.

Sophia and William associate the meaning of Ceremony with a personal encounter with Christ outside of the instruction they received. Such encounters led to purposeful and intentional thought during Communion as Ceremony. Similarly, Victoria associates the meaning of Ceremony with a personal expectation to encounter Christ; again, outside of the instruction she received. This led to affectionate imagery within Ceremony. In all three cases, understanding the meaning of Communion did not come through instruction about receiving the bread and wine as Ceremony. It came through participation in it. In contrast to the other three students, Samuel does not state any personal encounter with Christ or expectation of affecting a continued lack of understanding of Communion as Ceremony.

Belief: Relationship to the Church

The third lived experience involved Belief. Sophia, Victoria, and Samuel received formal education about Communion in church Sunday schools. William received informal education from his parents. Despite educational efforts, all four students developed their own unique beliefs determined by their individual experiences indicating that formal and informal education did not develop meaning for them. Education that failed to form meaning became evident by going further than a descriptive response. A variety of reflective and evaluative responses were given to probing questions about their unique beliefs. "I like to separate my beliefs from the church" (Sophia). "I identify as a Catholic, but that doesn't mean that I am limiting my interpretation of God" (Victoria). "We don't have any proof that Communion is the body and blood of Christ, and we don't have any proof about any of this really" (Samuel). "I believe these things [bread and wine] deserve my attention because they are so important as a Christian" (William).

In each response to a probing question about Belief, students elaborated on their beliefs. For example, regarding Sophia's separation of Belief from the church, "I don't like that an organization can tell you that God, Jesus, a deity who is all loving, cannot love you, because you have a certain preference on who you love."[38] Regarding Victoria's inclusive beliefs, "We would go from one church to the other church, and I'd see the same comparisons, like these are the same kinds of people." Regarding Samuel's exclusive beliefs, "I feel like a lot of what the church says, you know, makes a lot of people feel unwelcome if they're not part of it to start with." Regarding William's belief, on time to contemplate, "I've been in several churches, and it's easy for church to put time restrictions on when you physically take the bread or the wine."

Interestingly, **a personal story lay behind their beliefs.** For example, what came to mind for Sophia was the thought of going to college, "It was when I came out to college that I kind of discovered more of my faith." After the death of her brother, Victoria remembered being disillusioned regarding her mother in the Catholic Church: "She kind of tried to lean on the Catholic Church, but they weren't really there for her." Unlike Sophia, Samuel reflected on beginning to lose the faith he had on his first day on campus at SEU: "Going to college, you know, there are definitely less times we end up going to church." What came to mind for William was emotional times of worship at church youth camps: "You're driven by emotion, and you are constantly having times of worship in services. You know, it just brought tears every service."

---

[38] Sophia was referring to students who are gay, lesbian, bisexual, or transgender.

Despite formal and informal education about what they had been taught about Communion, all four students elaborated on their beliefs, personal stories of faith, disillusionment, loss of faith, and emotional worship as the background for what they believed separate from the church. Formal or informal education from the church **failed to form meaning.**

Community: View of Self in Relation to Group

The fourth lived experience was **Community**, viewed by each student through his or her individual relationship to it. Answers came from various questions in my interview. For example, "When you celebrate Communion, how is the church service organized?" "Who serves the bread and wine during Communion, and how do they do it?" "How do you feel at various stages during Communion?"

"Seeing all these people participate in the same thing I think really meant something to me even from the early age" (William).

Sophia and William both described their relationship from within a Community that gathered to celebrate Communion. Both recognized the **sameness of faith and practice** within the group. For example, "It's something that a lot, a large group of us are doing together. All of us are believing in the same faith, and we're taking the same communion out of the same dishes and receiving Jesus Christ together" (Sophia). "Seeing all these people participate in the same thing I think really meant something to me even from the early age" (William).

While recognizing sameness within the group, Sophia and William distinctly focus on themselves during Communion, rather than the group. "I feel as though I experience it a little bit more individually for myself, because when I'm receiving it, I typically don't think, 'Oh look at all of us coming together and doing this.' I typically think of myself" (Sophia). "I go through my own ritual still listening to what's being said in the front. We all take it in unison, but I might not be ready to do that, so I take my time" (William).

Victoria and Samuel both described a Community that gathered for Communion from the opposite standpoint to Sophia and William. Their view was from outside the group. "It's kind of different because in Mexico I feel like the spiritual community is a lot stronger than it is here [SEU]" (Victoria). Talking about coming together as a Community of participants in Communion, Samuel commented, "It just seemed like another step, and not necessarily into anything larger." Though Victoria and Samuel are invited into the community to celebrate Communion, both preferred to **remain outside the group.**

For example, Victoria makes a clear distinction between communities who celebrate Communion at SEU and her home church in Mexico: "This is important to us [in Mexico]; this is the cornerstone of our foundation, whereas it is not the same here [SEU]." Though Samuel considers himself an outsider, he places very little value on being part of a Community to celebrate Communion: "I just feel like I am, you know, an outsider and then not necessarily an integral part to it really."

> "I just feel like I am, you know, an outsider and then not necessarily an integral part to it really."

In response to my questions, Sophia and William associate the meaning of a Community that gathers for Communion with sameness of faith and practice while remaining individually focused during the celebration. Victoria and Samuel attach the meaning of a Community that celebrates Communion at SEU as an inviting group, preferring to remain outside of it.

Remembering: Triggers of Remembrance

The fifth lived experience involved **Remembering**. All students were asked if anything specific came to mind while seeing the bread and wine: "How would you regularly remember Christ if there was no Communion?" All four students described the bread and wine as elements that **triggered past memories** of participating in the celebration. For example, when Sophia sees the bread and wine, she recalled the details of an altar cloth from childhood in Beaumont, Texas, using a combination of reflective and picturing comments:

"I picture in my mind...the church that I was in in Beaumont, which we were members of it for about almost ten years, ten years plus. On the altar there's this giant cloth with a picture of a lamb and bread and wine and, like, rays coming from the lamb. Every time I take it [bread and wine] the imagery comes back to me, so that's what I remember. I see communion as this giant green cloth and I go to it, and I think it symbolizes Jesus, you know, being our holy lamb, or the shepherd."

Likewise, Victoria recalls a process of farming while living in her agricultural community in Mexico. That process also triggers memories of Communion classes as a child on the sacramental nature of the bread, also using a combination of reflective and picturing comments:

"When I see the bread, I remember that it's Kosher, and I think about Jewish farms where they make it, and then I start thinking about the process of how they make the bread and how detailed it must be, because I remember learning that it can't be touched, it can't fall; like, it's wafers, but at this moment [before consecration], it's not. But I'm thinking about all that and then it goes back to the fact it still came from the ground, and it still came from earth, so it did still come from God. So, either way, this is a gift from God, or it is God."

In contrast, when Samuel was asked about a consistent recollection, his response was evaluative and reflecting. "Nothing really, I mean, I, as far as like a personal experience that I've had like with the bread and the wine, other than with the first communion the first time I ever had Communion like as a kid, I don't really think there's a personal effect that it really does have on me." After further probing questions, Samuel made a structured response, "I remember they [church] taught you this—you have to be—you have to be very respectful when you're receiving it."

William recalls the message of Communion, but also finds the bread and wine distracting. "There is time I find myself looking at the cup in my hands and the cracker [bread]. I don't think it's those physical things I'm thinking about. I think it's more just me trying to concentrate on something else" (William). When asked a probing question about what he was concentrating on, bread and wine are dismissed as "those things":

> "I think actually sometimes it can be a little bit more distracting taking those things. I guess it's just me thinking about it, of this physical being, this is Jesus, this is His blood, this is His body. I think those can be distracting for what the real message is. I start thinking about those as the physical things. I don't think it helps remind me."

Fascinatingly, Sophia and Victoria link the meaning of Remembering with images from their childhood that tell a story when pieced together. In a similar fashion, Samuel also ties the meaning of Remembering with connection to his childhood. However, his consistent recollection is a respectful performance of Communion. William associates the meaning of Remembering with the message of Communion while the bread and wine do not help him remember.

Family: Traditions

The sixth lived experience listed was **Family**. The common thread found in all the stories of each student involves the **parents' tradition** for receiving the bread and wine of Communion. I found the students went routinely to church as children with their families, all were given instruction about Communion, and all began following their parents' tradition. For example,

"I was fulfilling something from my mom or my family, and I was fulfilling Communion as something I had to do" (Sophia). "Because she [mom] would take me to a Protestant church, and then, the same day, we would go to another church on Sunday. Not fun" (Victoria). "But yeah, when I went with my family, they all get up for Communion. I went with them" (Samuel). "I guess my parents made the decision. It was just sort of some way my parents have always done it. So, I didn't even think about what we are doing" (William).

At some point, Sophia, Victoria, and William adopted their parents' Communion tradition as a personal practice of their own. Again, from the question in my interview—"Tell me how you came to want to celebrate the Communion?"—all three came to have a personal relationship with God beyond a Family tradition. This was in direct response to my question: "Can you tell me how you came to want to celebrate Communion?" For instance, Sophia remarked, "I have this relationship with Jesus; I have a special relationship with my deity;" and, "my relationship with God."

Victoria remarked, "Relationship takes work, work, and constant work. I've always tried to make the effort to go to church every Sunday, but it is only a fraction of the effort that I think I'm doing that is in some way thanking God who is always watching and protecting over me." William went further than Sophia and Victoria, explaining the process of beginning a relationship with God for himself, "I became a believer myself and accepted Christ for myself as being my Savior when I was a teenager."

In contrast to the other three students, Samuel gave no indication he had a personal relationship with God. In a reflective answer to a probing question, Samuel remarked, "I learned a lot about Communion and a lot about religion itself, but, like, it was not anything of my own accord, you know. It was something that was expected of me." When asked a more in-depth probing question about participating in Communion of his own accord, Samuel remarked, "No, it's my parents still."

In direct response to my questions, all four students related the **meaning of Communion from their adopted Family traditions.** However, Sophia, Victoria, and William also associate the meaning of Family with a personal practice of their own through a relationship with God.

Completeness: The Complete Self

The seventh lived experience that emerged was Completeness. All four students described themselves in terms of **incomplete and complete individuals.** Their responses came from asking, "How do you feel at various stages of Communion?" and follow-up questions. What made each student move from a state of incompleteness to completeness was a connection with Christ. For example, referring to Christ as her deity, Sophia remarked, "You feel incomplete until you have your deity with you." In Victoria's case, Completeness was a connection to Christ in her home church in Mexico, "Geography shouldn't play a part in my connection with Christ, I guess. But it does to me because, I think, I am complete." In a non-personalized fashion, Samuel acknowledged Christ could make a person feel complete, "He [Christ] suffered, so maybe He understands that we're all suffering in some -- maybe not the exact same way for sure, you know. We're all suffering in our own way, so maybe He recognizes that, and He then thinks of us to make us complete." On the process of connecting to Christ during Communion to feel Complete, William remarked, "It's just the whole act of doing it. Just the whole act of concentration on Christ is what is really effective in completeness."

Using follow-up probing questions on Completeness through connecting with Christ, each student highlighted the importance of Communion in a variety of descriptive, narrative, evaluative, comparative, reflective, feeling, and sensitive responses. For example, Sophia remarked, "I feel more complete, I guess, when taking it." Commenting on Communion at Easter, Victoria said, "I feel like that if you only go once a year, you kind of lose your completeness."

Despite depersonalizing a connection to Christ, Samuel admitted the necessity of celebrating Communion more than once a year at Easter, "If the Eucharist [Communion] itself is completely taken out, I think that's one of the most important parts of feeling complete." Reflecting on the frequency of celebrating Communion, William confessed, "I just want to change so badly in that moment because I felt like I'm kind of short since last time we did it." When asked a probing question about what he meant by "short," William responded, "By 'short' I mean incomplete. I think it is important for me to feel in some way."

> students also connect the meaning of Completeness to the frequency of celebrating Communion more than once a year at Easter.

Sophia, Victoria, Samuel, and William describe the meaning of Completeness in contrast to incompleteness determined by a connection to Christ while celebrating the Communion. All four students also connect the meaning of Completeness to the frequency of celebrating Communion more than once a year at Easter.

Imagination: Communicating with Christ

The final lived experience was Imagination. Though similar to Completeness, in that students sensed Christ, Imagination went further than sensing. In fact, Imagination presented itself as an overarching lived experience to accommodate the seven other experiences. Each student imaginatively described **communication directly with Christ before or during Communion**. Again, answers were given to my questions: "How do you feel at various stages during Communion?" In each case, there is no doubt that Christ communicated to them, as they communicated with Christ, explained by using their own imaginations.

For example, Sophia has to sense Christ in the church in order to communicate with Him, "I can tell you when I enter a church that I do sense Jesus." After sensing Christ, Sophia was able to hear an inner voice, "I feel like there is someone telling me to keep going." Victoria described three imaginative worlds: earth, middle sphere, and heaven. In the first world, she cannot communicate with Christ, "There are so many pressures that are put on us from, like, the earthly world." In response to a probing question about the pressures, Victoria remarked, "Pressures surround me from, like, my culture, my family, my surroundings." The second world was described as a shape that Victoria visits in her mind to communicate with Christ, "Like, a spiritual world. It's this sphere in the middle that as an earthly person I can go to with my mind." After a probing question about the sphere in the middle, Victoria explained it was a place to Imagine heaven representing the third world, "Where we are going."

In Samuel's case, he becomes consciously aware that Christ is present during Communion and watching him, "He sees that I am thinking of His suffering, and so He feels, 'Well, don't worry.'" When asked a probing question about why God would tell him not to worry, Samuel responded, "We're all suffering in our own way." William invests time communicating with Christ every day, confessing, "I become stagnant in some way if I have not talked to Christ throughout the day." However, "Having communion brings me back." In response to a probing question about what he is brought back to, William responded, "Back to Christian life."

Although the meaning of Imagination is communicating with Christ, the way communication takes place is different for each student. Sophia had to sense Christ before she could hear Him; Victoria had to mentally go to a sphere-shaped middle world; Samuel had to become conscious that Christ was watching him; and William had to communicate every day in order to not feel stagnant.

Summary Thought

Having followed the phenomenological, hermeneutical, and ideographic principles of IPA set out by Smith (2011, 9-27), the results were sufficiently transparent, coherent, plausible, and analytically interesting within a sample group of four SEU students to show the density of evidence for the three theoretical principles of IPA. By following the four epistemological principles set out by Yardley (2000, 215-228), the results were sensitive to the students' context, showed commitment and rigor from the students and myself as the researcher, were coherent in the way the results were written up, and were important towards theory development.

Eight distinct lived experiences were discovered.

In the following chapter, the experiences of Sophia, Victoria, Samuel, and William are summarized, noting the commonalities and differences in the meanings derived from the eight lived experiences that represent what the students experienced when they participated in the celebration of Communion.

CHAPTER 8

COMMONALITIES AND DIFFERENCES

All four students associate an identical meaning in two of the eight experiences. First, in the experience Belief, formal or informal education that each student received as a child failed to form meaning. Rather, meaning was formed in their personal stories. Admittedly, each story was different. For example, Sophia and Samuel told the story of moving to college. Sophia discovered faith whereas Samuel lost faith. Victoria told the story of her brother's death and how she became disillusioned with the church. William told the story of youth camps where his beliefs were discovered and formed during emotional worship. Though each story contains different elements, the commonality found in each story is that their formal education from the church **failed to form meaning.**

Second, in the experience of Completeness, an identical meaning was associated from all four students. They felt incomplete or complete determined by a connection to Christ that related to the frequency of celebrating Communion. The presence of Christ made the students feel Complete. However, the details are different. In order to feel Complete, three of the four students personalized their connection to Christ. Sophia felt that her deity (Christ) was with her each time she celebrated Communion, Victoria felt that Christ was more with her in a Mexican celebration, and William felt the presence of Christ as he concentrated on Him during Communion.

Although Samuel acknowledged the presence of Christ was important for him to feel complete in his infrequent celebration Communion, his remarks came across in a non-personalized fashion. Though the details in each student's connection to Christ are different, the commonality in the meaning associated with the experience of Completeness was determined by their **sense of connection to Christ** during Communion.

Six other commonalities are seen in the experiences of the students, but unlike the experience of Belief and Completeness, all four students did not associate the same meaning. This is understandable as meaning was not derived from the education the students received from the church but individually in their personal stories.

First, all four students were able to sense the Presence of God. Though they identify the experience of Presence with God, the meaning they associate with it is not the same. The meaning that Sophia and Victoria associate with their experience comes from feeling the maternal nurturing influence of their respective mothers. In their view, God is female. Similarly, the meaning Samuel associates with his experience is the feeling of paternal discipline represented in his father's influence. The meaning that William associates with his experience is different than the other three students. For William, meaning is an act of invocation in order to feel he can receive personal spiritual benefits from God. While the students' perception of God was different, the commonality between all four was their **ability to sense the Presence of God.**

Second, a commonality was also seen in the experience of Ceremony in three of the four students. Sophia, Victoria, and William had a desire to actually encounter Christ. Samuel did not. Sophia and William associated their experience of Ceremony with sensing a personal encounter with Christ, creating ceremonial purpose and intent to experience Him. Prior to personally encountering Christ in a personal relationship, there was no purpose to Communion for Sophia or William. Also, there was no intent in receiving the bread and wine until they encountered Christ. Now Sophia has a clear intent regarding the bread and wine, "I believe it is Jesus Christ I am receiving." The same intent was seen with William, "I receive Christ." They want to celebrate Communion, and also want to encounter Christ represented in the bread and wine.

A difference is seen in the experience of Ceremony with Victoria and Samuel. Victoria also wants to celebrate Communion, but she associates her experience of Ceremony with an internal performance in light of her family traditions noted as celebrating "with everyone else so it's like sharing a meal with everyone." Victoria wants to internally encounter Christ. Her heart is in it. In contrast to Victoria's internal performance, Samuel associates his experience of Ceremony with an external performance. He only wants to celebrate Communion when his family is present as "sort of one of those extra things I do." The commonality in the experience of Ceremony is a **desire to encounter Christ.** The only difference is seen in Samuel who does not appear to have any desire.

Third, all four students have a desire to maintain their individuality. However, a different commonality is seen in the experience of Community between Victoria and Samuel, and Sophia and William. Victoria and Samuel associate the meaning of their experience with an inviting group but choose to remain outside the group for different reasons. Victoria remarks that "faith [in Mexico] is a lot stronger than it is here [SEU Chapel]" (P1:11-12). Samuel remarks, "I just feel like, you know, an outsider and then not necessarily an integral part of it." Mexico, as opposed to the SEU, and placing little or no value on Community that gather for Communion are the differing reasons why Victoria and Samuel choose to remain outside the group.

A different commonality is seen in the experience of Sophia and William. They associate the sameness of faith and practice with the group while wanting to remain individual for similar reasons. Sophia remarks, "I typically think of myself," and William, "I might not be ready [to eat the bread and drink the wine]." While there are two commonalities for different reasons, what is common in the experience of all four students is their desire to **maintain their individuality.**

Fourth, in the experience of Remembering, the commonality between three of the four students is that past **memories are triggered** when they see the bread and wine. What came to mind for Sophia and Victoria were specific images recalled from their childhood when they celebrated Communion. In each case, those images also told a story. Different than Sophia and Victoria, Samuel recalled his respectful performance during Communion when he was a child. Different again was William's recall of messages he heard from the person serving the bread and wine. However, it was the messages that triggered what came to his mind and not the bread and wine. He remarks, "I think those [bread and wine] can be distracting." For Sophia, Victoria, and Samuel, the commonality was past memories from their childhood that came to mind when they saw the bread and wine. The outlier was William who recalled Communion messages unrelated to seeing the bread and wine.

Fifth, Sophia, Victoria, and William all had something in common in their experience of Family. Each one had adopted the **tradition of their parents** as young adults. "I was fulfilling the Eucharist [Communion] as something I had to do" (Sophia); "I went with them [family] (Victoria); and "My parents have always done it…I didn't even think about what we were doing" (William). Added to that adoption was a personal encounter with Christ that made Communion a personal ceremony for each one of them.

Without sensing Christ in their lives, Communion would remain a mere adoption of their family tradition. This was evident in the meaning Samuel associated with his experience. When asked about any desire to celebrate Communion, Samuel commented, "No, it's my parents still." Though he adopted the tradition of his parents by continuing to accompany them in a celebration of Communion, he did not claim to have any personal encounter with Christ. He did not sense or feel that Christ was in his life. This probably accounts for his lack of desire to celebrate Communion.

A commonality was seen in all four of the students' experiences of Imagination. They consciously **communicated with Christ.** For example, during Communion, Sophia had to sense Christ before she could hear Him; Victoria had to feel she was transported in her mind to a sphere-shaped world to hear Christ; Samuel was very conscious that Christ was watching him as he participated in Communion, and William had to feel stagnant in order to hear Christ communicate to him. All the students had an ability to communicate with Christ outside of the five senses.

Summary Thought

Common among all the students' experiences of Presence, Ceremony, Belief, Community, Remembering, Family, Completeness, and Imagination is that each of them had to sense, or feel, something for their lived experiences during Communion to have meaning. Such sensing, or feeling, stands in contrast to the education each student received as a child from the church regarding Communion. By identifying the commonalities, a typical experience of a student at SEU who participates in Communion can be summarized (see Figure 8.1).

Table 8.1. Summary of Typical Experiences and Commonalities

Experience	Meaning
Presence	Able to sense God's presence
Ceremony	Desire to encounter Christ
Belief	Formal or informal education from the church failed to form meaning
Community	Desire to maintain individuality
Remembering	Past memories come to mind
Family	Adoption of parents' tradition
Completeness	Completeness when connected to Christ
Imagination	Varying degrees of imagination to communicate with Christ

Initial Discoveries

At the beginning of this chapter, I stated that Webber, Radcliffe, Gittoes, and Hartman offer theological explanations as possible answers to what participants experience when they celebrate Communion. Those theological explanations tend to identify and interpret an experience and its meaning by examining cultural trends in the light of biblical text. However, the cultural/biblical method explained what ought to be experienced, not necessarily what was being experienced.

IPA differs from this cultural/biblical approach because it seeks to understand a lived experience and not offer a predetermined theological explanation. The experiences of all students were explored by engaging in their explanation, and my interpretation of their explanation, as a double hermeneutic and not an exploration of a religious belief system about God or ultimate reality within culture. Eight distinct lived experiences were categorized with associated meanings. By identifying commonalities and differences in those meanings, an initial discovery emerged towards understanding how celebrating Communion can communicate biblical truth to postmodern communities similar to the students at SEU with a post-Christian worldview by retelling the redemptive story: students had to **feel or sense something** in order for their eight lived experiences **to have meaning.** It was not what their churches had taught them but what they sensed for themselves.

A second discovery also emerged: Communion acts as a **communicating vehicle** in order for the lived experiences of each student to find meaning. For example, though Communion communicated the redemptive story through ceremonial words and actions (Mazza 1999, 21), it also communicated the eight experiences of the students in their own stories. However, all eight experiences were not uniquely communicated through Communion. For example, though the students experienced Ceremony, Community, and Family, all three experiences are necessary as the context for the unique experiences of Presence, Belief, Remembering, Completeness, and Imagination (Heidegger 1962, 95). Necessarily, Communion is a celebration with others from a variety of family traditions.

In addition to the two discoveries, three indicators of a postmodern environment emerged: (1) a need to experience, (2) autonomous interpretation of an experience, and (3) an experience starting with self. I will examine these indicators later through an investigation into Generation Z and Postmodernity.

> an experience of God is embedded in the biographies, or stories, of the regular people, and not the stories of the experts

In their collaborative work, Heinz Streib, Astrid Dinter, and Kirstin Soderblom (2008, ix-x) shed light on a theological explanation of God. They explore what is taught by experts and what the man on the street senses or feels.[39] In their view, an experience of God is embedded in the biographies, or stories, of the regular people, and not the stories of the experts (2008, 53).

Such embeddedness dwells within sub-currents of religious organizations where experts teach. However, the biographical sub-currents exist not because of the structure of a religious organization, but because people from the street congregate there. By default, the same embeddedness has to dwell outside religious organizations. Embedded biographies inside and outside religious organizations create an open space for a broader discussion about God beyond a theological explanation (Streib et al. 2008, xii). More importantly, this type of approach indicates a reliance on personal experience, showing that God can be encountered inside or outside religious organizations (2008, 65).

However, conscious awareness of God that emerges from personal experience cannot be validated or invalidated by the accepted concepts of what **constitutes evidence.** According to Bruce W. Speck and Sherry L. Hoppe (2007, 37), "There is no epistemology for authoritative self-knowledge beyond the self or what self knows—or thinks it knows" It is the paradox of Rene Descartes, "I think therefore I am." Though God can be encountered inside and outside a religious organization by the people

---

[39] Streib defines an expert as an official in religious organization with theological training, and people on the street as congregants with no theological training or official position.

on the street, an experience that is sensed is solely reliant on self. Webber (2003, 88-89) draws attention to the dangers of being solely reliant on self in what he calls a "spirituality of self." I will tackle a spirituality of self later through an investigation into the characteristics of the spirituality and religious beliefs and behaviors of Generation Z in Postmodernity.

The idea of being solely reliant on self is also seen in my IPA results. Each student interpreted his or her experiences autonomously, applying historical and biblical contexts in a way that was personally relevant, or not at all. Communion has a rich history, but, despite this history, it was not reflected in a lived experience of the students I interviewed at SEU. Later, I will explore the biblical context of Communion. But again, I found the biblical context was not evident in the students' interpretation of their experiences. Furthermore, all four students did not show any uniformity in their reliance on self. In short, **there is no epistemology for the students' authoritative self-knowledge.**

My historical investigation in the first section revealed the necessity of Communion in order for participants to experience the empowering actions and promissory words of Christ. This was particularly highlighted in the Middle Ages surrounding the Fourth Lateran Council in 1215 and the issue of sacerdotal power. Celebrating Communion did communicate Christ's empowering actions, "Do this in remembrance of me" (Luke 22:19) and His promissory words that He would "not drink from this fruit of the vine from now on until that day when I drink it new with you in my Father's kingdom" (Matt. 26:29). Retrospectively, Communion could be historically viewed as a vehicle for communicating the empowering actions and promissory words of Christ.

Though sacerdotal power did not emerge in this section, my IPA results show that Communion does act as a communicating vehicle in the lived experience of the students at SEU. What did emerge were eight lived experiences with meanings attached to them communicated through Communion, of which three a necessary context for the five unique experiences. Heidegger

(1962, 95) would say the necessary experiences cannot be separated from the other experiences. Again, the experiences that were communicated were sensed, and not taught by experts (Streib et al. 2008, 53).

The difference between sensing and teaching is also noted by Catherine Bell (1997, 82). She points out that theorists tend to explore what a ceremony actually communicates, rather than what it ought to communicate (1997, 53). This was certainly true regarding the students' lived experience. Though Communion as ceremony with others from varying family traditions was generally common between all students, their lived experience through Communion was unique.

Furthermore, although the church taught the students about Communion when they were children, the church failed to form meaning in them. This was evident in the experience of Belief. What they were taught they *should* experience did not happen in actual reality. While it is quite probable that the church taught each student that Christ can communicate outside the five senses, what they actually experienced was Presence, Belief, Remembering, Completeness, and Imagination communicated through Communion.

> What they were taught they *should* experience did not happen in actual reality.

One particular anthropologist, Eric W. Rothenbuhler (1998, 7), believes that communication is implicit in ceremonies and is highly subjective to the participant. Again, his view highlights the tension between what *should* be communicated through Communion and what is *actually* communicated. However, Rothenbuhler (1998, 27) also points out that any form of ceremony, from a handshake to the coronation of a monarch, communicates different experiences. While the bread and wine of Communion explicitly communicate the body and blood of Christ, my IPA results reveal that eight experiences were communicated as the bread and wine were presented and received. On one hand, it is predictable that Communion does communicate something. On the other hand, it is not predictable what is actually communicates.

When Christ introduced Communion, He asked that participants remember Him (Matt. 26:26-28). However, Christ did not predetermine what a participant should experience as he or she remembered Him. Therefore, Communion as Ceremony communicated something to the students that was **highly subjective and unpredictable.** Because an experience is subjective, any lived experience is best understood within the parameters of Communion as a Christian ceremony for meaning making shaped by the biblical text. I will wrestle with the biblical text shortly. Consequently, understanding Communion that functions to communicate biblical truth is vitally needed to work with experiential encounters already occurring during the celebration with people like the students at SEU.

Summary Thought

Ordinary people, or none experts, on the street experience God within their own biographies or stories. By default, it is these stories that broaden the discussion about the activity of Christ in the lives of people. Such activity is not exclusive to the church or, more specifically, Communion. However, Communion as a Christian celebration does act as a vehicle for communicating the redemptive story that engages individual stories. During Communion, some experiences are necessary but not predictable. Other experiences are unique and unpredictable.

CONCLUDING THOUGHT

Three sets of initial discoveries were stated in this section. First, students predominantly had to **feel or sense something** in order for their experiences to have meaning. Second, Communion acts as a **communicating vehicle** in order for the students to encounter the eight lived experiences and meanings attached to them. Third, three indicators of the characteristics of the spirituality and religious beliefs and behaviors of students with a postmodern/post-Christian worldview were also discovered: (1) a need to experience, (2) autonomous interpretation of an experience, and

(3) that an experience started with self. In the next section I ask the question, "In what way can lived experiences be understood within Communion as ceremony?" This question is important because the IPA findings do not go far enough to analyze the context in which an experience occurred— namely, within a Christian ceremony. So, I assessed lived experiences through the lens of four systems that show me how the students' experiences occurred within ceremony.

SECTION THREE

SORTING OUT A LIVED EXPERIENCE

In this section, I show what can be learned in what Heidegger (1962, 95) calls the **context,** or **background,** of a lived experience. Essentially, I am exploring the overlap or what Merleau-Ponty calls **"embeddedness"** (1962, ix) where Communion participants see themselves as individuals within a community. While IPA includes a descriptive account of the way an experience happened in its own terms (Smith et al. 2009, 12), it does not go far enough to analyze the context in which it occurred—namely, Communion as a Christian celebration. Examining the context goes further than IPA by assessing what the performance of Communion does towards communicating biblical truth.

Whereas, IPA examines a participant's actions in light of his or her spoken words, examining the context focuses on the participant's interpretation in light of his or her actions. This section involves the discovery and what was learned from the findings of IPA, and assessment of those findings in their context, towards a theoretical model of communicating biblical truth for retelling the redemptive story.

First, I describe the performative context by exploring what was said and done during Communion. Second, I briefly explain four systems that put the idea of words and actions into effect. These systems help in assessing the performance of Communion as a Christian celebration. Third, I discuss my IPA findings presented through the lens of the **four systems** in order to show what can be understood from the students' lived experiences. Finally, I reveal a key discovery that emerged, among other findings, towards a theoretical model of how Communion serves to communicate biblical truth to a postmodern community populated by Generation Z by retelling the redemptive story.

CHAPTER 9

TOOLS FOR SORTING OUT A LIVED EXPERIENCE

Daniel Albrecht (1999, 13) describes a particular discipline for assessing a lived experience: "Ritology [the study of ceremonies/celebrations or rituals][40] focuses most directly on enactment and performance, that is, it gives priority to the acts, the actions, and gestural activities of people. In a secondary manner, it may focus on written texts and spoken words but will do so in the context of the people's actions." Subsequently, studying the performative aspects seeks to **interpret the words** used during Communion in light of **certain actions.** This is important because students did encounter God but had little or no reference for Him in the written text of the Bible.

However, Bell (1992, 69-70) notes that studying the performative aspects does more than focusing on actions and words. In her view, distinctions are required to narrow down a specific context. For example, distinctions are routinely drawn between ceremonies that include religious and secular, political and civic, private and collective, rebellion and solidarity, formal and informal, or festival and holiday. In my case, the context is religion.

---

[40] In this section, I use the word *ceremony* alongside the word celebration as Communion is a celebration of Christ performed in a ceremonial way.

Ronald Grimes (2010, 6) takes Bell's distinctions further by pointing out secondary distinctions in the subject religion that include funerals, weddings, initiations, christenings, memorials, ordinations, baptisms, and so on. So, I am focusing on the Christian celebration of Communion that originated with Christ (Lk. 22:15-20). However, in order to make an assessment of my IPA findings, systems were needed as lenses to view the performative actions and words of Communion.

Systems that Put Words and Actions into Effect

The extensive studies of Bell (1992; 1997) were useful for locating which systems were the most effective as it related to Communion. They were: (1) a system of structured and unstructured community; (2) a system of participant and observer; (3) a system of ethos and worldview; and (4) a system of belief and ceremony. The systems were helpful in learning what can be understood from a lived experience because they focused on the students' performance in the distinctive celebration of Communion.

A Structured and Unstructured Community

British cultural anthropologist, Victor Turner (2011), makes a societal distinction between structured and unstructured communities when people participate in a ceremony. In both types of community, ceremony must have elders who officiate. On one hand, elders are hierarchical in a structured community. An individual's caste or class in the community determines his or her eligibility for the hierarchical position held for an indefinite period of time. We would say "the elder is from good stock." Consequently, a structured community tends to separate people into what Turner (2011, 96) calls **"more"** or **"less."** What this implies regarding Communion is that those who officiate Communion would be considered "more" while those being served would be considered "less".

On the other hand, elders in an unstructured community are what Turner (2011, 97) uniquely calls **"modelessness"** because eligibility is not determined by caste or class in the community. Consequently, the idea of "more" or "less" becomes redundant. Rather, all people in the community are considered equal. As we have seen so far, this is an important characteristic in the spirituality of postmoderns.

when a student participates in Communion, does he or she feel "less" than, or equal to the person officiating?

An elder emerges in an unstructured community through a rite of passage, and only for a period of time in order to maintain a sense of humility in the community. Consequently, an unstructured community "tempers the pride of the incumbent [elder]" (2011, 97). Turner's system for understanding ceremony helped me to analyze a lived experience during Communion by assessing the students' **perception of the community** in which the bread and wine are presented and received (see Figure 9.1). Subsequently, when a student participates in Communion, does he or she feel "less" than, or equal to the person officiating?

Figure 9.1. More, Less, and Equal

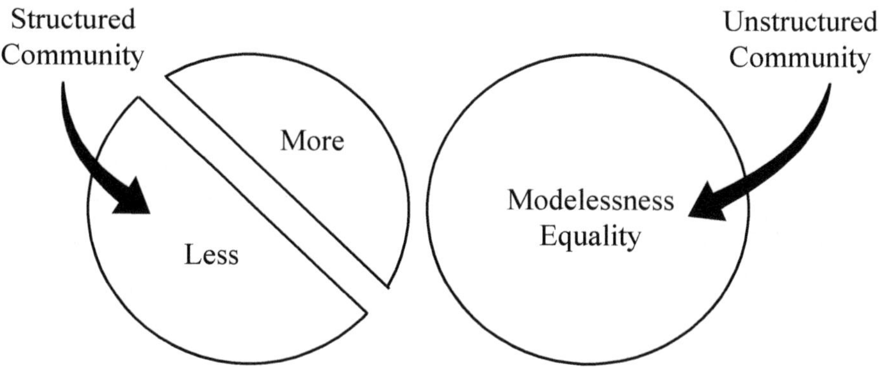

The Participant and Observer

Polish anthropologist Edward Singer (1959, xiii) explains a system in the relationship of participant and observer.[41] Singer

---

[41] An observer is someone who can physically see what is happening.

refers to the relationship between a **performance of culture**[42] for the participant's sake, and a performance for the sake of the observers. The participants are primary individuals who exhibit their culture through the performance of a ceremony. The observers, then, are secondary individuals who can see what is being exhibited and who may or may not have the same or similar culture. Consequently, Singer's system is not a private performance of culture through ceremony but a public one. He argues that heterogeneous cultures are secondary **"little traditions"** (1955, 27) framed within a unifying and primary **"great tradition"** (1955, 27) as a homogenous culture. This is important to assessing the performance of Communion.

On one hand, the homogenous culture of Communion unifies as a historical church tradition, or "great tradition." On the other hand, the heterogeneous cultures of participants are being exhibited acting like "little traditions" within historical church tradition. According to Singer (1955, 27-28), a "great tradition" cannot exist without "little traditions." Furthermore, the performance of "little traditions" within a "great tradition" "has a definitely limited time span, a beginning and end, an organized program of activity, a set of performers, an audience, and a place and occasion of performance" (1959, xiii).

Celebrating Communion requires all these elements. The lens of Singer's system helped me to analyze a lived experience by assessing the students' **perception of their own "little tradition," and the "little traditions"** of others, within the **great church tradition** of Communion (see Figure 9.2). Subsequently, in what way does each student's secondary culture relate to other cultures and the primary culture of Communion?

---

[42] According to Singer (1959, 71), a cultural performance contains "the elementary constituents of culture...they include also prayers, ritual readings and recitations, rites and ceremonies, festivals, and all those things we usually class under religion and ritual rather than with the cultural and artistic".

Figure 9.2. Performance of Traditions

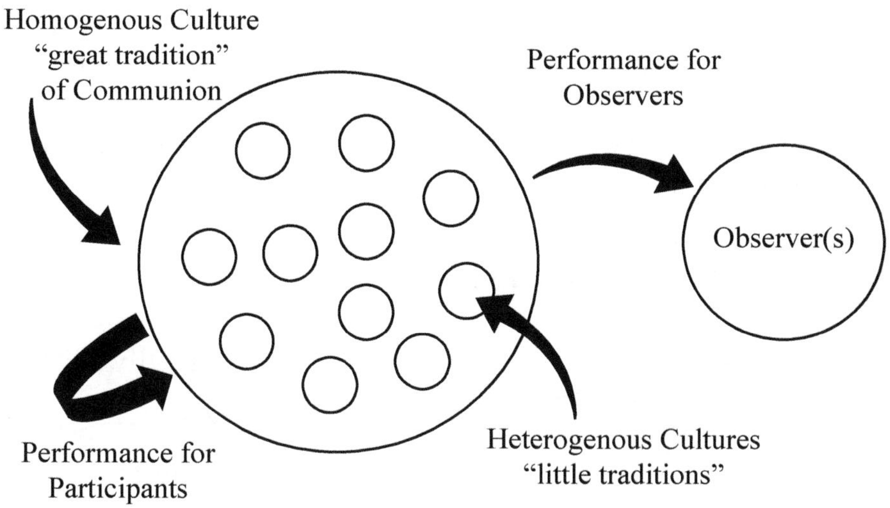

Shaping Ethos and Worldview

Symbiotic anthropologist Clifford Geertz (1973, 126-140) explains a system of ethos and worldview. He describes ethos as moral and evaluative, or the way people's lives **reflect their own realities.** In contrast, he describes worldview as existential and cognitive, or the way people sense what is **really real**, containing the most comprehensive ideas of order (1973, 126-127). Consequently, ethos represents a way of life implied by the actual state of affairs which the worldview describes, and worldview represents an image of an actual state of affairs of which such a way of life is lived.

> in what way is the student involved in shaping an experience as the experience shapes him or her?

Understood this way, the dialectical nature of Geertz's system, as it relates to Communion, is a **performance "of"** a lived experience [ethos] and a **performance "for"** an imagined experience [worldview] (Geertz 1973, 93-94). The dialectical nature is an important observation as the students are involved in shaping an experience as the experience shapes him or her. Or, as Geertz (1973, 112) puts it, "In a ritual [ceremony], the world as lived, and the world as imagined…turn out to be the same world." The lens of Geertz's system helped me analyze a student's **actual experience** with an experience he or she **imagines** (see Figure 9.3). Subsequently, in what way is the student involved in shaping an experience as the experience shapes him or her?

Figure 9.3. Real and Imagined

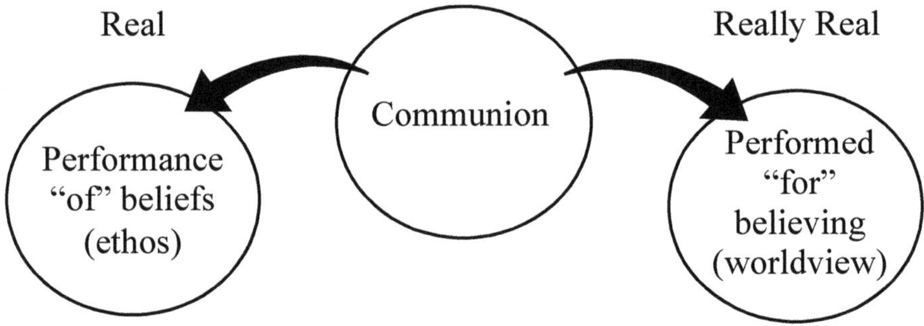

Belief and Ceremony

Distinguished Sociologist Edward Shils (1968, 736) explains ultimate things in a system of belief through ceremony. He believes an individual can renew personal belief of ultimate things through ceremony. Ultimate things go beyond the ordinary sequence of events, offering imperatives to action especially in times of crisis. Imperatives often include prayer (1968, 735). Articulating belief while praying can be a simple or complex act of self-protection, enabling the participant to confront and deal with crisis.

Consequently, ultimate things also get labeled as **"sacred things"** (Shils 1968, 735). "Ritual [ceremony] and belief are intertwined with each other; yet they are separable" (1968, 736). Because they intertwine as separate entities, it is conceivable that beliefs can be untwined from ceremony. "Logically, beliefs could exist without rituals [ceremonies]; rituals, however, could not exist without beliefs" (1968, 736). Consequently, in a time of crisis, a student can reinforce his or her belief in ultimate things by participating in Communion. The lens of Shils's system helped me to analyze a lived experience by assessing the way Communion **connects the student to ultimate things,** offering protection in a time of crisis (see Figure 9.4). Subsequently, does Communion succeed or fail in what it promises as it relates to ultimate things?

> does Communion succeed or fail in what it promises as it relates to ultimate things?

Figure 9.4. Renewal of Beliefs as Coping

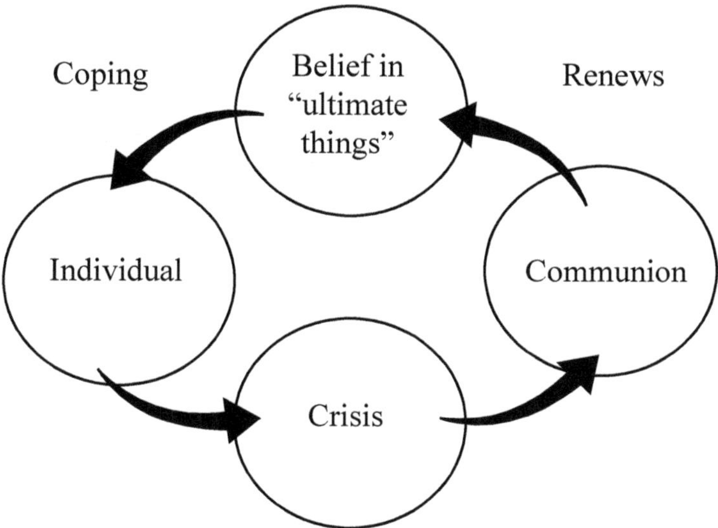

The enactment of a ceremony/celebration can be studied by focusing on the actions and words used, in that order. As such, studying the performative aspects seeks to interpret the words used during Communion in light of certain actions. Both can be assessed through at least six systems that act as lenses. The system of structured or unstructured community helps me understand if the student felt less or equal to the person officiating Communion. The system of participant and observer helps me see the individual traditions of students within the greater tradition of Communion as the celebration is performed for participants and observers. The system of ethos and worldview helps me see how Communion is a performance of beliefs, and for believing shedding light on what is real and imagined. Finally, the system of belief and ceremony helps me see how participating in Communion acts as a coping device in times of crisis.

CHAPTER 10

LIVED EXPERIENCE SORTED OUT

There were several commonalities found in the stories of the students. For example, the students participated in Communion as a Christian celebration, receiving the bread and wine. The students were all successive participants from their parents' traditions. However, what is not common in all four stories is the unique experience of each student. So, in this chapter I assess each story through the lenses of all four systems in order to analyze the students' interpretations of their experiences within Communion. Like **chapter seven**, verbatim extracts are cited from each interview. And, like the seventh chapter, each citation may read a little elementary.

Four questions guide my assessment as they relate to the four systems.

Essentially, I looked for answers to the following questions: (1) When a student participates in Communion, does he or she feel less than or equal to the person officiating? (Turner 2011); (2) In what way does the student's secondary culture relate to other cultures and the primary culture of Communion? (Singer 1959); (3) In what way is the student involved in shaping an experience as the experience shapes him or her? (Geertz 1973); and, (4) Does Communion as a Christian celebration succeed or fail in what it promises as it relates to ultimate things?

Sophia's Experience

Name: Sophia
Age: 19
Ethnicity: African American
Church: Raised in a variety of Protestant churches
Current: Now attending a Catholic church
Frequency: Celebrates Communion every week

In one particular segment of Sophia's story, she repeatedly made reference to "equality." "One of my moral compasses is equality." Drawing attention to the priest in her current church, Sophia made reference to "his very odd stance on gay people." His stance was to reject same sex marriage, but to include gay and lesbian participants in Communion. Sophia added, "I feel like love is equal, I guess, so when a man and a woman love each other that's equal; if a man and a man love each other, that's equal too; if a woman and a woman love each other, then that's equal as well." While Sophia does not feel "less" (Turner 2011, 96) than her priest as a participant in Communion, she recognizes that her priest does not think of himself as "more" (2011, 96) than those who sexually identify as gay or lesbian. Though the priest in her community takes a specific stance on same sex marriage, the lens of Turner's system helped me to discover that Sophia's **perception of her community that gathers to receive the bread and wine is not hierarchal.** Again, there was no indication that she felt less than her priest who was officiating Communion.

Sophia culturally identifies as African American, yet as she told her story there was no reference to her own culture ("little tradition") or the culture ("little traditions") of others who gather to celebrate Communion (Singer 1955, 27-28). Neither did she refer to how being African American related to the culture of Communion ("great tradition"). Consequently, Singer's system of participant and observer did not help me discover anything significant in assessing Sophia's **perception of her own culture, the culture of others, or the culture of Communion.**

The system of ethos and worldview (Geertz 1973, 126-127) was a particularly highlighted lens for assessing Sophia's lived experience in Communion. If Communion is a ceremony "of" believing God was present and a ceremony "for" believing God was present, it was verified in Sophia's story (1973, 114). Four of Sophia's comments highlight the "of" sense (ethos) or the way Sophia perceived reality. In a gentle tone she said, "I just know... entering a church," referring to "this energy" that was "present everywhere" and "you could feel it." In Sophia's story, her life reflects God's presence, but she has to invoke that presence for it to become really real (worldview, or what she imagines) during Communion. Consequently, Communion is a ceremony "of" what Sophia believes is God's presence.

Nevertheless, Communion is also "for" believing that God is present. Two comments highlight the "for" sense (ethos), or the way Sophia reflects reality: Again, in a gentle tone, Sophia remarked "It brings him a little more present," and "He is more present at Communion." Undoubtedly, Sophia believes that God is present during Communion, but again she has to invoke that presence for worldview (or what she imagines) to be real during Communion. This is what Geertz (1973, 93) calls "an intrinsic double aspect...by shaping themselves to it and by shaping it to themselves." An example of this is the feminization of God. If this is the situation, Sophia is **shaped by her belief "of" God's presence and "for" believing God can be present** through Communion as a female.

Bell (1992, 27) refers to Geertz's intrinsic double aspect of a ceremony shaping someone as a fusing of "people's conceptions of order and their dispositions for action." God's presence as a concept of order during Communion was undoubtedly nurtured in Sophia by the fact that her mother created routine in her life. For example, Sophia remarked that Communion is "a weekly thing you go off of." As a routine, celebrating Communion became "pretty hard wired."

However, Sophia moves from a weekly concept of order to a disposition for action. In other words, Communion is no longer a routine of God's presence, but a personal desire for His presence. She confessed, "Now it means completely something different." Though her story does not state specifics, the move from concept

> "I need to get Communion and I need, you know, to make sure I'm going to be a better person for the following week."

to action is seen in her passionate remark, "For me it's what I need to do when I wake up on Sundays; I know it's the day I need to be in church, and I need to go and I need to listen to the Gospel and I need to get Communion." Geertz's system helped me to discover that Sophia had the **capacity to move from the concept of God's presence to the reality of it.** Communion brings the presence of God into a sharper focus as a spiritually shaping ceremony.

Sophia made a particular statement in her story that momentarily brings into focus the lens of Shils' (1968) system. "I need to get Communion and I need, you know, to make sure I'm going to be a better person for the following week." Sophia equated participating in Communion with being a better person. This is what Shils (1968, 736) refers as the intertwining of beliefs and ceremony. Sophia believed that participating in Communion would actually make her a better person. Apparently, it works for Sophia.

> "For me, I guess it makes me feel like a bit of a better person. There are things that when I get out of celebrating Communion...the benefits are just, I watch what I say, watch what I do. I'm an awful driver. I like to swear a lot when I drive, and even when I'm getting out of church there will be someone who cuts me off and I want to, like, curse but I'm, like, 'No you need to watch yourself coz you just celebrated Communion.'"

The lens of Shils' system helped me to discover that **Communion as a ceremony succeeded for Sophia in what it promised** as it relates to becoming a better person.

Summary Thought

As a result of viewing Sophia's lived experience during Communion through all four systems, she has the capacity to move from the concept of God's presence to the reality of it, and Communion brings the presence of God into a sharper focus as a spiritually shaping ceremony (Geertz 1973); that she perceives her community that receive the bread and wine as unstructured (Turner 2011); and that Communion succeeds in her belief that celebrating it makes her a better person (Shils 1968) (see Table 10.1).

Table 10.1. Discoveries for Sophia

Theorist	Ceremonial Systems	What was Understood from a Lived Experience Within Communion as a Ceremony
Victor Turner	Structured and Unstructured Community	Perceives that her community that receive the bread and wine is unstructured where everyone is equal while celebrating Communion.
Milton Singer	Participant and Observer	
Clifford Geertz	Ethos and Worldview	The capacity to move from the concept of God's presence to the reality of it, and Communion brings the presence of God into a sharper focus as a spiritually shaping ceremony.
Edward Shils	Belief and Ceremony	Communion succeeds in her belief that celebrating the ceremony makes her a better person.

Victoria's Experience

Name: Victoria
Age: 20
Ethnicity: Mexican
Church: Raised in a variety of traditional Catholic churches
Current: Now attending Catholic chapel
Frequency: Celebrates Communion every week

Victoria makes only one reference to the priests who serve her the Communion bread and wine in the campus chapel and in Mexico where her family live. "He's the priest. He is representing Him [Christ] kind of thing." Victoria makes no other comment about what it means for either priest to represent Christ or about her relationship to them. She does compare the community who celebrate Communion on the campus with her home church in Mexico. However, Victoria does this in terms of connection to God and not connection to other participants. Therefore, the lens of Turner's system did not help in discovering **anything significant** in assessing Victoria's lived experience in Communion.

One lens that particularly helped assess Victoria's experience was Singer's (1959) system of participant and observer. Victoria consistently compares Mexican and American cultures in her role of participant and observer in her story. Singer (1959, 27) explains a participant and observer in the totality of a ceremony[43] and an exhibition of cultural performance. Within that exhibition, convergence takes place between the observer's culture and the participant's culture, or as Singer (1955, 27) puts it "between little traditions."

In Victoria's case, the totality of the ceremony is seen in her role as the participant and as the observer. For example, while participating in Mexican culture, she also observes from the stance of American culture. Also, while participating in American culture, she observes from the stance of Mexican culture. As a result, the little traditions of Mexico and the little traditions of America converge into a unifying "great tradition" (Singer 1955, 27) of Communion in church history.

Singer's (1955, 23-27) system particularly emerges in both geographical locations where Victoria has observed and participated in Communion: "I've had the Eucharist [Communion] in Mexico, and I've had it here [America]." Using biblical metaphors, Victoria remarked, "I compare the American culture to goats," and

---

[43] Strictly speaking, Singer's participant and observer are two different people; however, in Victoria's case, both can be found in her as an individual person.

"I feel like a sheep as a Mexican." The metaphor of "goats" is explained, "It doesn't feel like everyone is paying attention," and clarified, "As per usual of the American culture, it's very individual."

The metaphor of "sheep" is also explained, "I play my part of the little act [Communion]," and clarified, "I feel a lot more humble." Nevertheless, Victoria is not put off by the culture of goat individualism. While in America, Victoria confidently states, "I wanted to continue doing it [celebrating Communion]." Her comments reveal the dual role of participant and observer in both cultures.

A further example in Victoria's story reveals how Mexican and American little traditions converge within the great tradition of Communion. "So, it's like during this whole process we have been sitting in church, hearing the same liturgy and expression or, like, just, we've been through this the whole time, so this is like the final step. We're all partaking in this. So, I guess, it's feeling that togetherness with Him and with everyone else." This is where the great tradition of Communion unifies the little traditions of Mexican sheep and American goats in togetherness.

> "It feels different to me...you know, like when I am with them, I feel like one of them."

Nevertheless, when she participates in Mexico, "It feels different to me...you know, like when I am with them, I feel like one of them." If participating in Mexico is different, her experience is no longer converging. Rather, the image of a sheep takes precedence. However, at a later point while participating in America, the image of a goat takes precedence in her experience, seen in her comment, "I also feel like the lonely goat." Despite the metaphor change, Victoria is "homesick" while in America wanting to celebrate Communion back in Mexico. Her story shows a tension between Mexican and American cultures that is brought into focus by the great tradition of Communion.

Singer (1955) refers to the suspension of a cultural performance. Essentially, distraction suspends a cultural performance for the participant and observer where conflicting thoughts emerge. In Victoria's case, the culture of Mexico is largely suspended in America by the distracting thought of feeling more like a goat. At the same time, her experience of American culture is suspended in Mexico by the distracting thought of feeling more like a sheep. Either way, a cultural performance is momentarily suspended for Victoria in the great tradition of Communion. As a result of assessing Victoria's experience through the lens of Singer's (1955, 23-27) system of participant and observer, she was distracted by Mexican and American cultures as a participant and observer. Both cultures are brought into focus by Communion as a ceremony with no cultural bias as American and Mexican **cultures are suspended by each other.**

Another lens that particularly helped assess Victoria's lived experience during Communion was Geertz's (1973) system of ethos and worldview. Victoria makes a fascinating reference to three distinct locations: earth, a middle sphere, and heaven. On one hand, the first location, earth, represents ethos (Geertz 1973, 126-127) because it is the way Victoria reflects her own view of reality. The location requires little or no imagination. Victoria states "The earthly world, it's how you remember who you are like or what you are exactly."

On the other hand, the second and third location, a middle sphere and heaven, represents worldview (Geertz 1973, 126-127) because it is what Victoria senses is real. Both locations require imagination. Regarding the first location, "I feel like it's this -- it's this sphere in the middle that as an earthly people I can go to with my mind." She calls this middle sphere a "spiritual world." Identical to the middle sphere, Victoria calls heaven "a spiritual world," and she is assured, "It's where we are all going."

The dialectical nature of ethos and worldview show how Victoria is involved in shaping her lived experience, as the experience also shapes her while participating in Communion. For example, she makes a point of telling the story of when her brother died and went to heaven. When the priest talked about the resurrection during Communion, Victoria remembers who her brother was on earth and where she affirms, he is now, in heaven. She is able to do this when her mind can go to the imagined middle sphere location.

These three locations appear to come to mind specifically when she considers the resurrection during Communion. "He's [brother] not really dead, but it's really sad when I remember." Victoria shows that her participation in Communion is a performance "of" believing her brother is in heaven and "for" believing he is in heaven (Geertz 1973, 93-94). The lens of Geertz's system helped me discover that Victoria is **involved in shaping her lived experience, as her lived experience is also shaping her,** brought into focus by Communion as a ceremony specifically when the priest talked about the resurrection.

The lens of Shils' (1968) system helped me assess Victoria's lived experience regarding her comments on heaven as a spiritual location. Heaven can be classified as an ultimate thing (1968, 736). The crisis that caused Victoria to renew her belief in heaven was the death of her brother. As she told the story of her brother, it appears that Communion, as a ceremony of renewing a connection with ultimate things, does not fail her. At no point was there any doubt that her brother is in heaven.

However, any reference to her brother consistently centered around celebrating Communion. Though beliefs can untwine from a ceremony (Shils 1968, 736), this was not the case for Victoria. Her belief in heaven as a spiritual location is consistently connected to when she celebrates Communion. The lens of Shils' system helped me discover that Victoria renews her belief in heaven, as an ultimate thing, specifically when she celebrates Communion.

Summary Thought

As a result of viewing Victoria's lived experience during Communion through all four systems, she was distracted by Mexican and American cultures as a participant and observer, and both cultures were brought into focus by Communion with no cultural bias (Singer 1959); she is involved in shaping her lived experience, as the lived experience is shaping her, and this was brought into focus by Communion as a ceremony, specifically when the priest talked about the resurrection (Geertz 1973); and, she renews her belief in heaven as an ultimate thing, specifically when she celebrates Communion (see Table 10.2).

Table 10.2. Discoveries for Victoria

Theorist	Systems	What was Understood from a Lived Experience Within Communion as a Ceremony
Victor Turner	Structured Unstructured Community	
Milton Singer	Participant and Observer	Distracted by Mexican and American cultures as a participant and observer, and both cultures were brought into focus by Communion with no cultural bias.
Clifford Geertz	Ethos and Worldview	Involved in shaping her lived experience as the lived experience is shaping her, brought into focus by Communion as a ceremony specifically when the priest talked about the resurrection.
Edward Shils	Belief and Ceremony	Renews her belief in heaven as an ultimate thing, specifically when she celebrates Communion.

Samuel's Experience

Name: Samuel
Age: 19
Ethnicity: Caucasian
Church: Raised in a traditional Catholic church
Current: Now attending Catholic chapel
Frequency: Celebrates Communion infrequently

Turner's (2011) system of a structured and unstructured community helped me to assess Samuel's perception of the community that gathers to celebrate Communion. While his participation in Communion is infrequent, two issues stand out in his story that bring into focus Turner's system. First, there is a distance between the priest and Samuel that is seen in his relationship to the church. As a young boy, he accompanied his family to celebrate Communion stating, "And that's why I feel welcome."

However, now that Samuel is at college away from his family, he commented, "I feel like a lot of what the church says, you know, makes a lot of people feel unwelcome if they're not part of it to start with." He added, "and I tend to feel unwelcomed by the priest." A particular comment that shed light on the influence a priest has over Samuel: "Yeah, they [priests] pick a few certain people and bless them before they come up, and they'll serve the bread and the wine, but that's never me." From Samuel's perspective, the priest appeared "more" (Turner 2011, 96) than he was in the structured community.

Second, not only was there distance between Samuel and the priest, there was also distance between Samuel and the community that celebrate Communion. "I just feel like I am, you know, an outsider and then not necessarily an integral part to it really." Though Samuel is invited into the community that celebrate Communion on campus, he does not place any value on being part of it. His specific comments about the community make Samuel appear "more" (Turner 2011, 96) than the people who invite him:

> "Well, I mean, I know the intention of it is to make
> everyone feel welcome, feel a part of something
> bigger than themselves, but for me it's just more like,
> you know – again, I've gone to Catholic school for a
> while now; it just seemed like another step and not
> necessarily into anything larger, more like invited into
> a club, is kind of how I look at it now."

Whereas the distance between Samuel and the priest appears to originate with the priest, the distance between Samuel and community that celebrate Communion is in the opposite direction when viewed through Turner's lens. It originates with Samuel. The lens of Turner's system helped me to discover that Samuel's lived experience is like a two-sided coin. On one side, the priest appears "more" (Turner 2011, 96) than Samuel. On the other side, it is Samuel who appears "more" (2011, 96) than the community who invite him to celebrate Communion with them.

Because Samuel is infrequent in celebrating Communion, it was difficult to assess his lived experience through Singer's (1955) lens of participant and observer. Nevertheless, Samuel does talk about his performance in Communion. Recalling his childhood memories, Samuel notes for whom he performed. "It is really nerve wracking in front of my family with them watching." As a young adult at college, Samuel still performed during Communion as a ceremony, albeit infrequently, but the observer had changed. "He [Christ] sees." From a childhood experience to a young adult experience, Samuel's participation in Communion was a performance for the sake of the observer (1955, 27).

Samuel's performance, however, is not an exhibition of culture, or of little traditions, and there is no evidence in his story that convergence takes place (Singer 1955, 23). Samuel's performance was marked by nervousness as a child, with his family watching him receive the bread and wine, a process Samuel described as "really nerve wracking." It appears his experience carried over into his experience as a young adult, exchanging the observer from family to Christ. From a limited view, the lens of Singer's system helped me to discover that Samuel **exclusively performs nervously for an observer,** albeit infrequently.

The lens of Geertz's (1973) system of ethos and worldview also gave me a limited view of Samuel's lived experience. Because beliefs that surround Communion had been taught to Samuel as a child, they tended to elude him. It was difficult to determine his performance "of" belief and "for" (1973, 114). However, the lens helped me assess the way Samuel reflected reality (ethos) and what he sensed was real (worldview) to determine how he shaped his experience, as his experience shaped him.

Samuel sensed the presence of God as a child, "Like, I was sitting down with my dad like right before my first communion." He also sensed that God (or Christ) was watching him as a young adult. Samuel did not know why God was watching him, remarking, "Maybe he remembers us?" The lens of Geertz helped me assess that he is **being watched** as a young adult (ethos), and it is **God who is specifically watching** him (worldview).

A particular lens that helped me assess the lived experience of Samuel was the lens of Shils' (1968) system of belief and ritual. There was an intriguing play of beliefs and inconsistent participation in Communion as a ceremony. According to Shils (1968, 736), "Beliefs and systems of beliefs could conceivably be accepted without adopting the practice of rituals [ceremonies] associated with them...Logically, beliefs could exist without rituals; rituals, however, could not exist without beliefs."

What makes Samuel's case intriguing is the opposite of what Shils proposes. Samuel's random participation in Communion does not appear to be accompanied with personal beliefs. If this is the case, Communion as a ceremony does exist for Samuel without beliefs. Though he participated in Communion as a child, and was invited to participate at college, both imply beliefs were intertwined with Communion. At college Samuel's beliefs are random and disconnected from Communion.

Samuel casually mentions Communion is "one of those extra things that I do." Another example is Samuel's view of a gathering that celebrates Communion, "invited into a club is kind of how I look at it now." Despite his inconsistency in participating in Communion, Samuel articulates a set of beliefs seen in three specific comments: "I believe in God," "Yeah, I believe that Jesus died for all of us," and, "I really do believe the story of Jesus." Those beliefs are not consistent with his random participation in Communion.

Three significant issues give evidence that assess Samuel's lived experience. First, ceremony involves "a way of renewing contact with ultimate things" (Shils 1968, 735). Second, "Ultimate things are those which go beyond the ordinary, sensible evident sequence of events; they govern or are thought to govern these events and offer guidance and imperatives to action" (1968, 735). Third, "The strength of ritual [ceremony] practice, which according to theory affirms and renews solidarity of the community of participants, has not in the past proved sufficient to prevent the institutions within which they were practiced from floundering or falling into catastrophe" (1968, 743). In short, ceremony gives an expression of belief as a guiding and protective practice, especially in a time of crisis or challenge.

Samuel's story shows that his participation in Communion as a young boy was more important to his family than to him. "It was definitely a big deal." The "big deal" he refers to reflects family participation. At that same period in his story, Samuel mentions that making a mistake in the ceremony of Communion "was incredibly sacrilegious." If, "ultimate things are sacred things" (Shils 1968, 735), Samuel was connecting with something he considered sacred enough to become sacrilegious. His story lacks the recollection of a specific event where his belief and practice guided him through a particular crisis or challenge. For Samuel, participation in Communion as a ceremony neither guided him, protected him, nor renewed solidarity with his family tradition.

> "He [Christ] suffered so maybe he understands that we're all suffering in some way, maybe not the exact same way for sure, you know, we're all suffering in our own way, so maybe he recognizes that."

Revisiting earlier comments, "He [Christ] suffered so maybe he understands that we're all suffering in some way, maybe not the exact same way for sure, you know, we're all suffering in our own way, so maybe he recognizes that." During his comments on suffering, Samuel noticeably looked down with a distinct look I interpreted as sadness. The sacred that connected him to ultimate things had now become reduced to "just an act of remembrance now." When asked what it is that participants specifically remember during Communion as a ceremony, Samuel sincerely responded, "I can't remember." This implies that Samuel's set of beliefs are probably something the church had taught him as a boy, but they elude him as a college undergraduate.

Shils (1968, 736) explains how, "ritual [ceremony] is part of a complex act of self-protection from destructive, unintelligible, and immoral forces...ritual reinforces the beliefs which enable the actor [participant] to confront and deal with crises with some anticipation of effectiveness." At some unknown point in Samuel's story, there must have been a crisis in his life that separated his belief in God and that Christ died for him from the practice of those beliefs in Communion as a ceremony. The lens of Shils's system of belief and ceremony helped me to discover that Samuel's beliefs were untwined from Communion possibly because the ceremony failed him. When he participated in Communion, beliefs that accompany ceremony tended to elude him.

Summary Thought

As a result of viewing Samuel's lived experience during Communion through all four systems, the priest appears "more" than Samuel, but he appears "more" than the community who invite him to celebrate Communion with them (Turner 2011). He exclusively performs nervously for an observer, albeit very infrequently (Singer 1955). He senses being watched as a young adult (ethos), and it is God who is specifically watching him (worldview) (Geertz 1973). His beliefs were untwined from Communion possibly because the ceremony failed him, and when he did participate in Communion, beliefs that accompany the ceremony tended to elude him (Shils 1968) (see Table 10.3).

Table 10.3. Discoveries for Samuel

Theorist	System	What was Understood from a Lived Experience Within Communion as a Ceremony
Victor Turner	Structured Unstructured Community	The priest appears "more" than Samuel, and he appears "more" than the community who invite him to celebrate Communion with them.
Milton Singer	Participant and Observer	Exclusively performs nervously for an observer, albeit very infrequently (limited assessment).
Clifford Geertz	Ethos and Worldview	Senses being watched as a young adult (ethos), and it is God who is specifically watching him (worldview) (limited assessment).
Edward Shils	Belief and Ceremony	Beliefs were untwined from Communion possibly because the ceremony failed him, and when he did participate in Communion, beliefs that accompany the ceremony tended to elude him.

William's Experience

Name:	William
Age:	18
Ethnicity:	Caucasian
Church:	Raised in a traditional Baptist church
Current:	Now attending a progressive Evangelical church
Frequency:	Celebrates Communion monthly

The lens of Turner's (2011) system was particularly helpful in assessing William's lived experience during Communion. In William's story, the elder officiating the Communion appears casual. For example, "The preacher[44] tells everyone not familiar with it

---

[44] A preacher in William's church is also an elder who is elected from, and by, the church membership to serve for a period of time.

what it is that we are doing." There is little liturgy. "After communion is taken the preacher asks if anyone wants to talk about it, or they can talk to the elders or anyone, of course, you know, who wants to talk more about what it is that what we are doing here." In response to the casual approach of the elder, William remarked, "The preacher can be hindering." William explains, "The preacher continues to talk about why we do this." A crucial issue in William's story is that the elder was hindering his experience.

William states, "We are called to worship Him as a community." Corporate worship is a consistent theme in William's story, "I think it puts...let's see...puts everyone in the same page. I think it sort of brings everyone together and to recognize this is why we are here." Corporate worship, and not the elder, explains gathering for Communion in William's story. Such an explanation places the elder and participant in "liminality" (Turner 2011, 95).[45] In that temporary placement, "They are betwixt and between the positions assigned" (2011, 95). It is temporary because it designates a moment in time where the elder and participant have no specific assigned position; both are participating in the bread and wine of Communion.

In that temporary state, William referred to the function of the elder as "time filling." William's comment did not come across as disrespectful towards the elder. Though he described the elder this way, at no point did William feel "less" or "more" (Turner 2011, 96) than the elder during a period of liminality. William's story also reveals the importance of time during Communion as a ceremony. For example, "The prayer after is usually the time

---

[45] Turner (2011, vi) offers a unique view of liminality in the context of a ceremony. Bell (1992, 20-21), Driver (1991, 227-230), and Smart (1996, 86-88) believe his unique view is foundational for studying ceremonies. Waaijman (2002, 214) concisely states Turner's description of liminality in three phases: (1) separation from formal structure, (2) awareness of being separated from formal structure, and (3) reintegration back into formal structure. Liminality is mainly concerned with phase two (2002, 214). In this case, phase two is where the elders and participants become aware, they are an equal part of an unstructured community for a moment in time in Communion. Or, as Driver (1991, 213) puts it, a freedom from structure.

I'm given for reflection and then the prayer after that...I feel affected by it."

The delay of time affects William, "I might not be ready to do [eat the bread] that so I take my time." However, the time given to eat the bread and drink the wine is determined by liminality. "You are always given so much time to pray or reflect before you are cut short, and then they [elders] take over." Tom F. Driver (1991, 212) states, "Christian ritual [ceremony] is liminal and authentic when the people of God receive the Spirit of God into their midst."

William needs a measure of time for what Emmanuel Lévinas (1995, 65) refers to as something that "comes to mind" for it to become conscious thought. Without a certain amount of time, William's thoughts remain in what Wilhelm Dilthey (Rickman 1979, 210) refers to as "scattered." As a result of assessing William's experience through the lens of Turner's system, liminality is the time for his scattered thoughts to come to mind. The person officiating Communion as a ceremony has the potential to hinder that time.

The lens of Singer's (1955) system did not reveal anything significant about William's lived experience. William did not talk about his own culture (little traditions), the culture of others, or the culture of Communion (great tradition). Though corporate worship was a consistent theme in William's story, he talked about his experience in terms of personal reflection about himself. For example, "I go through my own ritual...we take it [bread and wine] in unison, but I might not be ready to do that, so I take my time." Consequently, there was nothing in his story that shed light on Communion as a ceremony that converges with the little traditions of its participants.

Another particularly helpful lens to assess William's lived experience was Geertz's (1973) ethos and worldview. Throughout

William's story, there were frequent remarks about what should be. The three comments that William made command attention. First, regarding worship during Communion, "Worship shouldn't be musically -- you know, we are always being call back to that heart of worship." Second, regarding communication with Christ, "I become stagnant in some way if I have not talked to Christ throughout the day."

Third, regarding the bread and wine of Communion, "I think actually sometimes it can be a little bit more distracting taking those things. I guess it's just me thinking about it -- of this physical being -- this is Jesus, this is His blood, this is His body. I think those can be distracting for what the real message is, because I start thinking about those as the physical things. I don't think it helps remind me."

In all three comments, it appears William compares reality (ethos) with something that should be or what he senses is real (worldview). Therefore, worship should originate from the heart of the worshipper and not the instruments; a believer should communicate with the unseen Christ in order to not feel stagnant; and, it is not the reality of the bread and wine as substances, but what they represent that is more real. William believes certain things, and Communion as a ceremony brings into focus those beliefs.

On one hand, it is a performance "of" what he believes about worship, fellowship with Christ, and the substance of bread and wine. On the other hand, it is a performance "for" believing those same things. By celebrating Communion, Geertz's (1973, 93) "intrinsic double action" is seen. William's lived experience shapes him as he shapes the experience. His concept of order, or what he believes is real (worldview), is his disposition towards reality in Communion actions (Bell 1992, 27).

The lens of Geertz's system helped me discover that Communion as a ceremony brings into focus what is **actually happening** with what William **believes should be happening.**

Similar to the lens of Geertz, the lens of Shils' system highlights William's beliefs in Communion. William is connected with ultimate things when he celebrates Communion and, at the same time, he is renewed in his personal beliefs about ultimate things (Shils 1968, 735). Christ is able to renew him, "clean" him up, bring him back to a Christian lifestyle, and restore "the heart of worship."

Evidentially, crisis that creates a sense of urgency to renew contact with ultimate things (Shils 1968, 735) in William's story concerns his spiritual life. He does not talk about something he did that was wrong. His comments surround what he feels about himself and the idea that Christ is the ultimate benefactor who renews, cleans, and brings William back to a Christian lifestyle. Communion is essential in William's lived experience. His beliefs are intertwined with the celebration, and the ceremony does not appear to fail in what he believes it promises (Shils 1968, 735). The lens of Shils' system helped me to discover that Communion connects William to Christ in times of personal crisis, and the **ceremony delivers what it promises to him.**

Summary Thought

As a result of viewing William's lived experience during Communion through the lens of all four systems, liminality is the time for his scattered thoughts to come to mind, and the elder officiating Communion as a ceremony has the potential to hinder that time (Turner 2011); Communion brings into focus what is actually happening with what William believes should be happening (Geertz 1973); and, Communion connects William to Christ in times of personal crisis, and the ceremony delivers what it promises to him (Shils) (see Table 10.4).

Table 10.4. Discoveries for William

Theorist	System	What Was Understood from a Lived Experience within Communion as a Ceremony
Victor Turner	Structured Unstructured Community	Liminality is the time for his scattered thoughts to come to mind, and the elder officiating Communion has the potential to hinder that time.
Milton Singer	Participant and Observer	
Clifford Geertz	Ethos and Worldview	Communion as ceremony brings into focus what is actually happening with what William believes should be happening.
Edward Shils	Belief and Ceremony	Communion connects William to Christ in times of personal crisis, and ceremony delivers what it promises to him.

CHAPTER 11

OBSERVING THROUGH FOUR LENSES

The following is a discussion regarding the discoveries I made when my IPA findings were viewed through the lenses of four systems. In this chapter, I wanted to know four things in the context of Communion as a Christian ceremony as they related to each system: (1) when a student participates in Communion, does he or she feel less than or equal to the person officiating? (Turner 2011); (2) in what way does the student's secondary culture relate to other cultures and the primary culture of Communion? (Singer 1959); (3) in what way is the student involved in shaping an experience as the experience shapes him or her? (Geertz 1973); and, (4) does Communion as a Christian celebration succeed or fail in what it promises as it relates to ultimate things?

Victor Turner: Structured and Unstructured

The lens of Turner's system revealed that the person officiating Communion really does matter in the students' lived experience. For example, Sophia's priest rejects the idea of same sex marriage; nevertheless, he includes gay and lesbian participants in Communion. Inclusion is very important to Sophia as seen in her value of equality in an unstructured community that gather to receive the bread and wine. Because her value of equality is emulated in her priest, Sophia's lived experience is unhindered by him. Though he held to a view about same sex marriage that differed from Sophia, she did not feel "less" (Turner 2011, 96) than him.

However, Samuel felt his priest appeared "more" (Turner 2011, 96) than he was, and this was fueled by the fact that he was not chosen to help serve the bread and wine. Also, William felt his elder got in the way of the time it took for his scattered thoughts to come to mind while receiving the bread and wine. In both cases, the person officiating hindered the lived experience of Samuel and William. If Communion is to succeed in functioning to communicate biblical truth, the **person officiating must be perceived as equal to, and not more than,** students who are participating in a postmodern environment.

Milton Singer: Participant and Observer

Nothing particularly significant emerged when viewing the experiences of Sophia and William through the lens of Singer's system. The experience of Victoria reveals that ceremony is, indeed, a performance of culture (little tradition) within a greater culture (great tradition) (Singer 1955, 27). Victoria's experience is complex in that she is both the participant and the observer with Mexican and American cultures (little traditions) influencing each other. Nevertheless, the primary culture of Communion (great culture) brings into focus Mexican and American cultures with no cultural bias. Communion places both cultures into a greater culture without removing Sophia's Mexican ethnicity while in America.

Undoubtedly, Sophia's cultures are involved in the performance of Communion as a ceremony. For different reasons than ethnicity, Samuel performed for his family, and also for Christ. Following the logic of the question that accompanies Singer's system in this section, it is difficult to identify his family and Christ as other cultures (or little traditions) in the greater culture (great tradition) of Communion. Consequently, the assessment is limited.

The relationship between his performance and the observers of family and Christ highlight his nervousness. The implications of Singer's system as a lens for the students' experiences points out the **need for their own cultures (little traditions) in the performance of Communion** in order to communicate biblical truth by retelling the redemptive story.

Clifford Geertz: Ethos and Worldview

The assessment of all four students' experiences through the lens of Geertz's system revealed their involvement in shaping their own experience, as their experience shaped them. In short, the dialectical nature of Communion as a ceremony had an "of sense" (Geertz 1973, 114) and "for sense" (1973, 114). For example, Communion was a ceremony "of" (1973, 114) believing God was present and "for" believing God was present in the experience of Sophia. When the priest talked about the resurrection of Christ, Communion was a ceremony "of" believing Victoria's brother was in heaven, and "for" believing he was in heaven. In the cases of Sophia and Victoria, Communion brought into focus vital aspects of their lived experiences. While it was difficult to assess Samuel's experience through the lens of Geertz's system, he shaped his experience as his experience was shaping him. Samuel sensed God was watching him as a child and continues to watch him as an undergraduate student.

The dialectical nature of Communion conveyed the thought "of" being watched and "for" being watched. In William's case, Communion brought into focus the thought "of" what was happening and "for" what should be happening. Undoubtedly, like Sophia and Victoria, Samuel and William were shaping their experience as their experience was shaping them. If Communion is to succeed in functioning to communicate biblical truth through retelling the redemptive story, a better understanding towards theory development **must appreciate the dialectical nature of ceremony.** As a result, meaning making can also be shaped by an experience informed by the biblical text through Communion as a ceremony.

Edward Shils: Belief and Ceremony

The final lens of Shils' (1968) system revealed that Communion as a ceremony does, indeed, deliver what it promises regarding ultimate things for three of the four students. This was not true for Samuel. In some undisclosed way, what Communion promised failed him. Sophia admitted to her anti-social behavior, especially when driving her car. However, she believed that participating in Communion made her a better person. Because her belief was intertwined with Communion, what she believed the ceremony promised was delivered. Her anti-social behavior was brought into line. Victoria held to a belief that was different than Sophia, but the principle of intertwining beliefs with ceremony was the same (1968, 736).

Victoria believed her brother was in heaven, and when celebrating Communion, that belief was renewed, causing her to feel reassured. Again, William held to a different belief than Sophia and Victoria; nevertheless, the principle of belief and ceremony intertwining was the same (Shils 1968, 736). Essentially, William believed that participating in Communion in times of spiritual stagnation renewed him. The assessment shows that his beliefs were also delivered. Beliefs and ceremony are intertwined, and **when the ceremony positively delivers those beliefs,** a participant will more than likely continue to celebrate Communion and, thus, reinforce those beliefs. Consequently, a better understanding of how Communion as a ceremony communicates biblical truth through retelling the redemptive story has the potential of developing and reinforcing the truth of the Bible.

> the students' beliefs approaching Communion shaped what they got out of the ceremony

Summary Thought

These four summary discoveries highlight a third key discovery: the students' beliefs approaching Communion shaped what they got out of the ceremony. Such an approach could have led to an empty celebration. This was not the case. The students did, indeed, experience Christ in some way while celebrating Communion. Sophia moved from the concept of God to sensing Him; Victoria became aware of the reality of the resurrection of Christ; Samuel felt God was watching him; and William felt connected to Christ. Again, there is a lot of genuine experience already happening during Communion. However, these experiences are currently based upon sub-orthodox beliefs.

Table 11.1. Summary of Discoveries

	Summary
1	The person officiating Communion matters in the experience of participants.
2	The culture of a participant is involved in the performance of Communion.
3	Communion has a dialectical nature of shaping the students' experience and for shaping it.
4	When personal beliefs are intertwined with ceremony, Communion tends to deliver what those beliefs promise.

CONCLUDING THOUGHT

Having discovered what the students experienced in section two and how that lived experience is understood within ceremony, in the next section I will deal with the characteristics of spirituality, religious beliefs, and behaviors of the postmodern students who participate in Communion. I narrow the idea of postmodern students to a specific identity: Generation Z. The ways that priests, faculty, and campus ministry at SEU influence the way Generation Z describe spirituality in relation to religion are investigated. At the end of section four, a clear picture is painted of (1) what Generation Z (represented by the students at SEU) experienced during Communion; (2) how those lived experiences can be understood within ceremony; (3) the characteristics of spirituality and religious beliefs and behaviors; and (4) a list of key discoveries moving towards a theoretical model of how Communion functions to communicate biblical truth through retelling the redemptive story to Generation Z.

SECTION FOUR

SPIRITUALITY, RELIGIOUS BELIEFS, AND BEHAVIORS AMONG LATE MILLENNIALS AND GENERATION Z

This section focuses on the characteristics of spirituality and its relationship to religion and behaviors of the students at SEU who participate in Communion. Using qualitative methods similar to those in the second section, four questions were asked. I wanted to know (1) the ways students at SEU describe their experience of spirituality and religion; (2) how faculty members and campus ministry influence the way students describe their experience of spirituality and religion; (3) in what way does the Communion facilitate the expression of an experience of spirituality through religion, if at all; and, (4) how students describe God.

The first two questions concern the students' lived experiences. In order to provide dimensions to the students' experiences, focus was given on interpreting what they think, feel, and sense for themselves—similarly to phenomenology that suspends, or brackets, predetermined language, allowing the students to define their own explanations. The last two questions concern Communion and how it facilitates the students' experience and description of God.

Investigating a lived experience during Communion among students at SEU not only helped me describe the characteristics of spirituality, religious beliefs, and behaviors, it also informed me about how late Millennials and Generation Z think about and practice spirituality.

There is some ambiguity about the characteristics of Generation Z probably due to the fact that clear information is still emerging. After all, Generation Z currently represent a group where much is still being discovered as the younger siblings of late Millennials. The book title of Seemiller and Grace (2016) sums it up: *Meet Generation Z: A Century in the Making.* Generation Z did not appear any more than the Protestant Reformation appeared. They emerged from Millennials.

One significant characteristic that remains a little vague among researchers is the period of time in which Generation Z began.[46] Identical to the generalizations in chapter one, periods of time are not an exact science. In many ways, the characteristics that define a period of time begin to emerge in the previous time period. For example, the 1960's was a particular decade that became representative of cumulative cultural changes prior to and following the 60's. There was a fading away of Modernity as Postmodernity emerged. For the sake of my purposes, I will use the beginning date from leading experts Corey Seemiller and Meghan Grace (2016)[47] and the end date from the research of the Barna Group and their partnership with the Impact 360 Institute (2018)[48] to represent Generation Z. So, in what follows, I refer to the time period of 1995-2015 as that representation.

---

[46] Though a period of time is not completely agreed upon, dates are only within a few years.

[47] "1999-2010" (2016, 6).

[48] "1999-2015" (2018, 10).

CHAPTER 12

BEFORE GENERATION Z

Generation Z emerged from Millennials. A brief view into what is happening with late Millennials on campuses across North America will help in understanding the spiritual, religious, and behavioral differences that are found in Generation Z today on the campus of SEU. Generation Z can be considered the children of Millennials, and as younger siblings to late Millennials.

Millennials

The Higher Education Research Institute (HERI 2003) reported an increased national interest in spirituality among undergraduate students in America. Michael Lipka and David Masci (2016), report the same national interest in their work for the Pew Research Center.[49] The interest focuses on the relationship of spirituality and religion (Speck and Hoppe 2007). The report of Lipka and Masci points out the relationship is not a balanced one. Americans have become less religious in recent years while,

---

[49] The HERI report (2003) is specific to undergraduate students in America, whereas the report of Lipka and Masci (2016) focuses on a much broader population. I use the latter to show that what happens in college, in terms of spirituality and religion, is carried into adult life.

at the same time, there is a significant rise in spirituality.[50] Thomas Plante and Allen Sherman (2001), W. R. Miller and C. E. Thoresen (2003), and Linda George, David Larsen, Harold Koeing and Michael McCullough (2000) examined the relationship of spirituality and religion in order to discover the impact it had when they overlapped in the **beliefs and practices** of individuals.

They found a number of commonalities that included spirituality and religion; social support and improved health (Plante and Sherman 2001, 41); longevity in life (2001, 66); optimism and purpose in life (2001, 142); spiritual development and well-being (Miller and Thoresen 2003, 25); and, a sense of coherence or meaning in life (George et al 2000, 102). Even with these commonalities, the studies revealed significant differences showing that spirituality and religion were **described as separate constructs.**

Similar results emerged in other studies. For example, in a study carried out by David Derezotes (1995, 1-15), 1,120 participants were asked to respond to definitions of spirituality and religion using a Likert scale. The level of agreement for a definition of spirituality was as follows: 91% meaning in life, 86% purpose in life, 79% acceptance of self and world, 71% appreciation of the transcendent, 66% highest levels of well-being, 61% highest levels of consciousness, and 49% sense of idealism. The results show that **spirituality can be defined** in seven different ways.

In the same study, the level of agreement for a definition of religion was as follows: 85% system of shared beliefs, 77% reverence for a supreme creator, 74% system of shared doctrines, 72% system of shared rituals, and 67% institutionalized form of worship. Again, though, the results show that **religion can be defined** in five different ways. Derezotes (1995, 1-2) points out a certain degree of overlap existed between spirituality and religion in what he calls "a complex, intrapsychic dimension of human development." Though the results of the study show definitional conflict

---

[50] The report (Lipka and Masci 2016) states that standard measures were taken to show the importance of spirituality and religion in day-to-day life. Measures included how frequent people attend religious services and prayer.

for spirituality and religion, Derezotes recognizes that **spirituality and religion overlap** in the minds of individuals in their **beliefs and values.**

Using one-word descriptors, the study of E. R. Canda, and L. D. Furman (2010), also describes spirituality as somewhat distinct from religion with a degree of overlap between them. From these descriptors, they conclude that practitioners "would be able to relate to the contrasts and overlap between the concepts of spirituality and religion" (2010, 68). Furthermore, several scholars have offered summary statements that describe spirituality as different from religion.

On one hand, Ronald Bullis (2013, 2) summarizes religion as "the relationship of the human person to something or someone who transcends themselves." Robert Barker (2003) describes it as "devotion to the immaterial part of humanity;" and M. M. Carroll (1998, 2) as "one's basic nature." On the other hand, K. I. Pargament (2001, 169) summarizes spirituality as "a search for the significant ways related to the sacred" Rebecca Gotterer (2001, 188) as "believing" and T. Cascio (1998, 524) as "acceptance of a particular set of beliefs and ethics." Spirituality and religion are described differently while, at the same time, a degree of overlap is found between them (Hodge and McGrew 2005, 5).

William Nicholls believes that all religions teach spirituality. Many religious people "remain much the sort of people they would have been if they had not belonged to a religion" (1996, 451). According to Nicholls, the main attraction people have to religion is its structured ceremonies: "I would speculate that the healthier the person psychologically, the more likely they are to employ their religion as an expression and reinforcement of their own innate spirituality" (1996, 452). Religion provides people with common ceremonies to express their individual spirituality. However, as Nicholls points out, personal transformation does not necessarily take place for those who are attracted to them.

> Religion provides people with common ceremonies to express their individual spirituality.

In contrast to Nicholls, Geoph Kozeny suggests that a close examination of how people embody spiritual values in everyday life in the practice of self-reflection, self-growth, honesty, mercy, kindness, compassion, love, and good works could lead to personal transformation. Kozeny observed, "These communities all have ceremonies and routines to bring people together, to challenge assumptions, to bring egos into line, to get the work done, and to explore the great mysteries of life" (2004, 125). The need to **gather together in order to explore life** is different from the need for religious structure and ceremony. Though the need is different, spirituality and religion overlap in both needs. Religion provides people with common ceremonies to embody their individual spiritual values. For Nicholls, personal transformation does not necessarily occur when individual spirituality is expressed through a formal religious ceremony. For Kozeny, personal transformation is possible when spiritual values are embodied in a formal religious ceremony.

The findings in the HERI report (2003) show that an overlapping point of spirituality and religion does exist for the 112,232 undergraduate students who took part in the study from 236 colleges and universities in the United States. For example, one primary research question asked to what religious ceremonies students attracted to (2003, 2). The results showed that 81% of the students attended religious services where a ceremony was a regular feature (2003, 5).[51] Another primary question asked about the connection of spirituality to religion (2003, 2). The results showed 76% of the students said their spirituality was expressed through a

---

[51] The HERI report failed to show what specific religious ceremonies the students were attracted to. However, after contacting the co-principle investigator (Dr. Alexander Astin) at the University of California Los Angeles (UCLA) on August 24, 2016 by telephone, I was given the following information. Communion was the most attractive ceremony. The reason for the attraction was because Communion is a repeated ceremony/celebration regarding the participant. Other religious ceremonies like baptism, ordination, weddings, and funerals only require an individual to participate as the primary candidate a single time. Other religious rituals outside of Christianity were not included in the report.

religious ceremony defined as a search for meaning and purpose in life (2003, 4-5). Students **searched for meaning and purpose** in life largely through discussion with peers before and after a religious ceremony.[52]

The report of Lipka and Masci (2016) paints a similar picture to the HERI report (2003). Though Christianity in America has seen a 7% increase between 2007 and 2014, there is a 17% rise in "nones" (Lipka and Masci 2016). While 36% of "nones" between the ages of eighteen and twenty-three eschew an affiliation with organized religion, 67% of "nones" in that age group typically do not become more religiously affiliated as they get older (Lipka 2015). This implies that college students are more likely to associate their spirituality with religion than later on in life.

The findings in the HERI report (2003), and the report of Lipka and Masci (2016) show that students have a need for religious structure and ceremony (Nicholls 1996, 451), and an equal need to gather together to explore life (Kozeny 2004, 125). Student developer, Kimberly Greenway (2006, 2), describes the overlapping point in the same way as the students in the HERI report. Furthermore, the theories of Sharon Daloz Parks (2011) and James Fowler (1995) suggest that a search for meaning and purpose in life is the only way of describing what happens when spirituality and religion overlap.

Data shows that scholars are, indeed, describing spirituality and religion as separate constructs. Scholars equally acknowledge that spirituality and religion overlap as seen in the students' need to gather together and explore life and their need for religious structure and ceremony. Both needs provide for the students' expression of personal spiritual beliefs and values through formal religion.

----

[52] The report (HERI 2003, 4) does show that student peer discussion was largely how the students searched for meaning and purpose in life. However, in my conversation with Dr. Alexander Astin from UCLA (August 24, 2016), it was conveyed to me that discussion took place before and after the religious ceremony.

The different ways that spirituality can be described point out that spiritual beliefs and values are personal; whereas, the formality of religious ceremony points out that religion is far more formal. Four characteristics that describe the spirituality and religious beliefs and behaviors emerge from the students who were surveyed in the literature, are: (1) gathering together, (2) searching for meaning and purpose, (3) believing in a supernatural God, and (4) participation in Communion as a religious ceremony/celebration (see Table 12.1). If so, the evidence in my data supports the same characteristics in the students at SEU.

Table 12.1. Characteristics of Spirituality, Religious Beliefs, and Behaviors

	Characteristic
1	Gathering together
2	Searching for purpose and meaning
3	Belief in a supernatural God
4	Participation in Communion as a Christian ceremony/celebration

Summary Thought

For Millennials, the literature shows that spirituality and religion are described differently. The literature also shows that a formal religious ceremony/celebration is seen in the overlap of spirituality and religion where beliefs and values are expressed. Does the literature show the same with Generation Z?

Generation Z

In 2019, the Barna Group in partnership with the Impact 360 Institute, ministry practitioners, and educators, published their findings on Generation Z (Barna 2018). What they discovered was surprising. For example, more than Millennials, Generation Z are drawn to "things spiritual" (2018, 26). So, how is spirituality currently defined?

In his recent publication, Arndt Bussing (2019, 2) notes on one hand that religion is often defined as adherence to beliefs, doctrines, ethics, texts and practices associated with a higher power that involve rituals or ceremonies. On the other hand, spirituality is defined from inner experiences seeking meaning and purpose (2019, 3). Using his definitions, it is not surprising that Generation Z are drawn to things spiritual. An experience of spirituality is far more personal, and even intimate, than religion.

As such, the starting point for spirituality among members of Generation Z is not a set of beliefs or values but more of a **blank slate open to the impressions of inward spirituality.** Despite the difference in definition and the varied attraction spirituality and religion create, Seemiller and Grace (2016, 166-180) recognize a continued merging similar to Millennials. James E. White (2017, 24) describes this merging as "far from waning." Interestingly, far more than Millennials, Generation Z have very little, if any, formal or informal religious education making them **a truly post-Christian generation** yet growing in spiritual awareness. Even so, there is an overlap between this growing spirituality and, to a lesser degree, religion (Bussing 2019, 3).

The overlap of spirituality and religion have value for Generation Z. For example, in a 2016 study by the Varkey Foundation, 54% of Generation Z said religion was actually important to their happiness (Seemiller and Grace 2016, 177). If spirituality and religion were a point of conversation for Millennials, the conversation is continuing for Generation Z. Nevertheless, in many ways, religion is "on the table but off the radar" (2016, 177). On one hand, the predominant religion in North America still on the table is Christianity. Generation Z have not opted out of the

Christian faith in favor of another dominant religion. On the other hand, Christianity is off the radar because Generation Z appear to have abandoned a definition of Christianity (White 2017, 24). For example, one particular member of Generation Z said, "I believe in God, in a higher power. I believe in Jesus. But I don't believe you necessarily have to follow the Bible step-by-step" (Barna 2018, 56).

> "I believe in God, in a higher power. I believe in Jesus. But I don't believe you necessarily have to follow the Bible step-by-step"

In fact, only 4% of Generation Z have a biblical worldview (Barna 2018, 25). It is no surprise, then, that spirituality and religion among Generation Z has little or no definition. Though spirituality is far more amplified than religion, both are on the table as the same thing but off the table as separate constructs. Whereas the popular phrase "I'm spiritual but not religious" tended to fit the beliefs and values of Millennials, it does not accurately describe Generation Z (White, 2017, 62). Rather, Generation Z are spiritual without the labels of religion. So, the phrase "I'm a Baptist" or "I'm not a Baptist" does not equate with "I don't believe in God" (2017, 62). While 58% identify as Christian, only 43% recently attended a church (2018, 26). In fact, "Most of those who say church is not important to them still consider themselves Christian" (2018, 61). Religion is not rejected, but Generation Z are far more apathetic towards it, or as Lipka (2015) points out, they are unaffiliated "nones."

However, when asked about the Christian religion, 35% said they preferred the symbol of the cross than a modern symbol, which was the majority preference; 77% preferred a sanctuary than an auditorium; 67% preferred a classic church service than a trendy one; and 67% preferred moments of quietness in a church service for reflection rather than noise (Barna 2018, 67-73). Also, 47% are attracted to religious ceremonies like Communion (Seemiller and Grace 2016, 43). Here is the point: **Generation Z are not religious, but they are drawn to things spiritual with traditional religious symbols and language.**

Similar to Millennials, Generation Z are concerned with meaning in life, purpose in life, self, and well-being with one exception. "The social issues that Generation Z students identify as caring about are we-centric, meaning that whatever the issue 'it affects all of us'" (Seemiller and Grace 2016, 122). This makes sense when the majority of Generation Z do not think about personal career goals as much as they focus on destiny statements that help them do deep reflection on their values, passions, beliefs, and life calling as a positive impact on the world (2016, 219). One could almost say that Generation Z, in general, is a deeper well than Millennials that preceded them.

The deepening affect is also seen in values held by Generation Z that were also held by Millennials. This affect is seen in emotional buy-in. Generation Z will buy-in to something if that something shares the same values (Seemiller and Grace 2016, 136). The same affect is seen in friendships. If there are shared values between people, friendships will ensue even to the point of calling those friendships the "good life" or "familial relationships" (Seemiller and Grace 2019, 109). Honesty, openness, and transparency are key values to Generation Z and foundational to friendships (Seemiller and Grace 2016, 166). As such, **sincerity is a valued marker for truth** (Barna 2018, 65).

However, caution is needed with Generation Z. "It is tempting to try to connect with a post-Christian culture by mirroring its post-Christian values" (White 2017, 93). Ministry practitioners that have tried to connect with post-Christian values this way tend to jettison the value of Scripture. Such an approach would be counter-intuitive with Generation Z. It would simply not be sincere of the ministry practitioner to jettison their beliefs. Added to this, one study found 78% of Generation Z believe in God (Seemiller and Grace 2016, 43). While belief in God is quite high, 37% believe it is not possible to know if God is actually real (Barna 2018, 64). This type of skepticism is supported by 46% who say, "I need factual evidence to support my beliefs" (2018, 65).

In addition to an overlap between spirituality and religion, the program manager at Fuller Youth Institute, Irene Cho (Barna 2018, 31), highlights the intersectionality in all parts of life for

Generation Z. "This intersectionality also creates one of the greatest opportunities for discipleship" (2018, 31). For Generation Z, diversity is not just about race. It is about all aspects of life that include spirituality and religion. There are no traffic lights or rules for the intersection. By default, the intersection creates a space for people to come together. According to Cho (2018, 31), the key for discipleship is to slow down at the intersection in order for dialogue to take place.

Summary Thought

There are many similarities concerning the spirituality, religious beliefs, and behaviors of Generation Z with their Millennial predecessors. The marked difference is one of depth and longevity. Generation Z tend to go deeper with their beliefs and focus on destiny statements rather than short term goals (see Table 12.2)

Table 12.2. Late Millennial and Generation Z Similarities

Late Millennials	Generation Z
Overlap of spirituality and religion	Intersection of spirituality and religion
Spirituality and religion defined differently	Spirituality and religion defined vaguely
Spirituality more dominant than religion	Spirituality more dominant than religion
Belief in an undefined God	Belief in an undefined God
Sub-Orthodox beliefs	Less than sub-orthodox beliefs
Shared belief values	Shared and differing beliefs and values
Overlap is where spirituality is expressed	Overlap is where discipleship can take place

CONCLUDING THOUGHT

Like Millennials, the literature shows that spirituality and religion are described differently. There is a similar overlap of **spirituality and religion** where beliefs and values are identified and shared. Within this overlap is an intersection where all aspects of life converge including spirituality and religion. Again, like Millennials, there are four characteristics that describe spirituality, religious beliefs, and behaviors: (1) gathering together, (2) searching for meaning and purpose, (3) the believing in a supernatural God, and (4) an opportunity to participate in Communion as a religious ceremony/celebration. The difference between Millennials and Generation Z is these **four characteristics go deeper into the culture where definitions become blurred.** In the next chapter, I give voice to the conversation of two student groups, faculty, and staff at SEU. What emerges is quite surprising.

CHAPTER 13

ON CAMPUS WITH LATE MILLENNIALS AND GENERATION Z

In this chapter, four similar stages of my research design were implemented. Again, I will not bore you with the details of my design as it would take at least another seventy pages. However, I will summarize, like **section two**, by stating that the design had: (1) two research instruments; (2) method for recruitment of students, tasks they performed, accomplishing tasks, and compensation; (3) staging interviews; (4) steps for data analysis; and, (5) establishing reliability and validity. Like previously, I assigned a gender relative pseudonym to each student, faculty and staff member, named from the history of British monarchy. Having got my **"Englishness"** in previously, I did not see any harm in amplifying the fact!

In order to show the students' perspectives, identical to the method in **section two** and **three,** verbatim extracts are cited from each discussion and interview. Like before, some citations may appear elementary in their written form.

The Students' Perspectives

To begin discussion with the first group, each of the students was asked what spirituality meant to them. Charles replied, "It's related to the Holy Ghost. Just like feeling the presence of God inside of you. It's more like how you feel on the inside, and how you manifest that to others." Following Charles, Anne responded, "I think in a way it ties into faith. I see spirituality as my relationship with God." In a similar response to Charles and Anne, Beatrice remarked, "It is your connection to your deity." In contrast to her peers, Kate explained, "It's the way a person interacts with the world around them on the level of what is a deity, on the level of what is infinite, not finite. It can be like anything and everything."

The same question was put to the second discussion group. Using similar language to Beatrice from the first group, Eleanor answered, "It all pertains to how you feel with yourself. It can be on any sort of level, but mostly it's on a basic level." Meghan's answer revealed her own narrative, "I don't know if it's just the way that I was brought up, but at the moment you said 'spirituality,' I automatically connected it to God."

In both discussion groups, spirituality meant different things to the students highlighting what personal spirituality looked like. Spirituality was defined in the Introduction of this book as "personal beliefs and values by which an individual relates to and experiences a supernatural God." The students explained that spiritualty: related to the Holy Ghost (Charles); tied to faith (Anne); connected to a deity (Beatrice); affected interaction with the world (Kate); influenced how one feels about oneself (Eleanor); and, connoted a connection to God (Meghan). The explanations of Charles, Anne, Beatrice, and Meghan could be classified as an expression of personal spirituality and religion. In each case, **spirituality was autonomously interpreted by the students** without any reference to the biblical text. Instead, their interpretation is based on sub-orthodox beliefs.

Spirituality and Religion

A successive question asked both groups about their experience of spirituality and religion. Anne was quick to respond stating, "I think spirituality is your relationship with God, and religion is your relationship with God as how the church expects you to have your relationship with God." Charles added, "Yeah, it's not tied to religion, it's how you act. It's based on your personal relationship with God. It's not a relationship with a religion then to God, it's directly to God."

After overtly nodding at the response of Anne and Charles, Kate remarked, "Spirituality is separate from religion because you don't necessarily need to have religion to be spiritual. Although spirituality can be in religion." Beatrice agreed with Kate adding, "I think that whatever divine presence is out there, it can be shown and displayed in multiple different ways. I don't think that one needs necessarily religion to recognize that spirituality."

In the second group, Meghan adamantly stated, "I believe religion and spirituality are completely different. There's a big disconnect. I feel like religion is just a set of do's and don'ts, and spirituality is more of a personal relationship with you and God." Agreeing with Meghan, Eleanor explained why spirituality and religion are separate, "Because you can have religion, you can have all this doctrine thrown at you, but if you don't get anything from it, like, if you just deflect it in your spirit, or how you're meant to be spiritual, it doesn't grow. There's nothing feeding it." Eleanor added, "I think we are born with religion, but spirituality is more of a choice to explore."

In both discussion groups, the students' experience of spirituality connects them to God and not necessarily to religion. Spirituality and religion are explained as relationally different (Anne);

not tied (Charles); separate (Kate and Eleanor); not the same (Beatrice); a deflection in the student's spirit (Meghan); and, disconnected (Eleanor). What begins to emerge is that spirituality, religion, and God are autonomously described without any reference to the biblical text and, yet, all three are connected. Again, this highlighted what personal spirituality looked like. It also highlighted what religion looked like. For the purposes of this book, religion is defined as a formal institutionalized system of beliefs and practices that concern a supernatural God.

Religion was for more formal than personalized spirituality. In particular, what also began to emerge helped me discover how the students describe a supernatural God with sub-orthodox beliefs. **Who the students refer to as a supernatural God does not appear to be the same supernatural God that the church has taught them about;** and, in the comment of Beatrice, God is merely a divine presence. A significant discovery is that the students are spiritually connected to a supernatural God based on sub-orthodox beliefs.

Overlap of Spirituality and Religion

Continuing along the lines of the students' experiences of spirituality and religion, they were asked if they overlapped, if at all. Again, if scholars are describing an overlapping point, I wanted to know if this was true in the experiences of the students. In the first group, Charles remarked, "I guess spirituality enhances religion when they meet, or the way you experience religion that expresses your purpose." Anne followed, "In a way, the overlap helps create purpose for me. To me, it's kind of like I know there's a heaven and I know that there's a hell, and I know that we are all meant to be here, not just to mess around but there's a purpose as to why we are all here and why we are all living." Describing her experience in the Methodist church, Beatrice remarked, "I am able to combine the two at some point, even though they are separate, as something intertwined to know who I am." Agreeing with Beatrice, Kate said, "I have also just noticed in myself that it is the place where your true purpose is revealed. I like to serve, and I am at my best when I serve others." The students' comments highlighted what meaning and purpose look like as part of a post-modern community.

In the second group, Meghan described an overlap of spirituality and religion as "more of a choice to explore where we discover who we are." In a lengthy explanation, Eleanor described how an overlap of spirituality and religion has the potential of destroying meaning in life. For example, Eleanor described her homosexual friend as a man who loved God (spirituality), but his church believes homosexuality is a sin (religion). For Eleanor, if spirituality and religion did overlap, it would create an opportunity to "rediscover meaning in life as a second chance." In her view, the homosexual friend would have to find another church (religion) that accepted his sexual identity.

All students in both discussion groups explained an overlapping point of spirituality and religion did exist in their experiences. This highlighted how personal spirituality is expressed through formal religion when the students gather together as a community to participate in Communion. Common among these responses was an emphasis on what took place. Religion was enhanced (Charles), purpose was expressed, created, and found (Charles, Anne, and Kate), personal identity was explored and discovered (Meghan and Beatrice), and an opportunity for personal rediscovery was found. The students appear to have a **need to individually experience something seen in the overlap of spirituality and religion.** Also, the students autonomously interpreted their experiences in the overlap with no reference to the biblical text. Once more, their views appear to be sub-orthodox.

Communion in the Overlap

Another commonality I found in both groups was in response to a question about Communion facilitating the expression of an experience of spirituality through religion. Communion, as a religious ceremony, did facilitate experiences in the overlap when the students gathered together to participate in the bread and wine. Prioritizing the ceremony brought into focus two characteristics of postmodern spirituality, religious beliefs, and behaviors of the students at SEU: gathering together and prioritizing a religious ceremony. In each case, the students felt a sense of overall completeness as they participated in Communion.

For example, building on his remarks that his spirituality is enhanced by religion, Charles recognized "love and compassion" among those gathered together. Likewise, Anne remarked, "Communion also enhances our purpose." Building on her comments about identity, Beatrice mentioned, "I'm connected to the community through Communion." Unrelated to her previous comments on the overlapping point of spirituality and religion, Kate believed Communion facilitated her ability "to think outside of the box of God being a man, or God being a woman or possibly something." Kate's comment ties in to expanded remarks about her own search for meaning and purpose.

In the second group, Eleanor felt her spirituality was "empowered" in the celebration of the Communion in community. Likewise, Meghan commented, "It [Communion] gives me a sense of hope; it reminds me of why I believe what I believe, why I am where I am." Experiences in the overlap were facilitated by Communion within a community of peers. Once again, the students' explanations highlighted what gathering together Communion look like as characteristics of spirituality and religious beliefs and behaviors. Though the students' experiences are explained in the context of a community, they begin with self and interpret their experiences autonomously. Hence, the community is a postmodern community.

Two important observations shed light on the indicators of a postmodern environment at SEU. First, when the students refer to God, it is based in sub-orthodox beliefs without any reference to the biblical text. Second, although the students experience love, compassion, enhancement of purpose, connection to others, empowerment, and hope in community, personal transformation does not take place despite their need to experience something.

Though all the students view spirituality and religion as different things, they place a greater importance on the former than on the latter. Spirituality and religion overlap where Communion as a religious ceremony facilitated their experiences. Both highlight what the ceremony looks like in a postmodern environment. Another significant discovery is that **Communion provides for the students' spiritual connection to a supernatural God.** If so, overlap is not a coincidence as there is a real need for religious structure and ceremony as an expression of personal spirituality.

Need for Religious Structure and Ceremony

Beatrice referred to Communion as a "spiritual monopoly" that includes or excludes participation in the ceremony based on church teaching. Charles made an impersonal reference to "the teachings they [church] have, and the way they [church] want you to act." Kate attributed her understanding of Communion to the teachings of her church stating, "I don't know that it changed me as a person." Likewise, Anne remarked,

> "We get so caught up with life, that we don't really see ourselves change, as we look back."

"I have grown up in the beliefs. But someone who hasn't can go into those beliefs and start learning them. Learning them does not change you."

Commenting on what the church taught her about the benefits of celebrating Communion, Eleanor stated, "I learned that when it comes to something like this it is for your own good, even though you don't change." Similar to Eleanor, Meghan commented on being taught by the church, "We get so caught up with life, that we don't really see ourselves change, as we look back." Though each student had been taught about Communion in some form of church education, personal transformation did not take place in their lives as a result of that teaching. Nevertheless, each student continued to celebrate the religious ceremony of Communion.

Continued participation in Communion as a religious ceremony provides far more meaning to a lived experience than what the church teaches. This fact alone may shed light on why the **stu-**

dents appear to have a need for religious structure and ceremony as a practice and not a teaching. There is continued desire to find meaning. If so, the students have a real need to gather together in order to explore life.

Need for Gathering Together to Explore Life

The students also talked about their attraction to Communion as a point of gathering together that gave an appearance of transformation in a reoccurring phrase, "I see." This phrase summarized what they valued in the gathering. For example, Charles said, "I see inspiration"; Anne, "I see the God of hope"; Beatrice, "I see interaction"; Kate, "I see others"; Meghan, "I see more of a symbol of love"; and, Eleanor, "I see partnership." Gathering together as students was less about personal transformation than the act of gathering together. This helped me further answer what gathering together looked like.

Each student simply made an observation of the gathering, stating what they personally valued and not their perception of transformation. For example, Meghan valued a symbol of love in her observation of the gathering. Her observation was not in contrast to a lack of a symbol of love at the commencement of their gathering. If this was the case, transformation would have taken place during the gathering. Communion as a religious ceremony frames the students' values, symbolized in elements of community observed by them as they gather together. The need to experience something is seen in their need for formal religious structure and ceremony and their need to gather together to explore life.

These needs shed light on all three indicators of a postmodern environment at SEU and also on the overlap of spirituality and religion—the overlap is not a coincidence. Both needs give rise to two significant discoveries towards theory development that explains how Communion serves to communicate biblical truth through retelling the redemptive story. First, a **personal lived experience is connected to positive aspects of community; and second, continued connection to God and positive aspects of community provide meaning for a lived experience.**

Summary Thought

The questions asked in this chapter helped me discover that the observations made by scholars about students in their research are also true about the students at SEU. Four characteristics emerged that describe the spirituality, religious beliefs, and behaviors: (1) gathering together, (2) searching for meaning and purpose, (3) believing in a supernatural God, and (4) participation in Communion as a religious ceremony (see Table 10.1).

CONCLUDING THOUGHT

Spirituality meant different things to the students, so spirituality is highly personal at SEU. No matter how the students described it, spirituality connected them as a community that gathered together to encounter a supernatural God where Communion facilitated their experiences. The students did not reference the biblical text in how they described spirituality or God. Rather, their views are sub-orthodox. These answers shed light on how the students described a supernatural God and led to a significant discovery: a spiritual connection to a supernatural God.

> the religious ceremony of Communion provided for the students' spiritual connection to a supernatural God.

Though the students connect with a supernatural God, they do not necessarily connect with religion. This highlighted that religion is formal and not personal to the students. The students' experience of spirituality and religion show an overlap exists where the religious ceremony of Communion facilitated their lived experiences. They had a need for religious structure and ceremony, albeit formal. These observations led to another significant discovery: the religious ceremony of Communion provided for the students' spiritual connection to a supernatural God.

The students' lived experiences are contextualized in a community of peers where positive aspects of that gathering are observed by the students. Their observation lined up with values that are individually important to them. This led to another significant discovery: a personal lived experience is connected to positive aspects of community.

The students continued with their participation in Communion despite negative encounters with church teaching. Two things emerged that shed light on continued participation. First, a lived experience in Communion provided more meaning and purpose than the teaching of the church. Second, the students had a need to gather together to explore life. These observations led to another significant finding: continued spiritual connection to a supernatural God and positive aspects of community provide meaning for a lived experience (see Table 13.1).

Table 13.1. Summary of Student Perspectives

Perspective	Interpretation
Spirituality	Means different things
Spirituality	Connects students to an undefined God
Overlap	Spirituality and religion
Lived Experience	Autonomously interpreted
Biblical	Sub-orthodox
Communion	Necessary for a lived experience
Communion	Necessary to discover meaning
Religion	Necessary for ceremonial structure
Community	Lived experience helps see positive aspects

At this point, I was beginning to grasp what a postmodern community looked like. I was also able to see the connections of the characteristics of the spirituality and religious beliefs and behaviors of the students at SEU who participate in Communion.

CHAPTER 14

CAMPUS INFLUENCE ON LATE MILLENNIALS AND GENERATION Z

Professor Blanche and Professor Edgar both responded to questions in order to determine how they influenced the way students describe the spirituality, religious beliefs and behaviors, a supernatural God, and in what way Communion as a religious ceremony facilitates an expression of spirituality through religion, if at all.

Influence of Professor Blanche

The dual profession of Professor Blanche as a faculty member at SEU and an ordained minister was seen throughout the analysis of her interview. After asking questions about the combination of teaching and ministry, Professor Blanche responded, "I still do feel called to preach and to preside over the sacraments and then, hopefully, to the students on campus." The idea that ministry and teaching are one and the same profession is important to understanding the influence Professor Blanche has on the students. For example, she presided over Communion in a make-shift chapel on campus at SEU for an entire year while the current sanctuary was being remodeled.

At the most, twelve to fifteen students participated with an average of five to six each week. Also, one of the students would regularly bake bread to use for the Communion bread. When asked further questions about how and when she invited students to participate, Professor Blanche replied, "I would say a few words in class or on campus about the meaning of the celebration and that all are welcome." She continued, "And that this table is not ours here at St. Ed's and it doesn't belong to the pastors, but it is God's table and God extends this welcome."

Professor Blanche also made some insightful comments about religion in her observations of the students. "I started talking to some students just about, especially non-Catholic students, about his or her experience of religion or lack thereof here on campus and whether they were wanting, desiring spiritual resources. And several of them said 'yes.' My idea was to provide a resource for the student community."

After talking about her observations of religion among the students and the need for resources, Professor Blanche talked about her observations of spirituality among the students. For example, in her basic questions class she teaches **"spirit experience."** "Often, spirit experience gets undervalued as an epistemological category, and so the experience of, say, taking communion or, in this case, if I were to say for the giving of the communion, it's certainly a real experience of spirituality. It's not like it's exclusive of rationality and intellect. **It's just so much deeper."**

The idea that ministry and teaching are one and the same thing emerges in the analysis of Professor Blanche's interview. This is an important observation about Professor Blanche as it relates to her influence over the students in the classroom. A connection between spirituality and religion is seen in her influence. In response to the students' religious experiences, she provides spiritual resources. Professor Blanche does not provide religious structure but a location for the students to gather together in order to celebrate the Communion as a religious celebration.

The extent of her influence on the way students describe their experience of spirituality and religion is seen in her theoretical ideas in the classroom and in the practice of those ideas through Communion. By placing ownership of Communion in the hands of God, Professor Blanche minimalizes meeting the students' need for religious structure stating it is "God's table" with few rules. At the same time, she maximizes meeting the need for the students to gather together to celebrate by providing a time and place for Communion. These observations highlighted how the Communion facilitates the expression of an experience of spirituality through minimized religion at SEU. This fact alone also highlighted how spirituality is personal and religion formal.

Summary Thoughts

Professor Blanche's provision for the students also sheds light on the indicators of a postmodern environment at SEU: the students have a need to **experience something**; their experience is left to their own **sub-orthodox interpretation**, guided by few rules; and their **experience begins with self.**

Influence of Professor Edgar

Professor Edgar was not as transparent as Professor Blanche about his influence on the student body. Nevertheless, he was open about Communion. After analyzing the transcript, several things emerged that show how Communion facilitates an expression of personal spirituality through formal religion. For example, "I think I would use a meal to categorize how Communion is organized or put together. It's like me inviting people in, sitting down, and sharing stories. It's coming together for a meal. It's being grateful for what we've been given. In that meal, communion is established." Pursuing his line of thought, Professor Edgar was asked to illustrate his views from his observations in the student body at SEU:

> "Whenever I talk to my students, they tell me you don't know your friends when you come to school the first week and you're looking for someone to go to dinner with. You're embarrassed but you find a few people and grab a slice of pizza. You get a couple beers, and there's five or six of them around the table who are just individuals who didn't know who else to

hang out with on a Friday night when they started, but at the end of the night they are communicating. The meal itself created that communion - in a particularly unique way that meal created the communion, and the Communion, as in celebrating in the Christian community, it's a unique particular way, and a beautiful way of doing it."

Professor Edgar's observations highlight the students' need for gathering together to explore life where Communion acts as a celebration for communication between the students. He acknowledges that "students are longing for some depth in their life, and one of the great traditions is that Communion is a profound place to experience that." In response to why students at SEU tend to gather as a community to celebrate Communion, specifically on a Sunday evening, Professor Edgar quickly responded, "In my opinion, it's because the students want to, not because they feel obliged to."

Again, the students need to gather together is highlighted. Gathering together is more of a need than an obligation. A later comment also reveals his approach to Communion that meets his own need for religious structure and ceremony: "My theology of the Eucharist [Communion], as communion and intimacy, facilitated my experience of intimacy in the Eucharist." A **theology of intimacy** was something he had been taught as a child. Since that time, he maintains this teaching in his own participation in Communion. Any **deviation from his theology of intimacy was not acceptable to him**. Professor Edgar's observation of spirituality and religion among the students recognizes their need for gathering together to explore life where Communion acts as a communicating celebration in that gathering. His own need is for religious structure and ceremony highlighted by the longevity of what he was taught as a child.

Summary Thought

Professor Edgar's influence on the SEU students' description of their experience of spirituality and religion or a supernatural God was unclear. Consequently, I was only able to partially answer what the spirituality and religious beliefs and behaviors of the students looked like in Professor Edgar's influence over the students as a celebration for the students to gather together and explore life. Thankfully, I was able to obtain more observations from two priests on campus.[53] Father Brown and Father Ted officiate over Communion on the campus of SEU in Our Lady Queen of Peace chapel. They are also involved in campus ministry and teach classes. In both interviews, questions were asked that related to all three roles. I gave them pseudonyms from my own influence from G. K. Chesterton's *Father Brown* series, in which, Father Ted makes an appearance.

Influence of Father Brown

Spirituality plays more of a significant role in Father Brown's life than religion. For example, he recalled teaching from his childhood, regarding Communion, "The teaching on the real presence made a big impact on me." The church's teachings created a **meaning in him** that differed from the **meaning students discussed.** The impact had a lasting effect that was seen in his comment on personal preparation to serve the student body in a chapel service, "I kind of let the Spirit move me because we are dealing with the presence of Christ and people gathering together."

> "I kind of let the Spirit move me because we are dealing with the presence of Christ and people gathering together."

Commenting on a chapel service, Father Brown remarked, "I'm a little more about the moving of the spirit among the students than script."[54] Father Brown's view of the student body as a community also includes the Holy Spirit. He remarked, "I don't

---

[53] Though St. Edward's University is a Catholic school, there are forty-nine different church denominations that can be called Christian, and eight other faith traditions that can be called non-Christian.

[54] Father Brown's repeated term "script" refers to strict guidelines regarding the priest, celebrant, and the Communion celebration.

see a division between the Spirit and the physical human body." He continued, "There can be all kinds of chemical reactions going on or neural pathways that are being formed; that is still the Spirit that script does not necessarily connect with." His comments highlighted why spirituality is personal and religion, in the use of set liturgy, is far more formal.

Father Brown invests himself in the students' lives in order to effectively communicate with them, "I think I'm sensitive to picking up different moods in the community of students that may not fit my beliefs." Regarding spirituality in the student body, he remarked, "It's something that's being *expressed both naturally but also culturally* and also something that's meant to be personally involving." Again, his comments highlighted why spirituality is personal and not formal like religion. He continued, "You're always being *careful not to intrude on the conscience* of other people." Being careful not to intrude also emerged in Father Brown's inclusive comment on receiving the Eucharist [Communion], "I would commune people because they are coming up and because I'm in no position to judge them or to make distinctions at that moment."

From personal conversations with the students, Father Brown added, "I think that there's a yearning for a mystical connection in that they are experiencing God at some level." Again, from the same conversations, he noted a dilemma in the student body, "When they're having trouble with religion, it's because they're lining their behavior up with certain Christian ideals, but the ceremonial part of it [Communion] gives them a space where they don't have to reconcile everything." In his view, Communion removes religious rules and replaces it with a spiritual experience because "truth, I think, is **embedded in the ceremony.**"

His observations highlighted what two specific characteristics of the spirituality and beliefs and behaviors of the students looked like. First, in the way Communion **facilitates an expression of personal spirituality through formal religion;** and second, in the way students could **describe God, different from how Father Brown may describe God** because, in his view, a description is open to personal interpretation.

Father Brown has a unique role by intentionally influencing the way students describe their experience of spirituality and religion. Undoubtedly, he identifies far more with spirituality than religion in his own life and ministry. His own spirituality is informed by the work of the Holy Spirit. He is less concerned with religious rules and more interested in creating an opportunity for the students to explore spirituality. That opportunity is seen in his practice of an inclusive Communion. In his view, the **spirituality of the students is a natural and personal thing**. Though Father Brown influences the spirituality of the students, he does not want to intrude on their lived experience while celebrating Communion.

> "If spirituality is the part that is malleable and moveable, how do I know the meaning of it? How do I create a meaningful world for myself to be in relationship—and this is the transcendent part—in relationship to a world that's bigger than me? It's about being related to a lot of people that are different."

Summary Thought

As a priest, Father Brown's influence and observations can be seen in his belief that Communion is a **point of inclusively gathering** students together. His observations reveal that the students do, indeed, gather together to explore life. Though students may have a need for religious structure and ceremony, Father Brown's emphasis on this need is minimal. His willingness to **not get in the way** of the students' lived experience in Communion stands out. Under this influence, all three indicators of a postmodern environment at SEU come into play. Students have a need to experience something, but they are left to **interpret their lived experience based on sub-orthodox beliefs** beginning with self.

Influence of Father Ted

Father Ted succinctly described his understanding of spirituality, "I would put it very simply: it's about one's being in the world. Who you are and how you are embedded with the world is ultimately your spirituality. It doesn't have anything to do necessarily with **religion or God or theology.**" He continued, "Students generally believe spirituality doesn't need to be all that clearly articulated." Commenting on his observations of a student definition of spirituality, Father Ted pointed out, "If spirituality is the part that is malleable and moveable, how do I know the meaning of it? How do I create a meaningful world for myself to be in relationship—and this is the transcendent part—in relationship to a world that's bigger than me? It's about being related to a lot of people that are different."

> "I teach the students that they will always be in process learning more about spirituality all their lives."

His comments highlighted personal spirituality, because, in his view and influence, spirituality is malleable. It also highlighted a gathering of diverse people. He was asked to elaborate on how he influenced a student's understanding of spirituality. Father Ted replied, "I teach the students that they will always be in process learning more about spirituality all their lives." A similar question was asked about religion, "I think generally the students question what they were formally taught about religion." Father Ted continued, "You know, when I teach world religions, I often have a student ask me why they were not taught about other religions when they were kids." By teaching other religions and encouraging the students to question what the church has taught them, his influence helps answer the way students could **describe God.**

> "We talk about the gathering of the church for Communion so that we can scatter from there for mission. We don't stay there at Communion. This is not a warm basket of puppies. We are here so that we can be nourished, Word and Sacrament, and then go forth in mission."

Intentional encouragement for the students to think about their understanding of religion in light of their own life experiences emerges in the analysis of Father Ted's interview. This was seen in his comments on a class he teaches about world religions. "I have them write a paper where students articulate who they are in the world and how experiences change them, like the death of a parent, the death of a sibling, or just that simple thing of boyfriend and girlfriend breaking up, and what that means." Tying the mission of SEU[55] to Communion, Father Ted explained:

> "As long as we are a Catholic institution, Communion is important on campus in terms of the mission in educating the mind and helping people grow responsibly by doing social justice so they can make a difference in the world. If a student comes out of this environment with those things, then we have been successful whether they're Catholic or not."

He continued, "We talk about the gathering of the church for Communion so that we can scatter from there for mission. We don't stay there at Communion. This is not a warm basket of puppies. We are here so that we can be nourished, Word and Sacrament, and then go forth in mission."

Summary Thought

Father Ted overtly influences the way students describe their experience of spirituality and religion and the way celebrating the Communion is an expression of personal spirituality through formal religion. This helps me answer what the specific characteristics of the spirituality and religious beliefs and behaviors looks like at SEU in how Communion facilitates the expression of personal spirituality

---

[55] St. Edward's expresses its identity by communicating the dignity of the human person as created in the image of God, by stressing the obligation of all people to pursue a more just world, and by providing opportunities for religious studies and participation in campus ministry. St. Edward's seeks to provide an environment in which freely chosen beliefs can be deepened and expressed (SEU 2015).

through formal religion. Surprisingly for a priest, his influence over the students does not highlight their need for religious structure and ceremony. He expects the students to **question what they were taught** about religion as a child.

He encourages the **development of personal beliefs and values** from the students' life experiences and not necessarily from the biblical text. The idea that spirituality has nothing to do with religion, God, or the biblical text, but a meaningful world developed in a community of others stands out in Father Ted's influence over the students. Under this influence, spirituality is highly personal. All three indicators of a postmodern environment at SEU come into play. Father Ted teaches that the students need to experience something that begins with self and is autonomously interpreted outside of religion, God, or the biblical text.

Influence of Arthur

Arthur is a key member of campus ministry. As you can tell, I gave him the pseudonym after the English king, Arthur. He described spirituality in a similar fashion to Father Ted, "I think it's the lived presence one feels in a lived experience. I would say in Christ, but for me it would probably be more strongly resonated of understanding God and God's role of my life and in the world but not in the religious sense." Arthur continued, "Spirituality and religion can be different things. They don't have to be different things, but they can be. So, as I study religion, I tend to separate the two. So, when I think of spirituality, I do not necessarily think about religion."

Commenting on his direct role with the student body as a key part of campus ministry, he remarked, "We [campus ministry] are **educators in the faith, not of the faith,** but in the faith. So, I believe that we are here to assist the students in their personal faith development and whatever that means for them." He continued, "We do not impose Christianity. We walk with them [students] because we are Christian. We believe that is our role and our purpose as Christians—to help people grow to the fullest that God created them to be...I think that's the role of campus ministry. We also want to be in dialogue with students of non-faith and in all traditions." His comments on the dialogue with the students help me answer how the students describe God outside of the biblical text or the Christian faith.

Arthur was asked if Communion played any part in his role in campus ministry. His response was personal. "Communion is still an elusive thing for me. I don't know if I would ever say that there's been a prolonged period of my life when Communion had any effect on me." Further questions were presented that juxtaposed his experience in Communion with students who participate in the celebration.

"For many of them, they come from backgrounds where it's kind of a requirement. Many come because it's their seeking, and some come because they find it part of who they are." Arthur continued, "But I would say our younger students[56] are more attuned to Communion." Arthur was asked to expand on his comment about students being attuned to ritual. "They want to see a priest, and they want to see a priest and a collar, not in a polo shirt. They are often kneeling. There are parts of the mass where you can either kneel or stand. In the evening mass, the students are kneeling." His comments highlighted why religion is formal.

Summary Thought

Though Arthur's role in campus ministry is not to convert students to the Christian faith, he positively influences the way students describe their experience of spirituality and religion by his **ecumenical approach to all faiths as well as non-faith.** Arthur's inclusive approach helped me further see what the characteristic of gathering together looked like. His role in campus ministry does not appear to influence the way celebrating Communion could facilitate the expression of spirituality through religion. Consequently, it could be said that Arthur's influence meets the students' apparent need to inclusively gather together to explore life. Regardless of a specific faith or non-faith, Arthur's inclusivism reveals

---

[56] Arthur refers to undergraduates as younger students. There are mature students at SEU that attend evening classes that are beyond the scope of this study.

all three indicators of a postmodern environment at SEU. The students' need to experience something must be interpreted by themselves, beginning with self.

CONCLUDING THOUGHT

I discovered five things that summarize the way both faculty members (Professor Blanche more than Professor Edgar), priests, and campus ministry members influenced how the students describe their experience of spirituality and religion. These discoveries not only helped me see what the characteristics of the spirituality and religious beliefs and behaviors of the students looked like, they also informed me that faculty, priests, and campus ministry do not necessarily teach or guide the students to reference the biblical text, but they allow for autonomous interpretation of a lived experience that begins with self. With this in mind, a fourth key discovery emerged: when late Millennials and Generation Z gather to celebrate or observe Communion, the gathering is composed of **individual interpretations of a lived experience that begins with self** (see Table 14.1).

Table 14.1 Summary of Campus Influence

	Summary of Discoveries
1	Influence was intentional, focusing on spirituality far more than religion.
2	Students were encouraged to be self-guided through their lived experiences with no reference to the biblical text.
3	Role that religion played was in the student's participation in Communion and how that celebration facilitated the student's spirituality.
4	Influence was unobstructed, seen in a lack of religious rules.
5	Their influence sheds light on the indicators of a postmodern environment at SEU.

CHAPTER 15

CHARACTERISTICS OF A POSTMODERN ENVIRONMENT

Essentially, I discovered the postmodern environment at SEU for late Millennials and Generation Z has four characteristics that describe the spirituality and religious beliefs and behaviors of the students who participate in Communion: gathering together, meaning, believing in a supernatural God, and Communion as a religious ceremony/celebration. In this brief chapter I show that the characteristics actually connect to each other. These connections provide an overview of what a postmodern community populated with late Millennials and Generation Z looks like (see Figure 15.1).

If the environment of late Millennials and Generation Z is made up of individual interpretations of a lived experience that begin with self, the four characteristics that connect work a particular way. Beginning with the community of individual students, or self, the religious ceremony/celebration of Communion provides for the students' spiritual connection to a supernatural God, in which a lived experience connects with positive elements of community, valued by the students. Therefore, the four characteristics work in a circular fashion, returning to the students in their continued connection to God and community, providing meaning for a lived experience.

Figure 15.1. Four Connecting Characteristics

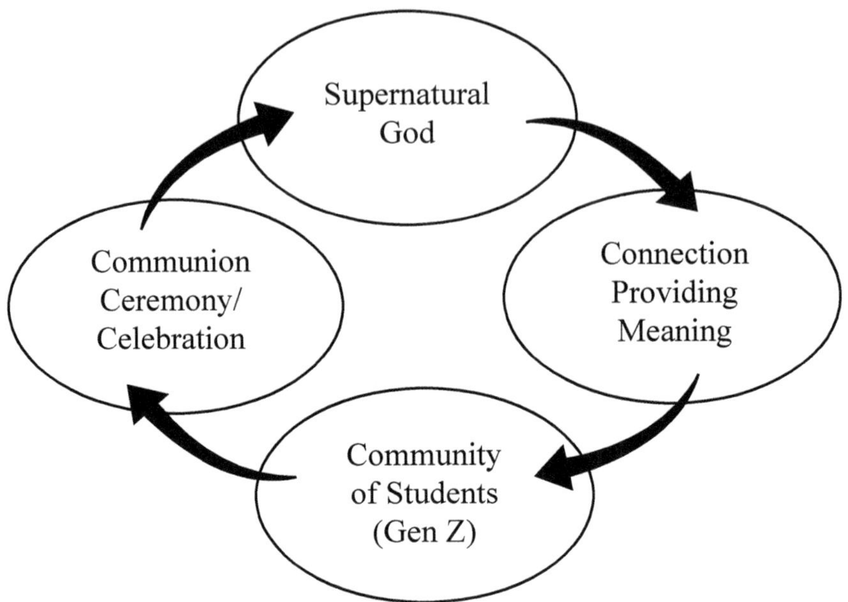

This implies that meaning is not fixed but subject to ongoing interpretations of lived experiences as the students continue to gather together to celebrate Communion. A non-fixed meaning is precisely what Father Ted stated: "I teach the students that they will always be in process learning more about spirituality all their lives." This is important towards theory development in how Communion serves to communicate biblical truth through retelling the redemptive story to late Millennials and Generation Z who participate or observe the celebration.

The first key discovery I made in **chapter eight** showed students needed to **sense or feel something in order to associate meaning** with their lived experiences. The process of learning about personal spirituality involves sensing. If the community of late Millennials and Generation Z that celebrate Communion is a continual cycle of four connections, the introduction of biblical truth that students can sense or feel during Communion becomes possible simply because meaning is not fixed but always in process.

The second key discovery also emerged in **chapter eight** showing **Communion acted like a communication vehicle** for the students' lived experiences. This is a vital component towards theory development to communicating biblical truth. Communion in itself is biblical. It tells the story of God. The students did, indeed, experience Christ during Communion as a religious ceremony/celebration in some way. In **chapter eleven**, the students' **beliefs shaped what they got out of Communion** in their approach to the celebration. Even with an experience of Christ in a celebration that was exclusively Christian,[57] the students made no reference to the biblical text. Rather, their views were sub-orthodoxy.

In **chapter thirteen**, the students' description of a supernatural God and their explanation of an experience of spirituality and religion also made no reference to the biblical text. If a postmodern community populated by late Millennials and Generation Z who celebrate Communion is made up of individual interpretations of a lived experience that begins with self, it is quite possible the influence of faculty, priests, and campus ministry led to students not mooring their experiences in the biblical text. Rather, influence over the students focused on spirituality, self-guidance, participation in Communion, and the lack of obstructing religious rules. Furthermore, the attitude of late Millennials and Generation Z towards spirituality is more like a blank slate. This reveals that the self can be greatly influenced (see Figure 15.2).

---

[57] The exclusivity of Communion as a Christian ceremony is set against religious pluralism seen in chapter two (Miner 2003, 45).

Figure 15.2. Influence Over the Students

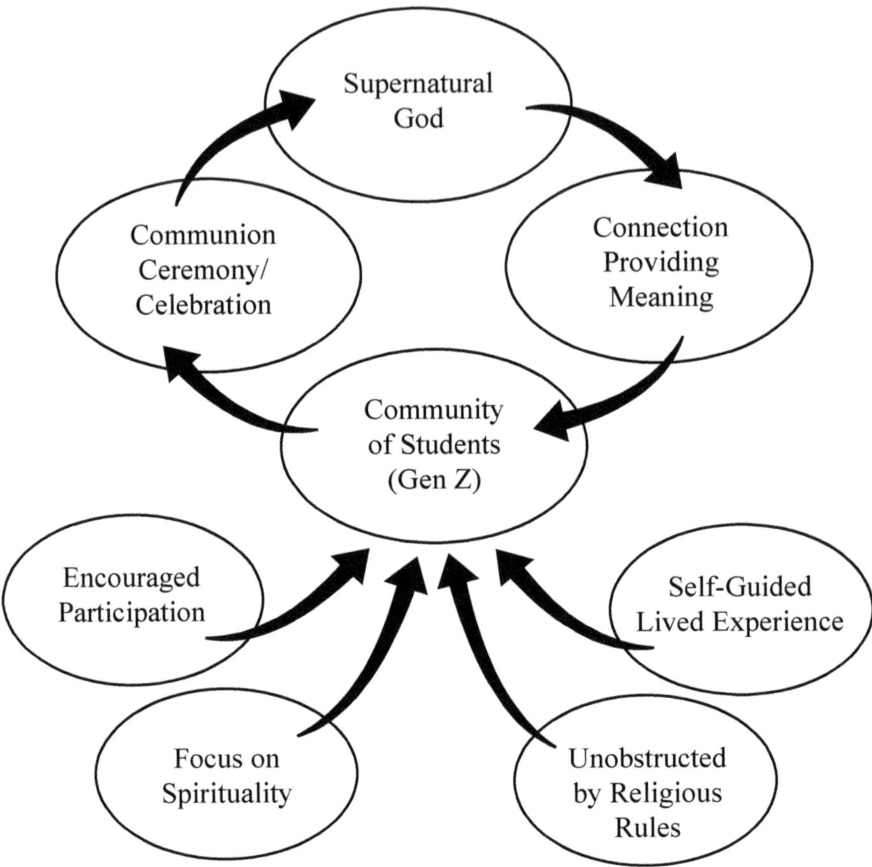

In this chapter, I discovered the characteristics of the spirituality and religious beliefs and behaviors of Late Millennials and Generation Z represented in the students at SEU who participate in Communion. The four characteristics that were discovered began with self, influenced by others, where meaning and purpose in life were communicated through words and actions in the students' lived experience during Communion as a religious ceremony/celebration. The challenge posed is to bring biblical truth into this postmodern community.

In the following section, I deal with the biblical text from the perspective of Communion to show how God was experienced in the Bible. The experience of each student at SEU **was not in-**

formed by the biblical text; neither was the way each one described God as a supernatural God. With this in mind, the next section helps explain an experience through the biblical text, developing a sound biblical explanation of God while moving towards a theoretical model of how to communicate biblical truth to late Millennials and Generation Z.

SECTION FIVE

EXPERIENCING GOD AT THE TABLE IN THE BIBLICAL TEXT

The focus of this section involves how God was experienced as expressed in the biblical text from the perspective of Communion. From this perspective, **a connection is seen with the Passover and the Wedding Supper of the Lamb.** For example, Robert Sokolowski (1994, 3) connects the Communion table to the Passover table by historically remembering the Exodus; and, from the same perspective, he also connects the Wedding Supper of the Lamb eschatologically, anticipating the fulfillment of redemption. Though Sokolowski (1994, 8) examines the biblical text, his primary concern is examining the appearance and structures related to how God is revealed to a participant, calling it a "theology of disclosure." Appearance and structure depict an expression of God and not the biblical text itself.

Fr. Roch Kereszty (2004, vii-ix), makes the same connections as Sokolowski regarding the Passover and Wedding Supper of the Lamb from the perspective of Communion as a theologian. He examines the gospels, Paul's letters, Hebrews, and Revelation using

Communion as a hermeneutic tool to shed light on God's love for the world as well as the mystery of faith that is needed to discover the purpose of human existence (2004, 19-90). However, he does not depict an experience of God as expressed in the biblical text without a Communion tool for interpretation.

Chris Green (2012) also connects the Passover and the Wedding Supper of the Lamb to Communion through the biblical text. He draws on documented testimony that explains how people experienced God while participating in the bread and wine of Communion (2012, 74-180). He pursues a strictly Pentecostal understanding of those testimonies. He does not explain how God was experienced as expressed in the biblical text separate from those documented testimonies.

Three table celebrations are considered: The Passover, Communion, and the Wedding Supper of the Lamb. An exegesis of biblical passages from Exodus, the gospels, Acts, 1 Corinthians, and Revelation determined in what way an experience of God was emphasized in the text at each table celebration.

CHAPTER 16

EXPERIENCES OF GOD IN THE FIRST PASSOVER CELEBRATION

The primary exegesis in this chapter is limited to Exodus 12 focusing on the first Passover, as opposed to the Passover in general. H. L. Ellison (1982, 62-64), classifies the rites of the Passover into two groups. First, the one-time rites that apply to those who were being delivered from Egypt. For example, the blood smeared on the door posts and lintels. Second, rites that apply to successive generations who were already delivered from Egypt. I examine four relationships of the first Passover to the **tenth plague, preexisting ceremonies, Egyptian polytheism,** and the **Egyptian calendar.**

In Relation to the Tenth Plague

Patrick D. Miller (1987, 248) makes a point of highlighting the significance of God announcing the tenth plague through Moses who functioned as both prophet and mediator (Exod. 11:1-10). Also, Douglas K. Stewart (2006, 264) notes that Moses began his announcements to **Pharaoh** with a typical messenger formula saying, "This is what the Lord says," so the Egyptian king had no doubt **Moses** was speaking on behalf of the Israelite God. Between the announcement and execution of the plague, regulations for the first Passover were given (Exod. 12:1-28). However, Peter Enns (2000, 244) is quick to point out that the Passover regulations were not "merely legal baggage tacked onto the narrative of the departure from Egypt"; rather, they are integral to the narrative.[58] If this is the case, three things are seen in relation to the tenth plague: (1) salvific blood; (2) the theological message; (3) and the sovereignty of God. I will explore them.

> Passover regulations were not "merely legal baggage tacked onto the narrative of the departure from Egypt"; rather, they are integral to the narrative.

Salvific Blood

Salvific blood can be viewed in opposite ways. On one hand, the **presence of blood** in the Passover preserved life during the plague (Exod. 12:13). On the other hand, the **absence of blood** resulted in death because of the plague (Exod. 12:13). The presence or absence of blood cannot be a legal matter or the preservation and loss of life, because the plague then makes no sense regarding the supremacy of God. The **Passover blood is essential to the overall narrative.** Consequently, James K. Bruckner (2012, 108) believes that Exodus 11-13 should be read as a singular literary unit. In doing so, the reader is able to make sense of the salvific substance of blood. "The tenth plague was not a divine temper tantrum... [but was] the necessary complementation of a redemptive pattern, one that requires death as a means to fuller life" (Enns 2000, 253).

The substance of blood is seen in five elements in Exodus 12. First, it is specifically seen in a year-old male lamb (Exod. 12:5). Second, the death of that lamb gave life by exempting the Passover participants from the horror of sudden death (Exod. 12:13). Third, more than exemption, the death of a lamb meant liberation from bondage (Exod. 12:31). Fourth, it also meant material blessing (Exod. 12:36). Fifth, more than blessing, the death of a lamb marked the inception of Jewish national identity as "a constant re-

---

[58] Similar views are expressed by Victor Hamilton (2011, 190), C. F. Keil and F. Delitzsch (2006, 335), Marc Vervenne (1996, 127) and Thomas Dozeman (2009, 248-259).

minder to Israel that their life came from death" (Enns 2000, 254). Hence, the presence of blood not only required death, resulting in a fuller life, but also a new national identity.

Theological Message

A theological message of redemption is seen when Exodus 11-13 is read as a singular literary unity. A brief survey of the New Testament shows that the five elements in the substance of blood can also be seen in the **fulfillment of Christ's sacrifice in His shed blood** as the Lamb of God.[59] First, He was required to die as "a lamb without blemish or defect" (1 Pet. 1:18-20). Second, His required death exempts the Christian from the same type of death (Rom. 6:23). Third, the Christian is liberated from bondage (Rom. 8:2). Fourth, the Christian is materially blessed (Phil. 4:19). Fifth, the Christian finds a new eternal identity (Phil. 3:20). Therefore, reading Exodus 11-13 as a salvific narrative, as Bruckner (2012, 108) suggests, highlights the theological redemptive message through the theme of blood fulfilled by Christ, the Lamb of God (1 Pet. 1:19).

Sovereignty of God

The theme of God's sovereignty is seen in salvific blood and the theological message of redemption. For example, Moses states to Pharaoh, "Israel is my firstborn son" (Exod. 4:21). Moses later continues, "But you refused to let him go; so I will kill your firstborn son" (Exod. 12: 23). The death of Egypt's firstborns explains the sovereignty of God over all the Egyptian gods. For example, Victor P. Hamilton (2011, 168-169) notes that everything firstborn, human or animal, belonged to God (Exod. 13:2). Enns (2000, 245) expands on the sovereignty of God by noting that **Pharaoh was considered a god** among Egyptians gods.

---

[59] Though Peter implies that Christ is the paschal Lamb, Paul does not. However, Andreas Köstenberger, L. Scott Kellum, and Charles Quarles (2012, 114) point out that what was accomplished in the sacrifice of Christ in His shed blood can be seen as a fulfillment of what was promised to Israel.

In his book *Pharaoh: Life and Afterlife of a God*, David Kennett (2008, 4) discusses the deity of a Pharaoh. The Egyptians looked to Pharaoh as the mediator of the will of the gods and as the supreme ruler and holder of all power. The death of Pharaoh's firstborn son and all Egyptian firstborns, human or animal, not only challenged the king's power as a deity, but also all Egyptian deities. As a result, **Egyptian gods were rendered powerless** before the sovereignty of God. Powerlessness is seen in the inability of the Egyptian magicians to reverse the effects of the tenth plague. The magicians of Egypt could not replicate or reverse the tenth plague. Previously, they had replicated several miraculous phenomena (Exod. 7:11, Exod. 11:22, Exod. 8:7).

Regarding the Egyptian magicians, Carol Meyers (2005, 80-82) notes that they were more like a priest with magical powers. Ann Jeffers (1996, 48) also describes Egyptian magicians as a powerful **cast of sorcerers,** similar to dream interpreters in the stories of **Joseph and Daniel.** Evidently, in the Exodus narrative, **the use of magic was not uncommon.** Interestingly, **God did not discriminate** among the Israelites, Egyptians, or other ethnicities.[60] Israel's exemption from the effects of the tenth plague was the result of the presence of blood,[61] not the result of their new national identity.

Summary Thought

God was experienced by Egypt and Israel as the indiscriminate[62] sovereign God who sheds the blood of firstborns in the absence of the shedding of the innocent blood of a lamb, resulting in Israel's redemption.

---

[60] The distinction of Israel in Exod. 11:6-7 must not be confused with Exod. 12:13. The absence of wailing among the Israelites was because of the presence of blood, not because they were Israelite.

[61] The theological and sociological implications of Christ's blood are evident in the New Testament: "He did not discriminate between us and them, for he purified their hearts by faith" (Acts 15:9).

[62] I am using the word indiscriminate to highlight that it was not Israel's national identity that saved them, but the presence of blood.

In Relation to Preexisting Ceremonies

It is quite probable the table celebration of the Passover borrowed from preexisting rituals. For example, Enns (2000, 248) is certain the Exodus generation did not need further clarification on the ceremony of the Passover because it borrowed from preexisting **Near Eastern** ceremonies.[63] Commenting on the historicity of the Passover, Bernard M. Levinson (2002, 58) believes that the Passover "originated as an apotropaic [power to avert evil] ritualized slaughter with no inherent connection to the plagues or the events of the Exodus."[64] Its purpose was to simply **ward off evil by the use of blood**. This may have been true in preexisting Near Eastern ceremonies but cannot be completely true in the Passover.

Israelites must have grown up around blood ceremonies in Egypt that had power to avert evil.

The protection of God from the effects of the tenth plague and the departure from Egypt are essential to the narrative (Enns 2000, 244). Quoted in Stuart (2006, 289), G. Dell'Orto argues the Israelites must have grown up around blood ceremonies in Egypt that had power to avert evil.[65] "Such an understanding makes a certain degree of sense of the biblical evidence, for sacrifice and other rituals [ceremonies] were commonplace in the ancient world" (Enns 2000, 248).[66] According to Menahem Haran (1977, 319-320), the use of hyssop branches (Exod. 12:22) to frequently apply blood in non-Passover apotropaic preex-

[63] Enns (2000, 248) does not list Near Eastern ceremonies that Passover may have borrowed from, but he affirms the high probability that such borrowing took place.

[64] Levinson (2002, 58)legal history, and literary theory, Deuteronomy and the Hermeneutics of Legal Innovation shows how the legislation of D

[65] Like Enns, Orto does not list what those Egyptian blood rituals were, but he affirms the high probability of such rituals.

[66] Enns points out that scholars argue that the Passover was not founded as a response to the tenth plague but adapted from preexisting rituals that preceded the exodus generation. Though he points this out, he does not list the names of preexisting ceremonies.

isting ceremonies was also commonplace. L. Rost (Haran 1977, 321) believes the Passover adapted an apotropaic ceremony from nomadic shepherds who sacrificed a lamb once a year when the moon was full.

In addition to rites in preexisting ceremonies that may have been reflected in the Passover, the name "Passover" may also have come from preexisting ceremony. For example, "slaughter the Passover lamb" (Exod. 12:21) has no detailed explanation for the slaughtering process. The lack of slaughtering detail is explained by Fr. James Plastaras (1966, 150-151) who argues that the name **Passover came from Akkadian culture,** in an appeasing ceremony. An appeasing view seems to fit with, "and when I see the blood, I will pass over you" (Exod. 12:13). It seems to fit the response to future generational questions by explaining how God "passed over" (Exod. 12:27).

From the evidence, if the Passover reflected rites in preexisting ceremonies, it only reflected a protective element.[67] Understanding the Passover only as a reflection of preexisting ceremonies[68] fails to account for all five elements in the theological message. It does not reflect the full narrative of being set free from bondage. If this is the case, experiencing God in the first Passover in relation to preexisting ceremonies only expresses the preventative or protective side of God. However, Israel reflected preexisting ceremonies, in name and rite, transformed by God, into a fully redemptive ceremony (Enns 2000, 248).

Summary Thought

Therefore, if preexisting ceremonies were reflected in the first Passover, God is experienced as the transformer of pre-existing ceremonies and the God who protects.

---

[67] Jewish author, Elon Gilad (2015), in Israel's oldest daily news publication *Haaretz* argues that Passover was derived from an ancient Canaanite ritual. If he is correct, his argument supports a protective and preventative experience.

[68] Jonathan Cook, Rob Haskell, Ruth Julian, and Natee Tanchanpongs (2010, 175) point out how new theological meaning can be attached to preexisting rituals in indigenous cultures.

In Relation to Egyptian Polytheism

Richard Bauckham (1993, 50) defines monotheistic worship as acknowledgement of the "ultimacy and incomparability" of God, not given to any finite beings. **Monotheistic worship** was the goal set by God for Moses and therefore Israel (Exod. 3:12). The first Passover marked the beginning of that goal (Keil and Delitzsch 2006, 236). Using Bauckham's definition of monotheistic worship, Israel did not qualify as a monotheistic nation. For example, Wright (2006, 137) points out that Israel's religion transitioned from polytheism, through henotheism, and eventually to monotheism throughout their Old Testament history.

Regarding Israel's religion, "The essence of Israelite monotheism lies in what it affirms dynamically about YHWH, not primarily in what it denies about other gods" (Wright 2006, 138). For example, Bauckham (2013, 196) notes how Israel affirmed God by acknowledging other gods were impotent and **unable to deliver their own people.** For Israel, monotheistic religion did not deny the existence of other gods, it just called the other gods impotent in comparison to their God. Therefore, Israel's religion was more henotheistic (one God). In contrast, their worship alternated between monotheism and polytheism throughout Old Testament history.[69]

> For Israel, monotheistic religion did not deny the existence of other gods, it just called the other gods impotent in comparison to their God.

If this is the case, the literary structure of Exodus 12:1 brings together evidence of three monotheistic issues: (1) God, the sovereign deity; (2) two monotheistic leaders (as Bauckham describes monotheism) in Moses and Aaron; and (3) Egyptian polytheistic

---

[69] Israel was still wrestling with monotheism under Joshua's leadership. He commanded the Israelites to throw away other gods that were worshipped (Josh. 24:14). Other examples are Jer. 7:30, Ezek. 14:3-4:7, and Hosea 8:4.

worship.[70] First, "The Lord" (Exod. 12:1) is parenthetical in the sense that God is not explained. In a previous revelation, God may not have told Moses His name, but He explained it (Exod. 3:12). In the explanation, God revealed Himself. In doing so, God not only declared Himself as Lord of Moses' forefathers (Exod. 3:15) but also the Lord of all gods (Keil and Delitzsch 2006, 287).

Second, H. D. M. Spence and Joseph S. Exell write, "neither Moses nor Aaron introduced any legislation of their own, either at this time or later" (Spence and Excell 1985, 258). The implication is that all Israelite religious systems, including the Passover, came from God and were merely established by Moses and Aaron. Hamilton (2011, 76) disagrees, noting that Aaron's eloquence was so compelling that he later crafted an idol in the form of a golden calf (Exod. 32). In Hamilton's view, Aaron did introduce, albeit momentarily, a polytheistic legislation of his own. It is doubtful that Aaron's eloquence persuaded the people; rather, he was pressured by the people (Exod. 32). Aaron was monotheistic in the way that Bauckham describes, momentarily drifting towards polytheism by creating an idol.

The issue of monotheism is seen in Aaron's life, and the same can be said of Moses, who "was educated in all the wisdom of the Egyptians" (Acts 7:22). Simon Kistemaker (1990, 525) describes the education of Moses taking place in the great center of Egyptian learning (1 Kings 4:30). Such learning would include exposure to Egyptian gods and how they are worshipped.[71] Also, Moses' marriage to Zipporah (Exod. 2:21) was an exogamous[72] union of Jew and Midianite (Hamilton 2011, 27). Such a union

---

[70] George Hart (2006), lists the gods and goddesses of Egypt. In his dictionary, Hart admits that his list is not exhaustive, but it exemplifies the polytheistic nature of Egyptian worship (G. Hart 2006, ix-xi).

[71] There is no evidence in the biblical passages that Moses worshiped any Egyptian god.

[72] Most exogamous marriages in biblical passages were disastrous: Samson (Judges 14); Solomon (1 Kings 11:1-13); Ahab (1 Kings 16:31); and Esau (Gen. 26:34-35). However, fewer exogamous marriages succeeded: Joseph (Gen. 41:45) and Boaz with Ruth (Ruth 1:4).

would bring Moses into contact with Midianite gods. Like Aaron, Moses was also monotheistic in the way that Bauckham describes, with first-hand knowledge of polytheism from his Egyptian and Midianite experiences.

Third, Egyptian polytheism is juxtaposed with the monotheistic goal of the exodus to "worship God on this [Sinai] mountain" (Exod. 3:12). Evidently, after the tenth plague, and before their exodus, Israel "bowed down and worshipped" (Exod. 12:27) God while in an environment of Egyptian polytheism. Interestingly, **Israelite worship prior to the exodus demonstrates monotheism** by making obeisance towards God (Spence and Excell 1985, 275) and expressing faith in God alone (Keil and Delitzsch 2006, 335).

Though Israelite monotheism did not deny the existence of other gods, to suggest monotheistic worship was a significant rite built into the ceremony of the Passover. It would also be correct to suggest the same rite was future-oriented with successive generations in mind. For example, Herbert Danby (2012, 151) points out specific text from the Jewish *Mishnah*, "In every generation a man must so regard himself as if he came forth himself out of Egypt."

Summary Thought

Therefore, God is experienced in monotheistic worship where the Passover serves as a perpetual reminder that God requires spiritual fidelity from His worshippers even in an environment of polytheism.

In Relation to an Egyptian Calendar

At first glance, the Passover simply commences a new religious calendar year for Israel, in addition to its preexisting civil calendar (Exod. 23:16). "This month is to be for you the first month, the first month of your year" (Exod. 12:2). A new religious calendar does more than mark a new beginning for Israel. For example, if all ten plagues, especially the tenth, challenged and rendered powerless the Egyptian deities, establishing a **new religious calendar** would do the same. For example, Egyptologist Jan Assmann (2001, 79) notes that Thoth, the Egyptian moon god, was "the reckoner par excellence of time."

Not only was Thoth perceived by the Egyptians as a god controlling their calendar, but he was thought to control and to influence everything lunar — "calculation, planning, counting, measuring, weighing, distributing and so forth" (Assmann 2001, 80), significantly relating to a fruitful agricultural harvest. With this in mind, it could be said that a new religious calendar year, marked by the Passover, challenged and rendered the Egyptians gods powerless, not only on earth but also in the heavens.

> Freedom created room for a covenant with God independent of any form of political statecraft designed to govern Israel..

A new religious calendar year does more than mark defeated Egyptian gods. The first Passover distinguished itself from later Passovers as the **birthday of a new liberated nation.** That birthday, in a new month, naturally lends itself to a time not occupied by agricultural concerns. Israel's civil calendar began in Tishri (September/October) (Exod. 23:16). Ellison (1982, 63) notes that the soil in "Tishri" was baked hard and in need of rain. In contrast, he notes "Aviv" marked a fruitful time of harvest where the soil was naturally more fruitful (Exod. 23:15) (1982, 63). Therefore, Aviv naturally lacked agricultural concern in light of a new harvest for the present and near future.

The birthday of a new nation needed more than a lack of agricultural concern to hold perpetual national thinking. Deliverance from servitude, resulting in freedom, held their thinking. Freedom created room for a covenant with God independent of any form of political statecraft designed to govern Israel.[73] As a result, a new religious calendar year also demonstrates God's governance over the dominance of an imposed Egyptian calendar.

Summary Thought

Therefore, God is experienced not only as the liberator from servitude, but also as a God who is celebrated in a

---

[73] Freedom from statecraft also came into conflict during Roman occupation in the New Testament.

time of annual thanksgiving, in the absence of agricultural concerns, and in the birth of a new nation.

CONCLUDING THOUGHT

God was experienced as expressed in the biblical text in four ways in the Passover. First, in relation to the tenth plague, God was experienced in Egypt as a discriminating deity who kills firstborns where there was no blood. To Israel, He was experienced as the indiscriminate Sovereign Deity who redeems the firstborn through the shedding of innocent blood, resulting in a fuller life and identity. Theologically, God was experienced in both ways when personified in Christ.

Second, in relation to preexisting rituals, God was experienced in the first Passover as the transformer of preexisting rituals and the God who protects. Third, in relation to Egyptian polytheism, God was experienced in monotheism where the Passover serves as a perpetual reminder that God requires spiritual fidelity from His worshippers even in an environment of polytheism. Fourth, in relation to an Egyptian calendar, God was experienced as the liberator from servitude, clarified as a God who is celebrated in a time of annual thanksgiving, in the absence of agricultural concerns, and in the birth of a new nation (see Table 16.1).

Table 16.1. Four Ways God was Experienced in the First Passover Celebration

Celebration	In Relation to	Expressed in the Bible
The Passover	Tenth plague	Indiscriminate
	Preexisting ceremonies	Transformative
	Egyptian polytheism	Monotheistic
	Egyptian calendar	Liberator

CHAPTER 17

EXPERIENCES OF GOD IN THE CELEBRATION OF COMMUNION

The gospels collectively offer three accounts of Communion when it was first appointed by Christ (Matt. 26:26-29; Mk. 14:22-25; Lk. 22:14-20; Jn. 13:1-30). Subsequent celebrations of Communion are found in the **writings of Paul** (1 Cor. 11:23-26), and **Luke** (Acts 2:42-46, Acts 20:7-11). In this chapter, the gospels, 1 Corinthians, and Acts were primarily examined. Similar to the first Passover, the first Communion had elements not found in subsequent celebrations. The most significant element was the physical incarnate presence of Christ. While present, Christ announced his imminent absence from subsequent celebrations of Communion until an undisclosed eschatological time[74] (Mk. 14:25; Lk. 22:16, 18) when the fullness of His Father's kingdom had come (Matt. 26:29).

Prior to the first Communion, Christ had intimately related Himself to His Father.[75] An example is seen in His question to Phil-

---

[74] Craig Kenner (1999, 590) points out in Matt. 24:36 that undisclosed time is authentic because it is not known by Christ or angels, only the Father. The authenticity of an undisclosed time is not robbed by the fullness of His father's kingdom (Matt. 26:29).

[75] Matt. 7:21; 10:32; 11:27; 12:50; 16:17; 18:10; 18:19; 18:35; 20:23; 26:29; 26:53; Mark 8:38; and Luke 2:49; 9:26.

ip, "Anyone who has seen me has seen the Father. How can you say, 'Show us the Father'?" (Jn. 14:9). After the first Communion, and prior to His death, Christ reinforced His intimate connection to His Father (Jn. 14:23). To conclude, **experiencing Christ was also to experience His Father.** I examine Communion in relationship to the incarnate presence of Christ, His resurrected presence, and His ascended absence.

The Physical Incarnate Presence of Christ

Though an intimate connection was made by Christ and His Father, the same connection cannot be made with Christ's body and blood in relation to the bread and wine of Communion. The bread and wine were distinctly "my" body and blood (Matt. 26:26, 28; Mk. 14:22, 24; Lk. 22:19-20), not my Father's and mine, or ours. Furthermore, eating human flesh and drinking (or eating) blood of any kind was unthinkable to a Jew (Lev. 17). Christ had already **stated the unthinkable** to a number of Jews (Jn. 6:54-56). Did the disciples understand what Christ meant by "my" body and blood (Matt. 26:26, 28) while physically present with them at the first Communion? Luke may shed light on the answer.

Luke records two separate accounts where the disciples did not understand Christ, and they were afraid to ask what He meant (Lk. 9:45; 18:34).[76] The fact that Luke records both accounts must be contrasted with the absence of any record of their ignorance at the first Communion. Evidentially, if the disciples did not understand any words or actions of Christ, the gospels record their questions, or fear of asking (Matt. 13:36; Mk. 9:32; Lk. 9:45; Jn.13:7). However, at the first Communion, there is a complete absence of questions, or fear of asking questions, regarding the bread and wine.[77] Ironically, the time to ask a question about what Christ meant by "my" body and blood was at the first Communion where He was physically present.

---

[76] Also found in Mark 9:32.

[77] Because it is not known whether the disciples did not ask questions, or whether the writers did not record the questions, caution is needed as it is an argument from silence.

R. T. France (2007, 992) draws attention to the sense in which the bread "is" the body and the wine "is" the blood of Christ. In his view, any discussion "cannot be settled by the choice of the verb, since "is" can have a range of meaning from complete identity to symbolic equivalence" (2007, 992). Symbolic equivalence is seen in the parable of Christ where "the good seed is the Son of Man" (Matt. 13:37, italics mine); "The field is the world" (Matt. 13:38, italics mine); and, "The harvest is the end of the age" (Matt. 13:39, italics mine). In each example, the sower, field, and harvest are symbolically represented as Christ, the world, and the end of the age.

it would be ambiguous to suggest Christ intended the bread and wine as His literal body and blood when His physical body was reclined at the table with the disciples.

Regarding complete identity, it would be ambiguous to suggest Christ intended the bread and wine as His literal body and blood when His physical body was reclined at the table with the disciples.[78] If not His literal body, which one was His body: the physical body or the bread? Darrell Bock (1994, 1724-1725) notes the verb "is" in Aramaic indicates representation and not an identification. If the first Communion took place post resurrection but pre-ascension, the verb "is" could be an identity. If that was the case, the body of Christ would be different from his former **pre-resurrected body.**[79]

By contrasting the first Communion with the Passover, it can be seen why the disciples may have understood what Christ meant in the bread and wine. For instance, the bread eaten at the Pass-

---

[78] However, though the Greek verb "is" has a range of meanings, the Roman Catholic view understands "is" as a point of refocusing from the bread to the literal body of Christ (Sri et al. 2010, 337).

[79] Different in the sense that people who encountered the resurrected Christ did not recognize him at first (Lk. 24:13-35), (Jn. 20:11-18; 21:1-13). However, Christ would still be human, as A. W. Tozer writes in *Jesus, Our Man in Glory* (2009). Also, the "flesh and bones" (Lk. 24:39) of Christ were different to His former flesh and blood. Also, His body could have been prophetically identified which was fully understood as the meaning after the crucifixion and resurrection.

over commemorated the affliction of Israel[80] (Deut. 16:3). John Nolland (2005, 1075) suggests the Passover bread of affliction was transplanted from those who ate it to Christ who was the bread of affliction at the first Communion. If Nolland is correct, a further relocation also takes place. Affliction is transferred from the disciples' Israelite ancestors to Christ who was physically present with them at the table. In both cases, Christ is represented in the bread of affliction and identified as the afflicted One (Isa. 53:4).

Staying with the comparison of Communion and the Passover, Bock (1994, 1725) suggests the disciples also understood the sacrificial language Christ used while at the table, albeit different from the traditional Passover language. Specifically, in Luke's gospel, Bock (1994, 1725) notes the theological force in "given for you" (Lk. 22:19) and "poured out for many" (Lk. 22:20) as new elements to the **preexisting Passover language.** In another language connection, France (2007, 991-993) connects "gave thanks" (Matt. 26:26-27; Mk. 14:22-23; Lk. 22:17, 19) with the traditional Passover blessing over the bread and wine.[81]

Further evidence may be found in Christ repeatedly referring to His death prior to the first Communion (Matt. 16:21; 17:22; 20:17; Mk. 8:31; 9:30; 10:32; Lk. 9:21-43; 18:31). Repetition does not always translate to full comprehension, cognitively and emotionally. The disciples may have understood the words of Christ without emotionally accepting what they meant. This may account for why they resisted His arrest (Lk. 22:49-50).

Summary Thought

Therefore, God is experienced at the first Communion, in the physical incarnate presence of Christ, **without the post-resurrection clarity.**

---

[80] Peter Craigie (1976, 243), notes the Passover bread of affliction symbolized fearful haste with connotations of speed and anxiety.

[81] In his book, *The Concise Guide to Judaism: History, Practice, Faith,* Rabbi Roy Rosenburg (1994, 89) cites the sacrificial language of Passover, "Blessed are you Lord God king of the world who brings forth bread from the earth... Blessed are you, Lord God, king of the universe, who creates the fruit of the vine".

The Physical Resurrected Presence of Christ

Caution is needed to locate a Communion celebration between the resurrection and ascension of Christ because Christ said He would not celebrate the bread and wine again until an undisclosed eschatological time (Lk. 22:16, 18). However, not eating or drinking the bread and wine does not rule out officiating over Communion. Without being conclusive, William Hendriksen (2002, 1066) speculates over the realization of two disciples[82] and "how Jesus was recognized by them when he broke the bread" (Lk. 24:35). Christ and the two disciples did not celebrate the Last Supper again.

Bock (1994, 1919) rejects the idea that Jesus and these two men participated in Communion at the climax of the Emmaus road journey. For example, why was Christ the host when He was an invited guest, and where was the Communion wine? Bock may have overlooked Jewish tradition as noted by R. J. Dillon (1978). The oldest man, an expositor of Scripture, or simply someone special to those that have gathered around a meal table could be the host. R. C. H. Lenski (2001a, 1192) also notes the same Jewish tradition as a reason for Christ to host the meal.

Undoubtedly, Luke makes a strong connection between breaking the bread and the two disciples realizing it was Christ (Lk. 24:35). Furthermore, a liturgical sequence is seen (Lk. 24:30) to not completely rule out a celebration of Communion.[83] Christ used a similar liturgical sequence when two large crowds were miraculously fed (Mk. 6:30-44; 8:1-10). Luke's apparent use of liturgy may or may not designate a Communion event, however, transformation took place at the table.

---

[82] Scholars abound with theories on who Cleopas and the other disciple were (Lk. 24:18). As the only named disciple, Cleopas is not mentioned elsewhere in the NT (Bock 1994, 1911). Cleopas and the other disciple are probably among more unnamed disciples Luke mentions as, "all the others" (Lk.. 24:9).

[83] Bock (1994, 1919) notes that Luke distinctly describes the evening meal in a worshipful way in keeping with Communion (Bock 1994, 1919). Also, John Carroll (2012, 487), notes the proleptic use of liturgy could denote a Communion celebration.

On one hand, the two disciples were walking away from Jerusalem (Lk. 24:13). Bock (1994, 1908) suggests they were returning home after the annual Passover.[84] In addition, Jean-Luc Marion (2002, 146) suggests **Jerusalem had become too dangerous** for followers of Christ after the crucifixion and death of Christ. Therefore, the disciples in Jerusalem met together "with the doors locked for fear of the Jews" (Jn. 20:19).

On the other hand, after the meal, "They got up and returned at once to Jerusalem" (Lk. 24:33). There is a definite transformation seen in the redirection of the disciples' journey. If the house in Emmaus was their home, it became **unimportant to them**. If they feared the Jews in Jerusalem, it **no longer inhibited them.** Furthermore, Hendriksen and Kistemaker (2002, 1066) suggest it was common practice to share good news on the day it was received. Therefore, the testimony of both disciples added to a growing number of eye-witness accounts on the same day they encountered Christ (Lk. 1:1-2). Undoubtedly, transformation took place at the table (Lk. 24:30-31). A closer examination may shed light on their transformational experience through a possible Communion celebration.

Luke writes, "They were kept from recognizing him" (Lk. 24:16) and "their eyes were opened, and they recognized him" (Lk. 24:31). Whether he intended it or not, Luke juxtaposes blindness with sight. Bock (1994, 1910) supports the view that God blinded them because the disciples were not ready to comprehend Christ at that point (Lk. 24:27). Hendriksen (2002, 1060) believes God restrained their sight for similar reasons. Lenski (2001a, 1180) also points out, "The passive verb connotes an agent, namely God, just as the passive verb does in verse 31." With this in mind, the evidence points to God who prevented the disciples from recognizing Christ.

Evidently, they were discussing what had just happened to Christ (Lk. 24:15/18), downcast (Lk. 24:17), without hope (Lk.

---

[84] Though Luke does not state the disciples had a personal home in Emmaus, Hendriksen and Kistemaker (2002, 1060) point out the implication of one (Luke 24:28-29).

24:21), and without concrete evidence of the resurrection (Lk. 24:22-24). All four factors informed their blindness.[85] Consequently, a combination of natural blindness caused by preoccupied emotion and supernatural blindness caused by God veiled the disciples from identifying Christ. However, as a result of the meal in Emmaus, both **natural and supernatural veils were removed**. The meal was transformative, removing any fear of returning immediately back to Jerusalem. Therefore, God is **progressively experienced** through the whole episode.

Summary Thought

Only two disciples personally experienced a possible Communion with Christ at Emmaus. Furthermore, both disciples were not part of the remaining eleven disciples who had been chosen by God for Christ (Jn. 17:6).

The Physical Absence of Christ

Successive celebrations of Communion are found in the writings of Luke (Acts 2:42-46, Acts 20:7-11), and Paul (1 Cor. 11:17-26). The passage in Paul's first letter to the Corinthian church relates to celebrating Communion. There has been much dispute over the passages in Acts. For example, researcher and Anglican minister David Peterson (2009, 161) believes Luke's use of breaking bread (*klasai arton*) could refer to Jewish tradition around a meal table or Communion. Others, like Joachim Jeremias (1966, 215-218) firmly believe Luke intended Communion. I. Howard Marshall (1998, 204) agrees with Jeremias in the sense that breaking bread was not just a Jewish meal tradition but a religious intention. Lenski (2001a, 116) also points out that Luke was attempting to record a reliable account for **Theophilus**; therefore, it was Communion.

---

[85] Bradley Chance (2011, 365), suggests the two disciples could not reconcile their hopes in Christ with the death of Christ and the stranger with them who was Christ.

The Account of Luke in the Book of Acts

Luke records, "On the first day of the week we came together to break bread" (Acts 20:7). According to Kistemaker (2002, 718), the first day of the week fits a calendar used by Jews, God-fearers, and Christians at the time Luke wrote Acts. Since the Romans and Greeks did not practice a day of rest,[86] the gathering had a distinct cultural and Christian tone. Furthermore, a seven-day calendar numbered five days Sunday to Thursday[87] followed by named days -- the "Preparation Day" (Friday) (Mk. 15:42) and the "Sabbath" (Saturday) (Jn. 19:31).

Early Christians adopted this nomenclature, but at some point, Sunday was adopted as the first day of the week, commemorating the resurrection of Christ.[88] Some believe Luke had already made that adoption (Kistemaker 2002, 716). Lenski (2001a, 824) notes Luke literally meant a Sunday. In addition, Luke also refers to a Sunday identical to his gospel account, "On the first day of the week" (Lk. 24:1). Either way, Kistemaker (2002) and Lenski (2001a) point to a Sunday.

Culturally, Communion as a religious ceremony had **not yet separated from a general meal.** This would account for a second mention of breaking bread in the same narrative (Acts 20:11). The purpose of gathering together was to break bread as a possible Communion within a general meal (Acts 20:7). A precise time of the day cannot be stated. However, Paul finished his discourse around midnight and intended to leave early the next day (Acts 20:7). It would appear strange if people had collectively brought

------

[86] Erich S. Gruen (2002, 556) notes how Seneca mocked the Jews for not working on the Sabbath.

[87] The first day, second day, and so on.

[88] Irving L. Jensen (1990, 4), notes the first day of the week would become known as "the Lord's Day" (Rev. 1:10) (Jensen 1990, 4). Also, *Didache* acknowledges the adopted, "And on the Lord's own day gather yourselves together and break bread and give thanks, first confessing your transgressions, that your sacrifice may be pure" (Milavec 2003, 35). In his epistle to the Ephesians Ignatius adopts the same term to describe Communion (Roberts, Donaldson, and Coxe 1999, 57).

food and not eaten it, delayed by Paul's lengthy discourse. Therefore, Lenski (2001b, 830) locates the commencement of Paul's discourse after the gathering had celebrated Communion within a general meal.

However, after the miracle of Eutychus's resurrection, Luke moves from one pronoun, "we," to another, "he," meaning Paul (Acts 20:11). In this case, Lenski (2001b, 831) believes breaking bread applied to eating the food that was left over from the previous meal and not Communion. Furthermore, "After talking until daylight" (Acts 20:11) is distinguished from "Paul spoke to the people" (Acts 20:7). It is probable that Paul, and those gathered, were talking about the miracle of Eutychus's resurrection. It seems to fit the flow of narrative concluding, "The people took the young man home" (Acts 20:12).

While breaking bread in Acts 2:42-47 and Acts 20:7-11 remains disputed, the absence of the physical incarnate and resurrected presence of Christ is not. Strangely, Luke makes **no reference to the presence of God, Christ, or the Holy Spirit** in the narratives that contain breaking bread. In contrast, Luke is apt to note the power of the Holy Spirit working through the apostles at many episodes recorded in Acts.[89] Therefore, it could be argued that these breaking bread incidents were not a celebration of Communion.

Summary Thought

Presupposing that these incidents were Communion, celebrating it would be an act of thanksgiving towards God. Such an act would be void of any notable divine presence or power. Therefore, God is experienced as the recipient of thanksgiving void of any notable divine presence in direct relation to Communion in Acts 2:42-46 and Acts 20:7-11.

---

[89] Several examples are found in Acts 1:8, Acts 4:33, Acts 6:8, Acts 19:20.

The Account of Paul in the First Letter to the Corinthian Church

Paul uses the term "Lord's Supper" (1 Cor. 11:20) and not breaking bread. Gordon D. Fee (2014, 598) believes such a term originated with Paul. However, the idea of a religious supper did not. Anthony Thiselton (2000, 757) quotes J. Behm and his thoughts on the noun "supper" (*dipenon*) as a traditional term used for any supper that **honored pagan deities.** Paul inserts the possessive adjective "the Lord's" (*kyriakon*) (Fee 2014, 598) to the traditional term. Whether he intended it or not, Paul juxtaposes a "private" (*idiom*) supper with "the Lord's" (*kyriakon*) Supper (1 Cor. 11:20-21). Consequently, the Lord's Supper is distinct from any other supper, private or otherwise.[90] With this in mind, Paul suggests Christ is spiritually present.

Previously, Paul had explained how he could be physically absent from the Corinthian Christians, yet present at the same time:

"For my part, even though I am not physically present,
I am with you in spirit. As one who is present with
you in this way, I have already passed judgment
in the name of our Lord Jesus on the one who has
been doing this. So when you are assembled and
I am with you in spirit, and the power of our Lord
Jesus is present, hand this man over to Satan for the
destruction of the flesh, so that his spirit may be saved
on the day of the Lord." (1 Cor. 5:3-5)

In a similar fashion, Paul writes to the Christians in Colossae, "For though I am absent from you in body, I am present with you in spirit" (Col. 2:5). Contrasting body and spirit enables more than an idiom. Paul emphasizes his presence with them. Three other letters to the Christians in Corinth reveal Paul's emphasis that may help in understanding Christ's presence in His physical absence.

---

[90] George Hunsinger (2014, 71-72), makes an interesting observation that Paul is not trying to teach the Corinthians about the Lord's Supper. On the contrary, he was comparing their supper with the Lord's Supper.

First, the Christian has received the "Spirit who is from God" (1 Cor. 2:12); second, the Christian is "one with him [Christ] in spirit" (1 Cor. 6:17); and third, the Christian is the "temple of the Holy Spirit...received from God" (1 Cor. 6:18). The Christian receives, is made one by, and becomes the house of the Holy Spirit. With this in mind, Paul does not mean the Corinthians should act in a way as though he were present, like a well-behaved child in the absence of a parent. Rather, because Paul has received the same Spirit as the Corinthian Christians, both are already uniquely together.

For this reason, Fee (2014, 514) argues that fellowship (*koinonia*) speaks to the inherent nature of Communion seen in the juxtaposition of the "Lord's table" and the "table of demons" (1 Cor. 10:21). If fellowship indicates participation with Christ in His spiritual presence, it would be unthinkable for a Christian to fellowship at other tables. Wayne Meeks (2006, 164), in an article called *Social and Ecclesial Life of the Earliest Christians* notes, "A banquet in the name of the Lord Jesus would not in itself seem more unusual than a banquet of the Lord Sarapis."[91] For

> it was taken for granted by the Greco-Romans that an invitation to a banquet did not come from the host, but the god of that particular host

example, it was taken for granted by the Greco-Romans that an invitation to a banquet did not come from the host, but the god of that particular host.[92] Therefore, Paul draws a distinct line, "You cannot have a part in both the Lord's table and the table of demons" (1 Cor. 10:21).

The problem in the Corinthian church was not the neglect of assembling together as a church (Heb. 10:25), but their **failure to represent fellowship with** Christ and each other specifically as participants in the Communion celebration (1 Cor.

---

[91] Third century B.C. Greco-Egyptian god.

[92] Larry Hurtado (1999, 27), quotes a surviving papyrus invitation found in an Oxyrhynchos text: "The god invites you to a banquet being held at the Thoereion tomorrow from the 9th hour."

12:13). Paul is not focused on the implications of separateness as opposed to togetherness.

Implications of separateness and corporateness were common in Greco-Roman culture. D. E. Smith (1981, 323) outlines a list of seven unacceptable behaviors for banquets held by clubs and associations during the Greco-Roman era: (1) quarreling and fighting; (2) taking the assigned place of another; (3) speaking out of turn without permission; (4) fomenting factions; (5) accusing a fellow member before a public court; (6) specific trials within the club for inter-club disputes; and (7) specific worship activities. Paul could have adapted **existing club and association rules** applying them to the church. The Corinthians Christians were breaking club rules and, in doing so, they misrepresented the togetherness of the church.

Fee (2010, 595) draws attention to a separation in the Corinthian church: the "have-nots" and the "haves." Evidently, the have-nots who felt humiliated by the haves petitioned Paul (1 Cor. 11:22). Further insight into sociological separateness is seen in **two Roman authors** who comment on an invitation to a banquet. **Martial** writes, "Since I am asked to dinner...why is not the same dinner served to me as to you? Why do I dine without you, although, Ponticus, I am dining with you?" (O'Connor 2005, 185). **Pliny** writes, "The best dishes were set in front of himself and a select few, and cheap scraps of food before the rest of the company....One lot was intended for himself and for us, another for his lesser friends" (O'Connor 2005, 184).

Two views are represented in these quotes. On one hand, Martial implies the have-nots should eat the same food as the haves. On the other hand, Pliny implies the haves should eat the same food as the have-nots. Both address the community from different vantage points. Paul is not concerned with adopting one view over the other. He is concerned with a unique view that **radicalized a hierarchal Greco-Roman culture** by reintroducing the institutional and historical words of Christ (1 Cor. 11:24-26).

Summary Thought

God is experienced as **invisibly present by His Spirit,** made visible by Christian togetherness.

CONCLUDING THOUGHT

God was experienced through celebrating Communion in three ways. First, in the physical incarnate presence of Christ at the first Communion, God was experienced without post-resurrection clarity. Second, in the physical resurrected presence of Christ prior to His ascension, God was experienced progressively to the two disciples on their way to Emmaus. Third, in the absence of the physical presence of Christ after the ascension, God was experienced in the breaking bread incidents in Acts as the recipient of thanksgiving. In contrast to Acts, God was experienced in first Corinthians as present by His Spirit (see Table 17.1).

Table 17.1. Four Ways God was Experienced in the Celebration of Communion

Celebration	In Relation to	Expressed in the Bible
Communion	Incarnate presence	Without post-resurrection clarity
	Resurrected presence	Progressively
	Ascended absence (Acts)	Recipient of thanksgiving
	Ascended absence (1 Corinthians)	Present by His Spirit

CHAPTER 18

EXPERIENCES OF GOD IN THE WEDDING SUPPER OF THE LAMB CELEBRATION

There are many New Testament passages that analogously present the Church and Christ as a bride and groom (Matt. 9:15; Jn. 3:29; Rom. 7:3-4; 1 Cor. 6:15; Eph. 5:23-32). There are also a number of Old Testament passages that present a similar relationship (Isa. 54:5, 6; 62:5; Jer. 3:20; Hosea 2:19). However, this chapter primarily examines Revelation 19:6-9 where the bride of Christ is present at the table celebration called the Wedding Supper of the Lamb. I look at **cultural setting** of the celebration, its prophetic genre, and **appropriate clothing** for the occasion.

Cultural Setting

John sets the passage against the cultural background[93] of a Jewish wedding, historically and culturally very different to weddings in the West (Hendriksen 1998, 514). Professor of Jewish Studies, Ivan Marcus (2013, 124-192), describes **a seven-stage nuptial sequence** of events that would take place in Jewish culture during the time period when John wrote Revelation: (1) choosing a bride;

---

[93] Anita Diamant (2007, 135-205), presents a unique view of a traditional Jewish wedding bringing together theology, Jewish history, and traditional customs.

(2) announcing the wedding; (3) betrothal; (4) paying a dowry; (5) waiting for an interval of time; (6) collecting the bride; and (7) celebrating the union. Similarly, Peter Williamson (2015, 310) does the same in a six-stage sequence by reducing Marcus' final two stages into one.

Marcus (2013, 124) points out many cultures can trace some form of matrimonial text or custom back to a Jewish wedding. These cultures include the following: Greco-Roman; pre-modernity; various forms of Christian and Muslim cultures in Asia, Europe, and North Africa; modernity; and postmodernity. Consequently, though John presents the Wedding Supper of the Lamb in a Jewish setting, the matrimonial aspects of the celebration can be understood in other cultures. For example, the Wedding Supper of the Lamb can be likened to a wedding reception, or dinner, in the West.

Prophetic Genre

Similar to Marcus (2013), Hendriksen (1998, 181) uses a seven-stage nuptial sequence **prophetically applying** it to Christ and His Church: (1) the bride was chosen from eternity; (2) the wedding was announced throughout the entire Old Testament; (3) The Son of God assumed human flesh and blood; (4) the betrothal took place; (5) the dowry was paid on Calvary; (6) an interval of time must pass, which in the eyes of God is but a little while; and (7) The Bridegroom returns[94] and "the wedding of the Lamb has come" (Rev. 19:7).

In the past tense, the "wedding of the Lamb has come" (Rev. 19:7) assumes all seven sequential steps have occurred (Hendriksen 1998, 181). In the present tense, "Blessed are those who are invited" (Rev. 19:9) goes back two steps to a waiting interval of time. Although the past and present tenses appear confusing, Lenski (2001c, 541) points out both are acceptable within a prophetic vi-

---

[94] The seventh sequential stage differs between Marcus (2013) and Hendriksen (1998) in that the former celebrates the union while the latter returns ready to be united.

sion. Since the genre of John's text is a prophetic vision (Rev. 1:10), "It presents so much and no more" (2001c, 541). **Five of the seven sequential steps are assumed in Revelation** 19: 6-9 but not detailed in their accomplishment.

Another assumption is the use of the word "blessed" (Rev. 19:9) in reference to "the bride." The parable of the wedding banquet (Matt. 22:1-14) may shed light on both assumptions.[95] The parable focuses on invited guests and does not mention a bride. The invitation to the banquet was sent out twice to the "invited" (Matt. 22:3-4) who refused. As a result, the same invitation was sent to "anyone you find" (Matt. 22:9). The parable focuses on a greater redemptive narrative rather than an attempt to fill empty seats.

More importantly, Gregory Beale (1999, 495) highlights "anyone" (Matt. 22:9) fits the prophetic vision: "Here I am! I stand at the door and knock. If anyone hears my voice and opens the door, I will come in and eat with that person, and they with me" (Rev. 3:20, italics mine). Although the prophetic imagery in Matthew is not exactly the same in Revelation, it does point to the celebration of the Wedding Supper of the Lamb (Lenski 2001c, 542).

Because the celebration is prophetic, an invitation remains active until the Second Advent, or the coming of Christ for His bride. In addition to Hendriksen (1998), Marcus (2013), and Williamson (2015), Lenski (2001c, 541) expands on the idea of a wedding procession led by the bridegroom to collect his bride. While John prophetically observed such a procession, Christ the bridegroom is still actively knocking on the door to invite anyone who opens to Him. In John's prophetic vision, the invitation is closed (Rev. 19:7). However, within the same vision, the invitation remains open while in an interval of waiting for the bridegroom (Rev. 19:9). The relationship between past and present invitations is one of yearning for a predetermined celebration.

---

[95] Williamson (2015, 311) points out the parable should not be taken as a literal description of the wedding supper of the Lamb; rather, a resemblance of it.

Appropriate Clothing

The Wedding Supper of the Lamb could not take place without the removal of Babylon (Beale 1999, 934). As a result, the fourth "Hallelujah" (Rev. 19:6) celebrates the destruction of Babylon paving the way for the supper (Williamson 2015, 311). However, a problem arises between the bride who "has made herself ready" (Rev. 19:7) and "fine linen, bright and clean, was given her [the bride] to wear" (Rev. 19:8). There are **theological implications** to the fact that she is ready (Rev. 19:7), but also is still getting herself ready (Rev. 19:8) and, at the same time, she is getting herself ready.

Beale (1999, 935) points to Pauline doctrine of justification to explain the clothing problem (Rom. 5:18-19). "Theologically, this would mean that justification is the causal necessary condition for entrance into the eternal kingdom, but good works [righteous acts (Rev. 19:8)] are a non-casual necessary condition" (Beale 1999, 935). If this is the case, the clothing problem is solved in two necessary realities: **justification** accomplished by God through Christ to acquit the bride of sin; and, the **righteous acts** of the bride as the evidence of that justification.

Righteous acts become pronounced in contrast to the unrighteous acts of Babylon. Prior to the removal of Babylon, the bride could not have "made herself ready" (Rev. 19:7) without the contrasting unrighteousness of Babylon as the oppressor (Phil. 1:28-30). On one hand, justification is given to the bride as "fine linen, bright and clean" (Rev. 19:8). On the other hand, the bride has made herself ready because she is given such linen. Without the appropriate clothing, expulsion from the wedding supper is absolute (Matt. 22:11-14).

John set the Wedding Supper of the Lamb celebration against a Jewish culture. Nevertheless, other cultures can understand the matrimonial aspects of the celebration. The prophetic genre of the supper, in light of the banquet parable, requires the correct clothing, called "justification." Dressing can be called a righteousness act.

Summary Thought

Therefore, God is experienced at the Wedding Supper of the Lamb in relation to the bride providing the appropriate clothing, and the one who **expels** the inappropriately dressed (see Table 18.1).

Table 18.1. Two Ways God was (will be) Experienced in the Wedding Supper of the Lamb Celebration

Celebration	In Relation	Expressed in the Bible
Wedding Supper of the Lamb	The Bride	Provider of appropriate clothing
	The Bride	Expeller of the inappropriately dressed

CONCLUDING THOUGHT

God was experienced in ten different ways through three table celebrations. First, in relation to the tenth plague, preexisting ceremonies, Egyptian polytheism, and an Egyptian calendar, God was experienced in four ways in the Passover celebration as: (1) discriminate/indiscriminate; (2) transformative; (3) monotheistic; and (4) liberator. Second, in relation to the physical incarnate presence of Christ, His physical resurrected presence, and His physical ascended absence, God was experienced three ways in celebration of Communion as: (1) without post-resurrection clarity; (2) progressively; (3) recipient of thanksgiving; and (4) present by His Spirit. Third, in relation to the Bride, God was experienced in two ways: (1) the provider of appropriate clothing; and (2) the expeller of the inappropriately dressed. As a result of this section of study, a sixth key finding that emerges: the God of the Bible can be depicted in many ways.

> the God of the Bible can be depicted in many ways.

In the next section, I take these experiences and assess them through the four ceremonial systems from chapter nine, looking for commonalities and differences. Such an assessment helps towards understanding how Communion can function to communicate biblical truth by retelling the redemptive story to people with a postmodern/post-Christian worldview called Generation Z.

CHAPTER 19

COMMONALITIES AND DIFFERENCES AT EACH TABLE

To focus on how God is experienced at each table celebration in the biblical text, in this chapter I assess commonalities and differences through four ceremonial systems from chapter nine: community and ceremony (Turner 2011); belief and ceremony (Shils 1968); participant and observer (Singer 1959); and, ethos and worldview (Geertz 1973). I summarize the way each system assesses how God is experienced from the perspective of Communion in the Passover and Wedding Supper of the Lamb as table celebrations and what this means towards theory development of how Communion functions to communicate biblical truth through retelling the redemptive story to late Millennials and Generation Z.

In a similar fashion to the **previous chapter**, primary focus was given to biblical passages from **Exodus** for the Passover; the **gospels, 1 Corinthians,** and **Acts** for Communion; and **Matthew** and **Revelation** for the Wedding Supper of the Lamb. Additional biblical passages support the primary focuses.

Ceremonial System of Belief and Ceremony

The ceremonial system of Shils (1968, 736) was evident in the narrative of the Passover. The narrative was filled with ultimate things beyond the ordinary, necessitating a ceremony to express and renew contact with them (Exod. 12:2). Though all ten plagues were extraordinary, Israel was only commanded to remember the tenth plague[96] (Exod. 12:26-27). Pharaoh's belief in God is vicarious (Exod. 8:9-10, 25, 28, Exod. 9:27-28, Exod. 10:16-17). It exemplifies Shils' ceremonial system that beliefs can exist without practicing the ceremony of those beliefs. For Moses and all the Israelites, the opposite was true (Exod. 12:24). The ceremony of the Passover could not exist without belief: therefore, they were commanded to celebrate it "as a lasting ordinance" (Exod. 12: 14, 17, 24). If not, the Passover as a ceremony would cease to exist. Therefore, celebrating the **Passover not only expressed belief, but it also annually renewed contact with the God of ultimate things.**

Similarly, belief and ceremony are also found in Communion. Paul's additional words to Christ's invocation renew contact with resurrection as an ultimate thing. "For whenever you eat this bread and drink this cup, you proclaim the Lord's death until he comes" (1 Cor. 11:26). Christ's death, resurrection, and promise to come again are certainly beyond the ordinary. Again, because **belief and ceremony intertwine,** it is possible to proclaim the Lord's death without celebrating Communion. For example, Simon the sorcerer "believed" (Acts 8:13), but Peter exposed him as "full of bitterness and captive to sin" (Acts 8:23). According to Kistemaker (1990, 305), Simon believed all that Peter said regarding Christ, and that included statements about his death, resurrection, and promised return. His heart was not right before God (Acts 8:21).

Kistemaker (2001, 515) theologically connects the parable of the wedding feast (Matt. 22:1-14) with the Wedding Supper of the Lamb (Rev. 19:7-9). However, a wedding feast is not beyond the ordinary. An eschatological wedding feast is beyond

---

[96] My point is not that heads of Israelite families were forbidden to remember all ten plagues at Passover but that they were commanded to remember the tenth.

ordinary.[97] A theological connection is seen in proper and improper wedding clothing. Such a connection reveals Shils' ceremonial system of belief and ceremony. For example, David L. Turner (2008, 524) makes two insightful observations that shed light on this system. First, the king calls an improperly dressed man "friend" (Matt. 22:11). He is a friend because the servants of the king had invited him, not because the king personally knew him (Matt. 22:9-10). Although the man had accepted the invitation, he had not prepared himself with proper clothing. Second, the man has no explanation or defense for his improper clothing (Matt. 22:11) (2008, 515).

By returning to Beale's paradigm that the bride had made herself ready (Rev. 19:7) and at the same time was making herself ready through righteous acts (Rev. 19:8), Shils' ceremonial system can be seen. In Matthew's parable, the bride has been invited because of all that the king has done on her behalf, or "the causal necessary condition for entrance" into the wedding feast (Beale 1999, 935). Because the bride has been invited, she is making herself ready for the wedding feast through her righteous acts, or "the non-causal necessary condition for entrance" into the wedding feast (1999, 935). The improperly dressed man undoubtedly believed he was invited. He had done nothing with the "fine linen" (or righteous acts) (Rev. 19:8) the king had provided for him. Evidently, **belief existed for the man, but he had not practiced his belief to prepare himself.**

Summary Thought

The ceremonial system of Shils in belief and ceremony, intertwining, yet remaining separate, are common in all three table celebrations. Belief existed in Pharaoh, Simon the sorcerer, and the improperly dressed man. Pharaoh did not participate in the Passover ceremony associated with belief in order to renew contact with ultimate things. The same can be generally implied to Simon regarding Com-

---

[97] It is beyond the ordinary in the sense that the guests and bride are the same (Beale 1999, 945).

munion, and the improperly dressed man regarding the Wedding Supper of the Lamb. In contrast, belief existed in Moses and the Israelites, and Peter, essential for the existence of the Passover and Communion respectively. The existence of the Wedding Supper of the Lamb is seen differently. If ceremony needs belief to exist, belief expressed through Communion can be seen as partly necessary for preparation and legitimate entrance into the Wedding Supper of the Lamb (see Table 19.1).

Table 19.1. Belief and Ceremony Commonalities and Differences

Ceremonial System	Ceremony/Celebration	Commonalities and Differences
Ceremony and Belief	The Passover	Belief exists without ceremony
	Communion	Belief exists without ceremony
	The Wedding Supper of the Lamb	Previous ceremonies are essential for legitimate preparation.

Ceremonial System of Community and Ceremony

Presupposed in the Passover celebration was **inquiry and succession.** Both are seen in generational questions (Exod. 12:26-27, Exod. 13:14). Consequently, expected questions of inquiry meant the responsibility fell on the oldest man in each family or family circle to answer questions and officiate over the Passover celebration (Keil and Delitzsch 2006, 335). Through natural succession, those who made the inquiry would at some later point be those who officiate and answer questions of inquiry. Turner's ceremonial system of community and ceremony are seen in the way succession occurs. For example, in an unstructured family community, the oldest male who officiates would have naturally come through his family as a younger man who inquired.

As the benefactor of deliverance from Egypt, the one who **officiates the Passover is not constant**. Each generation has a new officiant who has come up through the family. Consequently, the Passover as a ceremony was greater than the oldest man who officiated it. As a result, the community that celebrated the Passover also carried transient humility or **"modelessness"** to temper the possibility of pride in successive older men who may think themselves more important than the Passover (Turner 2011, 97).

The same cannot be said for Communion as a ceremony after it was first appointed. Susan White (2006, 79) critically notes the insincerity of the clergy who **officiated Communion in the fifth century.** This is what Turner (2011, 96) points out in ceremonies within a structured community. The biblical passages themselves do not read like successive church history. For example, in the absence of church buildings, Christians were "breaking bread from house to house" (Acts 2:42). Foley (2009, 67) points out a similar practice to the Passover in that the oldest member of the family officiated over Communion as a ceremony. Heidi Parales (1998, 149) is convinced that Christ's teaching rejects structured community by allowing women to officiate over the bread and wine of Communion.

Nevertheless, whether high positions were held by men or women, Communion generally had a structured community throughout church history, elevating those with high positions from those with low positions. High and low positions in Corinth did not relate to age or gender. Rather, assignment of positions related to the "haves" and "have nots" (Fee 2010, 595). The hierarchal principle of a structured community was certainly operating during **Communion at Corinth.** Evidentially, their division was rebuked by Paul, "When you come together to eat, you should all eat together" (1 Cor. 11:33).

The Wedding Supper of the Lamb may look like an unstructured community due to the communal aspect of the wedding guests that also comprised a singular bride (Beale 1999, 945). A strictly unstructured community would not be true to Turner's ceremonial system. On one hand, the community that gathers for the Wedding Supper is a structured community due to the **permanent high position of Christ.** There is and never has been or will be anyone else like Him (Phil. 2:9). His position had no **predecessor or successor.** On the other hand, His position was given to Him because He experienced what a low position was like (Phil. 2:6-8), that included his obedience to death on a cross (Phil. 2:8).

There is an absence of transient humility or "modelessness" to temper the pride of Christ in His unique high position because it is **totally unnecessary.** For example, "He humbled himself" (Phil. 2:8) by taking on the nature of a person in a low position and sacrificing himself for all people. Christ did not need a societal system to keep Him humble. Because the Wedding Supper of the Lamb is minimally structured, it is not automatically structured. Christ may have the high position, but the guests are His bride. The marital nature of "bridegroom and bride" (Rev. 18:23) void any fragmentation of cast, class, rank, or segmenting oppositions (Turner 2011, 96).

Summary Thought

Turner's unstructured community is common in the Passover due to presupposed generational inquiry. The Corinthian church made the ceremony of Communion structured by its practice of hierarchy. The same cannot be said for other house churches where the Communion took place. Therefore, community is both structured and unstructured in Communion as a ceremony. Turner's ceremonial system is different in the Wedding Supper of the Lamb. It is different in the sense that there is no more need for a structured or unstructured community (see Table 19.2).

Table 19.2. Community and Ceremony Commonalities and Differences

Ceremonial System	Celebration	Commonalities and Differences
Community and Ceremony	The Passover	Unstructured
	Communion	Structured and unstructured
	The Wedding Supper of the Lamb	Minimally structured

Ceremonial System of Ethos and Worldview

The dialectical natures of ethos and worldview are common in the Passover as a ceremony. Evidently, it is a ceremony **"of"** deliverance but also a ceremony **"for" deliverance** (Geertz 1973, 114). For example, the Israelites remembered that God had delivered them (Exod. 12:42) but also looked for His continued deliverance (Exod. 12:42). Therefore, the Passover is not only a ceremony of what the Israelites believed, but also a ceremony for believing. Without the "of" and "for" rite in Geertz's (1973, 93-94) ceremonial system, it is doubtful whether the Israelites would "attain their faith as they portray it" (1973, 114). Consequently, in the Passover, the dialectical nature of ethos and worldview looks back to the past reality "of" deliverance and into the present and future "for" continued deliverance.

Similar to the Passover, Communion appears to perpetuate its meaning in the dialectical nature of ethos and worldview. It is a ceremony **"of" proclaiming the death and resurrection of Christ and "for" proclaiming His return** (1 Cor. 11:26). Geertz's (1973) ceremonial system logically creates an opportunity for participants to attain faith as it is experienced in Communion as a ceremony. Similar to the Passover, Communion evaluates the past in that historically Christ died, was buried, and resurrected for the forgiveness of sins. It also senses that Christ will return again in the present or future with reassurance of continued forgiveness of sins until that time.

Difficulty arises in the biblical passages by comparing three of the gospels (Matt. 26:26-29; Mk. 14:22-25; Lk. 22:15-20) with Paul's first letter to the Corinthian church (11:23-26). Evidently, Christ's invocation did not have the words "lasting ordinance" (Exod. 12:14, 17, 24) or "for generations to come" (Exod. 12:42) impetus like the Passover. Even the biblical passages in Acts fail to deliver a direct command similar to the Passover. Christ does promise that He will celebrate once again in His Father's kingdom (Matt. 26:29; Mk. 14:25; Lk. 22:16/18). Paul's additional invocation words "until He comes" (1 Cor. 11:26) highlight the dialectical nature of ethos by historically looking back to what Christ has done as a basis "of" belief. At the same time, Paul's words highlight worldview "for" believing Christ will return in the present or future.

Geertz's (1973) ceremonial system is common in the Wedding Supper of the Lamb. For example, the fourth "Hallelujah" (Rev. 19:6) punctuates the victory of Christ and destruction of Babylon, "For our Lord God Almighty reigns" (Rev. 19:6). If the dialectical nature of ethos and worldview has two senses of belief — "of" and "for" — the Wedding Supper of the Lamb is a convergence of both in Geertz's ceremonial system. The supper is a celebration **"of" marriage,** but also a celebration **"for" the continued and eternal marriage** of bridegroom and bride. There is one significant exception to Geertz's system. The bride no longer has a need to attain her faith (1973, 114) by portraying it in the Wedding Supper (Rev. 19:7). Faith is no longer necessary. Therefore, the "for" sense in Geertz's system no longer anticipates the future because "the wedding of the Lamb has come" (Rev. 19:7).

Summary Thought

Geertz's (1973) dialectical nature of ethos and worldview are common in the Passover as a ceremony and to some degree Communion. Ethos and worldview are common in the Passover because both evaluate past deliverance and senses present and future deliverance. Ethos and worldview are also common in Communion as a ceremony for the same reasons. However, without Paul's additional words of invocation, Geertz's ceremonial system is different in the Passover. It is different because while sensing the present, it would lack a worldview sensing the future. For similar reasons, Geert's system is different from the ceremonies of the Passover and Communion in the Wedding Supper of the Lamb. It is different because the supper no longer anticipates marital status. Faith is no longer necessary so attaining it through the Wedding Supper is redundant (see Table 19.3).

Table 19.3. Ethos and Worldview Commonalities and Differences

Ceremonial System	Celebration	Commonalities and Differences
Ethos and Worldview	The Passover	Evaluates past deliverance and senses present and future deliverance
	Communion	Evaluates past forgiveness and senses present and future forgiveness
	The Wedding Supper of the Lamb	No longer anticipates the future or need to attain faith

Ceremonial System of Participant and Observer

God passed through Egypt with the tenth plague only in the first Passover (Exod. 12:12). Therefore, the first Passover had no observers, only participants.[98] After the first Passover during the Exodus, "Many other people went up with them [Israelites]" (Exod. 12:38). Enns (2000, 251-252) makes two distinctions regarding other people in the Exodus narrative. First, they were probably a mixture of ethnicities. Second, they are called Israelite slaves (Exod. 12:44), temporary residents (Exod. 12:45), and hired workers (Exod. 12:45). All three were classified as "foreigners."[99] In Singer's ceremonial system, the foreigners become the observers. A foreigner would not want to participate in the Passover unless he or she had been observing the totality of the ceremony performed by the Israelite (Singer 1975, 39). Provision was made for "a foreigner residing among you who wants to celebrate the Lord's Passover" (Exod. 12:48). Upon circumcision, "he may take part like one born in the land" (Exod. 12:48). Consequently, the Passover as a ceremony brings together the Israelite participant and foreign observer who wanted to participate.

As the Passover was an exhibition of God's saving power to the participant (Enns 2000, 251), so Communion as a ceremony

---

[98] It could be argued that some Egyptians observed the first Passover by looking into the open homes of the Jews. Also, it could be argued that surrounding nations observed the first Passover (Josh. 2:8-10). However, it would be more accurate to say surrounding nations heard about the disaster that came on Egypt rather than observers of the first Passover. An observer is understood as someone who is physically present and able to see for themselves what is happening among those who participate in the first and succeeding Passover celebrations.

[99] The Passover regulations in Exodus 12:43-49 were future-oriented. Israelite slaves, temporary residents, and hired workers are not applicable in the actual Exodus as the Israelites were slaves themselves (Enns 2000, 252).

publicly exhibits the saving power of God (Col. 2:15; Eph. 3:10) performed for the observer. From a public performance, an observer is exposed to the saving power of God. However, whereas the Passover requires physical circumcision to participate, Communion may require spiritual circumcision, or it may not (Rom. 2:25-29).[100]

On one hand, if Communion as a ceremony is only available to Christians, an observer must first become a Christian to participate by having his or her heart circumcised by the Holy Spirit. On the other hand, if Communion is available to Christians and the observer "who wants to celebrate" (Exod. 12:48), the observer is not required to become a Christian.[101] However, if circumcision of the heart is the requirement to become a Christian, Communion as a ceremony fails to bring together the Christian participant and observer. It also fails because circumcision of the heart is only performed by the Holy Spirit,[102] not by human hands who officiate the ceremony of Communion (Jn. 1:13). Proving **spiritual circumcision is far more difficult than proving physical circumcision.**

The Wedding Supper of the Lamb undoubtedly has observers. However, those observers are not redeemed humans but

---

[100] My point in this biblical passage is that a Christian's heart is spiritually circumcised by the Holy Spirit, but there is no concrete biblical evidence that such a circumcision is necessary to participate in Communion.

[101] Bradshaw (2012, 269) notes in John Calvin's Communion reform "the unworthy [observer], without faith, receive only bread and wine." Observers are welcome, but they not have the same experience as the Christian. For the Christian, the bread and wine are more than their substance. John Christopher Thomas (2005, 45-51), highlights the consequences of participants in Communion who approach and conduct themselves in an unworthy manner (1 Cor. 11:29-30). Unlike Calvin, Thomas (2005, 50) believes the unworthy receive "judgment" (1 Cor. 11:29). However, Thomas (2005, 47) is unclear on whether that judgment comes from God. He is clear that judgment is a direct result of not "recognizing the body of the Lord" (1 Cor. 11:29). Whether the unworthy receive only the substance of bread and wine (Calvin), or judgment (Thomas), the ceremonial system of participant and observer applies to both.

[102] It could be argued that water baptism is the outward sign of inward circumcision of the heart. However, water baptism is a sign, not a literal proof of spiritual circumcision.

celestial angels (Heb. 1:14). The bride can only be redeemed humans wearing fine, bright, and clean linen (Rev. 19:8). If, "Fine linen stands for the righteous acts of God's holy people" (Rev. 19:8), angels do not qualify because they do not perform righteous acts having been justified[103] (Rom. 5:18-19). Therefore, redeemed **humans and angels do not converge into a singular bride.**

Summary Thought

Singer's (1955, 23-27) ceremonial system is not common in the first Passover due to a lack of observers.[104] In successive celebrations, the system is explicitly common in the ceremony of the Passover. It is explicit because the biblical text anticipates observers and their desire to participate with celebrants through a prescribed rite of passage. It is common and different in Communion as a ceremony for opposite reasons than the Passover. It is common because observers are inevitable. It is different in the gospels because the biblical text is not explicit about observers, their desire, or rite of passage to participate with celebrants. Singer's (1955, 23-27) ceremonial system is common in the Wedding Supper of the Lamb with remarkable difference to the Passover and Communion. Celestial angels observe and join with participants in worship but not as a singular bride made up of redeemed human beings (see Table 19.4).

---

[103] See Beale's (1999, 935) comment on the relationship of the bride's fine linen clothing and Pauline justification.

[104] Again, an observer is understood as someone who is physically present and able to see for him or herself what is happening among those who participate in the first and succeeding Passover celebrations.

Table 19.4. Participant and Observer Commonalities and Differences

Ceremonial System	Celebration	Commonalities and Differences
Participant and Observer	The Passover	Intentional - performed with observers in mind
	Communion	Intentional - performed with observers in mind
	The Wedding Supper of the Lamb	Unintentional - performed with observers in mind

CONCLUDING THOUGHT

I discovered commonalities and differences in four ceremonial systems. The system of ceremony and belief (Shils 1968) was common in all three celebrations with preparatory difference in the Wedding Supper of the Lamb. The system of structured and unstructured community (Turner 2011) was common in the Passover, common and different in Communion, and neither common nor different in the Wedding Supper of the Lamb because the bride and groom are neither structured nor unstructured, common nor different. The system of ethos and worldview (Geertz 1973) was common in the Passover and Communion, but it was different in the Wedding Supper of the Lamb as sensing, anticipation, and faith are no longer necessary. Finally, the system of participant and observer (Singer 1959) was common in the Passover[105] and Communion with intentional performance, and it was different in the Wedding Supper of the Lamb with unintentional performance for celestial angels (see Table 19.5).

---

[105] Not the first Passover in Egypt, but all successive Passovers.

Table 19.5. Summary of Commonalities and Differences

	Ceremony and Belief	Structured and Unstructured Community	Ethos and Worldview	Participant and Observer
Passover	Common	Common	Common	Common
Communion	Common	Common and different	Common	Common
Wedding Supper of the Lamb	Different	Neither common nor different	Different	Different

Specific to this chapter, what I discovered showed me that the Wedding Supper of the Lamb has little in common with the Passover and Communion when assessed by the four ceremonial systems. Such a discovery is important towards a theoretical model than explains how Communion can function to communicate biblical truth through retelling the redemptive story to late Millennials and Generation Z with a postmodern/post-Christian worldview. It is particularly important because in **section four** I noted that community of students at SEU who gather to celebrate Communion express spirituality through religion in order to search for meaning. In short, **the Wedding Supper of the Lamb brings an end to searching for meaning.** While Communion finds its historical roots in the Passover, the same celebration finds its ultimate fulfillment in the Wedding Supper of the Lamb.

> While Communion finds its historical roots in the Passover, the same celebration finds its ultimate fulfillment in the Wedding Supper of the Lamb.

CHAPTER 20

COMPARING THE BIBLICAL TEXT, LIVED EXPERIENCES, AND CEREMONIAL SYSTEMS

In this chapter, I compare three aspects: (1) how God is depicted as expressed in the biblical text (see Table 20.1); (2) the students' lived experiences; and, (3) the four ceremonial systems (see Table 20.2).

Biblical Text and Lived Experiences

Sokolowski (1994, 3), Kereszty (2004, vii-ix), and Green (2012, 182-240) were able to make connections from Communion historically to the Passover and **eschatologically** towards the Wedding Supper of the Lamb, and all three described an experience of God. However, Sokolowski (1994, 3) was more concerned with the structure and appearance of God in a theology of disclosure. Kereszty (2004, 19-20) was concerned with God's love for the world and the purpose of human existence, and he uses Communion as a hermeneutic tool. He does not describe how God is depicted in the biblical text. Green (2012, 182-240) was concerned with a Pentecostal understanding of experiencing God and uses documented testimonies of how people experience God as participants in Communion. In his case, it is the testimonies, not the biblical text, that depict God.

Table 20.1. Experience of God in all Three Table Celebrations

Celebration	In Relation	Experience of God
The Passover	Tenth plague	Indiscriminate
	Preexisting rituals	Transformative
	Egyptian polytheism	Monotheistic
	Egyptian calendar	Liberator
Communion	Incarnate presence	Without post-resurrection clarity
	Resurrection presence	Progressively
	Ascended absence (Acts)	Recipient of thanksgiving
	Ascended absence (1 Corinthians)	Present by His Spirit
Wedding Supper of the Lamb	Bride	Provider of appropriate clothing
	Bride	Expeller of inappropriately dressed

Table 20.2. Four Ceremonial Systems

Theorist	System
Victor Turner	Structured Unstructured Community
Milton Singer	Participant and Observer
Clifford Geertz	Ethos and Worldview
Edward Shils	Belief and Ceremony

While all three describe an experience of God, they do not exclusively describe it as expressed in the biblical text. A depiction of God informed by the biblical text is essential for developing a thoroughly theological explanation towards communicating biblical truth to Generation Z who participate or observe Communion. The key discovery that emerged in chapters sixteen, seventeen, and eighteen is that the God of the Bible can be depicted in the biblical text in many ways. These biblical depictions give me points of comparison for how the students at SEU described God.

Though a depiction of God was largely influenced by the **maternal relationship**s of Sophia and Victoria in their respective experiences, the biblical passages that depicted God do not gender Him as female in any of the three table celebrations. He is Christ at Communion, and the Father of the bride and groom in the Wedding Supper of the Lamb. It could be argued that God has female characteristics because He required spiritual fidelity in the Passover, but this could also be argued as a male characteristic. Furthermore, **Moses consistently genders God male** in any dialogue with Pharaoh and the Israelites regarding the Passover.[106]

The **paternal influence** on Samuel's understanding of God created an imbalance between the positive and negative aspects of God depicted in the Bible. Though he fears his father, the biblical passages do, in fact, show that God has fearful characteristics. These were particularly seen in how God is experienced as the discriminator in the Passover and the expeller of inappropri-

---

[106] Hans Boersma (2001, 117-118), emphasizes that the theological tradition of gendering God in masculine language does not mean He is male or masculine. However, though Boersma makes this assertion, he does not reduce it to a linguistic issue but states there are theological problems when using inclusive language about God incompatible with the Bible.

ately dressed guests in the Wedding Supper of the Lamb. While Samuel may fear his father, the biblical passages also show that God is experienced as the **transformer giving new identity and liberation from bondage** in the Passover, and the provider of appropriate clothing in the Wedding Supper of the Lamb. Samuel may understand the threatening aspects of God, but he does not comprehend the transforming, liberating, and providing aspects of God.

William tends to allow the pendulum to swing in the opposite direction from Samuel. Though William feels the need for consistent renewal, God does not threaten him. God is his **personal benefactor.** Furthermore, the student discussion groups in **chapter eleven** described God as "deity," "something," "divine presence," and "whatever is out there." Though God was described in various obscure and impersonal ways, the students did **encounter God.**

A thoroughly theological explanation is necessary for students like those who were interviewed and involved in discussion groups to comprehend their experiences of God by informing them with the biblical text. Currently, God is depicted through external influences in the students' portrayal of Him, creating a **sub-orthodox view of God.** Without the biblical text, God can be anything a student espouses Him to be guided by what the student senses or feels is true. Without the biblical text, students would more than likely not comprehend the threatening and delivering aspects of God.

> Without the biblical text, God can be anything a student espouses Him to be guided by what the student senses or feels is true.

In **chapter seventeen**, Communion did **not discriminate** among age, gender, or wealth in the biblical passages. This was particularly seen in Paul's rebuke of the Corinthian Christians. The same could not be said for the Passover where **discrimination was seen** between those who had the lamb's blood on the entrances to their homes and those who did not. Also, the Wedding Supper of the Lamb **demonstrates discrimination** between those who were appropriately dressed and those who were not.

As a point of comparison, the issue of discrimination emerged in the interview with Sophia and group discussion with Eleanor. Both students were guarded **against any form of discrimination** from the church towards their friends. Aside from these two students, others did not feel they were directly discriminated against in any way. In short, they did not feel excluded from celebrating Communion as college students, which is also a reality of a postmodern spirituality noted at the end of **section two.** Another comparative point is that Christ is present by His Spirit in Paul's first letter to the Corinthian church.

All the students who were interviewed sensed the presence of God. Admittedly, the **memories of the students were triggered** by a variety of occurrences that included a remembrance of feeling God's presence. Remembering is not the only way they sense God. He was also currently present. There was no evidence of apparitions of God in the interviews but a progressive sense of His presence.

Progression brings up another comparative point in how the gospels depict Christ without post-resurrection clarity. The same could be said for Sophia, Victoria, and William, in that they form meaning in their progressive experiences of God as they continually participate in Communion. The same could not be said for Samuel who participates in the celebration to appease his family. A progressive depiction of God in the biblical text points out that any understanding **must be non-linear.** Introducing biblical truth to late Millennials and Generation Z who participate or observe Communion is not only progressive in meaning making but also continual until the ultimate fulfilment at the Wedding Supper of the Lamb.

Biblical Text, Lived Experiences, and Ceremonial Systems

The four ceremonial systems enabled me to discover how each table celebration communicated a depiction of how God was experienced, giving me further points of comparison with the students' lived experiences (see Table 20.3).

Here is where a seventh key discovery emerges. A depiction of God is experienced at each table celebration in a set of beliefs grounded in biblical truth. From the perspective of Communion, the depictions of God in the Passover and Wedding Supper of the Lamb connect the past and future to the present. The present celebration of Communion is ceremonially performed with the participant in mind as well as the observer who is not participating, informing them of the past and future. Again, from the perspective of Communion, each table celebration shows a God who wants to communicate Himself to people He can call His own and to others who He wants to call His own.

Considering all three table celebrations, the Communion table is central to the students' lived experience of God. Communion acts like a communication vehicle that brought into focus the students' experiences in communities that were largely unstructured. Without participating in the ceremony, there is enough data to show that students did have beliefs that existed outside of the Communion.

For example, Sophia believed in the concept of a supernatural God that was brought into focus by participating in Communion, enabling her to move from a simple concept to the reality of His (in Sophia's case it would be Her) presence. Also, her driving habits encouraged negative behavior in her towards other motorists. It seems that celebrating Communion reminded her that God had forgiven her in the past and will continue to forgive in the present and future. I am unclear who observed Sophia participating in Communion, therefore unclear if anyone was reminded about the forgiveness of God in the past, sensing present and future forgiveness in her performance. Because the community was largely unstructured, I can only assume her participation was observed, as her negative driving habits are undoubtedly observed.

Table 20.3. How Each Table Celebration Communicated a Depiction of God

Ceremonial System	Celebration	Commonalities and Differences
Ceremony and Belief	The Passover	Belief exists without ceremony.
	Communion	Belief exists without ceremony.
	The Wedding Supper of the Lamb	Previous ceremonies are essential for legitimate preparation.
Community and Ceremony	The Passover	Unstructured
	Communion	Structured and unstructured
	The Wedding Supper of the Lamb	Minimally structured
Ethos and Worldview	The Passover	Evaluates past deliverance and senses present and future deliverance
	Communion	Evaluates past forgiveness and senses present and future forgiveness
	The Wedding Supper of the Lamb	No longer anticipates the future or need to attain faith
Participant and Observer	The Passover	Intentional and performed with observers in mind
	Communion	Intentional and performed with observers in mind
	The Wedding Supper of the Lamb	Unintentional and performed with observers in mind

Victoria believed her **brother was in heaven** after his untimely death. This belief was brought into focus by Communion especially when her priest talked about the resurrection as part of the redemptive story of God. Victoria also believed certain things about American and Mexican cultures. Communion brought those beliefs into focus within a greater context of the redemptive story. Though Victoria has a set of beliefs about God, Communion functions as a ceremony that places those beliefs in a relationship with God and **enables her to feel close to Him.** Similar to Sophia, I am unclear who observed Victoria's performance in Communion. I can assume the death of her brother was not completely private and caused observers to note her performance. The same can be said for her performance in Mexico as an American student and in America as a Mexican student. The little traditions of both cultures were more than likely observed in the great tradition of Communion.

Participating at the Communion table appears to make little difference in focusing Samuel's beliefs in his lived experience in a largely unstructured community. However, it does highlight the fact that his **beliefs do, in fact, exist without a ceremony.** Samuel's beliefs about God negatively evaluate the past, believing it makes no difference to the present or future. God is simply watching and judging.

William had certain beliefs about what should happen in corporate worship. Participating at the Communion table brought into focus the thought **"of" what was happening and "for" what should be happening.** The bread and wine were what focused his thoughts or, as William put it, "I believe these things [bread and wine] deserve my attention…because they are so important." Like Sophia, William is reminded that he can be clean [forgiven] in the present and future based on how he has felt cleansed [forgiven] in the past. Without Communion it is doubtful whether William would feel continually cleansed.

The first two key discoveries emerged in **chapter eight.** The students had to **sense or feel something in order for their lived**

> "I believe these things [bread and wine] deserve my attention...because they are so important."

experiences to have meaning uninformed by the biblical text. Also, participating in Communion acted like a **communication vehicle** for the students' lived experiences. The eight experiences and meanings associated with them were also not informed by the biblical text. The third key discovery that emerged in **chapter eleven** showed what the students **believed approaching Communion and shaped** what they got out of the ceremony. The students did, indeed, experience Christ in the religious ceremony of Communion dependent on their approach.

But again, their experience of Christ was not informed by the biblical text. In **chapter fourteen,** the fourth key discovery showed a postmodern community at SEU populated by Late Millennials and Generation Z is composed of individual interpretations of a lived experience that begins with self. The fifth key discovery emerged in **chapter fifteen,** showing four characteristics of the students' spirituality and religious beliefs and behaviors that connect with each other moving in a circular and continued fashion. Once again, the four characteristics were not informed by the biblical text, but rather by sub-orthodox beliefs.

Considering the lack of reference to the biblical text in the five key discoveries, two final key discoveries emerged that address this lack. In **chapter eighteen,** an experience of the God of the Bible as expressed in the biblical text can be depicted in many ways. In **chapter twenty,** God is experienced in a set of beliefs grounded in biblical truth. From the perspective of Communion, the depictions of God connect the past and future to the present, ceremonially performing a set of beliefs in Communion with the participant in mind rather than the observer who is not participating. A better understanding of how Communion can function to communicate biblical truth towards theory development could inform a lived experience of Christ, thereby, influencing late Millennials and Generation Z as a post-modern community. In the next section, I bring together all seven key discoveries focusing on retelling the redemptive story.

SECTION SIX

SO WHAT?

In this section **I bring together the seven key discoveries** that have emerged throughout the book to better understand how Communion functions to communicate biblical truth by retelling the redemptive story to late Millennials and Generation Z who hold to a postmodern/post-Christian worldview.

An explanation of why the seven discoveries are important is briefly reviewed in **chapter twenty-one.** Following this review, **chapter twenty-two** paints the picture of the postmodern community at SEU that includes how Communion functions to communicate truth. How to bring biblical truth to Generation Z with a postmodern/post-Christian worldview through this vehicle is shown in three successive steps that predict a number of changes in the process of meaning making. The connection between ceremony and meaning making is shown by drawing on the perspectives of each ceremonial system described in chapter nine. Consideration is also given to liminality and its role in communicating biblical truth through Communion towards meaning making. Finally, I discuss theory development in light of other relevant ideas, showing how a Christian ministry practitioner can work in different settings where late Millennials and Generation Z gather as a community.

CHAPTER 21

____

OVERVIEW OF DISCOVERIES

The purpose of this book involved findings and key discoveries towards a better understanding of how Communion functions to communicate biblical truth by retelling the redemptive story to Generation Z who hold to a postmodern/post-Christian worldview.

In section one, I wanted to know the ways that participants in Communion experienced Christ as described in church history. In **section two**, I wanted to know what it was that late Millennials and Generation Z experienced when they participated in Communion. In **section three,** I wanted to know how each student's lived experience could be understood within a ceremony. In **section four,** I wanted to know the characteristics of spirituality, religious beliefs, and behaviors of late Millennials and Generation Z who participate in Communion. Finally, from the perspective of Communion, I wanted to know how God was experienced as expressed in the biblical text.

Church history provided the historical background for the current era of Postmodernity, indicating the realities of postmodern spirituality by which the meaning and function of Communion is approached. The historical background also explains how late Millennials and Generation Z came to celebrate Communion in the inclusive way that they do, self-guided in their interpretation of their own lived experiences (see Table 21.1).

Table 21.1. Realities of Postmodern Spirituality

Lens	Postmodern Spirituality
Access to Communion	Excluding people from Communion is not characteristic of late Millennials and Generation Z in the era of Postmodernity
Biblically explaining Communion	Including participants in interpreting the biblical text is attractive to late Millennials and Generation Z because it is full of experimentation.
Liturgy and Communion	Liturgy comes from the community using cultural elements that make sense to late Millennials and Generation Z who participate or observe.
Finding	Church history provides the background for the realities of postmodern spirituality and explains how late Millennials and Generation Z came to celebrate Communion in the way that they do.

The key discoveries in chapter eight showed the students had to sense or feel something in order for their eight lived experiences to have meaning. The vehicle for this sensory interpretation was Communion. Therefore, Communion functioned as a central communicating vehicle between the students and their lived experiences (see Table 21.2).

Table 21.2. IPA: Typical Experience

Experience	Summary Meaning
Presence	Able to sense God's presence
Ceremony	Desire to encounter Christ
Belief	Formal or informal education from the church failed to form meaning
Community	Desire to maintain individuality
Remembering	Past memories come to mind
Family	Adoption of parents' tradition
Completeness	Completeness when connected to Christ
Imagination	Varying degrees of imagination to communicate with Christ
#1 Key Discovery	Students had to sense or feel something in order for a lived experienced to have meaning.
#2 Key Discovery	Communion functioned like a communication vehicle.

The key discovery in **chapter eleven** showed that what the students believed approaching Communion shaped what they got out of the ceremony. The students did, indeed, experience Christ during Communion dependent on their approach. The fact that Christ was experienced in some way clearly points out the religious celebration of Communion is strictly a Christian ceremony (see Table 21.3).

Table 21.3. Typically Understood within Ceremony

Ceremonial System	Summary Understanding
Structured and Unstructured Community	Person officiating Communion matters to late Millennials and Generation Z
Participant and Observer	Culture of the student is involved in the performance ceremony
Ethos and Worldview	The dialectical nature of Communion shapes the experience of Generation Z as the experience shapes late Millennials and Generation Z
Belief and Ceremony	Communion delivers what late Millennials and Generation Z believes it promises when beliefs are intertwined with ceremony
#3 Key Discovery	What late Millennials and Generation Z believe approaching Communion shape what they get out of the ceremony.

In **chapter fourteen,** a picture of late Millennials and Generation Z emerged which showed that it is composed of individual interpretations of a lived experience that begins with self where the characteristics of that community move in a circular fashion. Consequently, a lived experience had no fixed meaning. Instead, meaning making was progressive. Biblical truth unassociated with a lived experience failed to provide meaning for the students. Rather, a lived experience informed by biblical truth must accompany the students' need to sense or feel that truth (see Table 21.4).

Table 21.4. A Picture of Generation Z who Participate in Communion

Students	Four Characteristics of Late Millennials and Generation Z as a Postmodern Community
Interviews and discussion groups	Spiritual connection to a supernatural God
Interviews and discussion groups	Communion provides for the connection to a supernatural God
Interviews and discussion groups	A lived experience is connected to elements of community valued by the students.
Interviews and discussion groups	Continued connection to God and community provides meaning for a lived experience.
#4 Key Discovery	The four characteristics connect, moving in a circular fashion.
Influence of Students	Summary of Influence
Two faculty, two priests, and a member of campus ministry	Intentionally focused on spirituality and not religion
Two faculty, two priests, and a member of campus ministry	Encouraged to be self-guided through lived experiences
Two faculty, two priests, and a member of campus ministry	Role of religion was Communion facilitating spirituality
Two faculty, two priests, and a member of campus ministry	Unobstructed by religious rules
#5 Key Discovery	Late Millennials and Generation Z is a postmodern community composed of individual interpretations of a lived experience that begins with self

From the perspective of Communion, the ten ways that God was portrayed show that the God of the Bible can be depicted in different ways. Assessed through ceremonial systems, God is experienced in a set of performative beliefs that show He wants to communicate Himself to people He can call His own and others who He wants to call His own (see Table 21.5). These biblical depictions gave me points of comparison for how late Millennials and Generation Z depict God through their sub-orthodox beliefs (see Table 21.6).

Table 21.5. Biblical Text

Celebration	In Relation	Experience of God
The Passover	Tenth Plague	Indiscriminate
	Preexisting Rituals	Transformative
	Egyptian Polytheism	Monotheistic
	Egyptian Calendar	Liberator
The Communion	Incarnate Presence	Without post-resurrection clarity
	Resurrection Presence	Progressively
	Ascended Absence (Acts)	Recipient of thanksgiving
	Ascended Absence(1 Cor.)	Present by His Spirit
Wedding Supper of the Lamb	Bride	Provider of appropriate clothing
	Bride	Expeller of inappropriately dressed
#6 Key Discovery		The God of the Bible can be depicted in the biblical text in different ways

Table 21.6. Lived Experiences and Ceremonial Systems

Ceremonial System	Celebration	Commonalities and Differences
Ceremony and Belief	The Passover	Belief exists without ceremony
	Communion	Belief exists without ceremony
	The Wedding Supper of the Lamb	Previous ceremonies are essential for legitimate preparation
Community and Ceremony	The Passover	Unstructured
	Communion	Structured and unstructured
	The Wedding Supper of the Lamb	Minimally structured
Ethos and Worldview	The Passover	Evaluates past deliverance and senses present and future deliverance
	Communion	Evaluates past forgiveness and senses present and future forgiveness
	The Wedding Supper of the Lamb	No longer anticipates the future or need to attain faith
Participant and Observer	The Passover	Intentional and performed with observers in mind
	Communion	Intentional and performed with observers in mind
	The Wedding Super of the Lamb	Unintentional and performed with observers in mind
#7 Key Discovery		God is experienced at each table celebration in a set of beliefs grounded in biblical truth connecting the past and future to the present, from the perspective of Communion by ceremonially performing beliefs with the participant in mind as well as the observer who is not participating informing them of the past and future.

Summary Thought

Developing and implementing these findings and key discoveries to better understand how Communion functions to communicate may have a causal effect on late Millennials and Generation Z: **collective change.** If biblical truth provides meaning for the lived experience of the students in the Christian celebration of Communion, by default students who participate or observe Communion will also be informed by biblical truth.

CHAPTER 22

LATE MILLENNIALS, GENERATION Z, AND COMMUNION

In **chapter fourteen,** a picture of a postmodern community emerged. The questions I asked helped me answer what the **characteristics of late Millennials and Generation Z looked like.** More specifically, answers to the questions highlight four characteristics that connected to each other moving in a continued circular fashion. These connections and circular movement described the basics of how a community of late Millennials and Generation Z who participate in or observe Communion works: [107] the community of individual students gathers together where the religious ceremony of Communion provides for their spiritual connection to a supernatural God in which a lived experience connects with positive elements of community valued by late Millennials and Generation Z providing meaning (see Figure 15.1).

---

[107] Research revealed far more than addressed here in the way a community of Generations works. However, at this juncture, the four characteristics provide a basic foundation to build the model that will include other empirical findings and key discoveries in what follows. Though Communion is key to communicating biblical truth, I rearranged the four characteristics placing meaning as the central characteristic. Essentially, meaning is the result of the other three characteristics. However, meaning is not an end result, simply a result in a continual celebration of Communion as a community of Generation Z who participate in or observe Communion (see Figure 22.1).

In general, the perception of the students was that their lived experiences connected to a supernatural God, but also reflected an autonomous interpretation that began with self, based on sub-orthodox beliefs. This provided meaning for their lived experiences. In order to lay the foundation for a theoretical model of Communion among students, the picture of a community emerged in **chapter fourteen,** and the characteristics are labelled accordingly. These labels and reasons for rearranging the characteristics are important to know how Communion serves to communicate biblical truth by retelling the redemptive story to late Millennials and Generation Z who hold to a postmodern/post-Christian worldview. Labelling and arranging the characteristics this way is the foundation of building a theoretical model (see Figure 21.1).

Figure 22.1. Foundation of a Postmodern Community

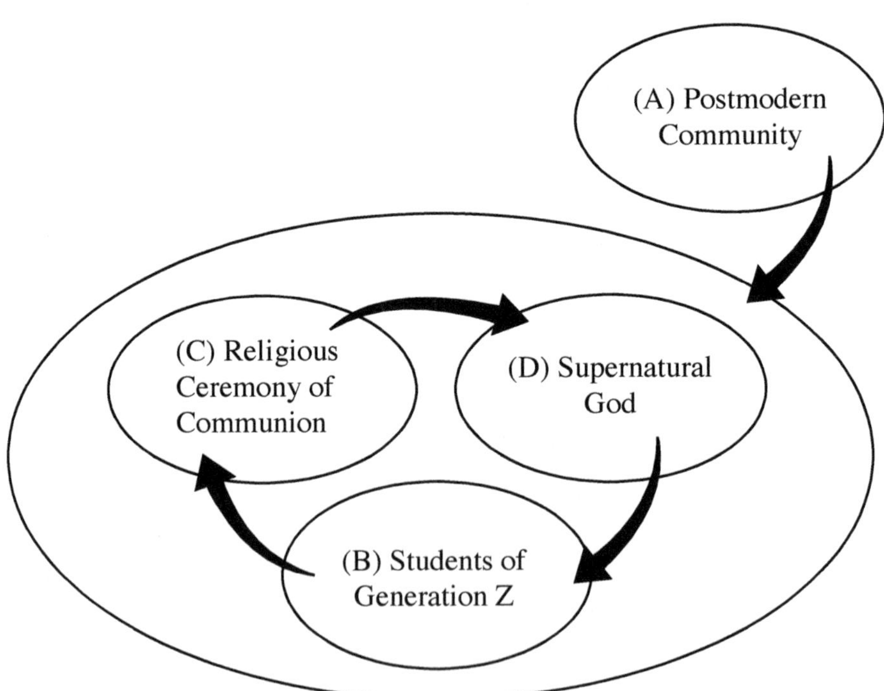

As a whole, the connecting characteristics of the postmodern community revealed that whatever meaning was autonomously provided was not fixed because the students of late Millennials and Generation Z continually celebrated Communion on a regular basis. A progressive meaning fits the stories that Sophia, Victoria, Samuel, and William told in **chapter ten** from their childhood experiences to young adult experiences. Therefore, **meaning was progressive** as the students continually celebrated Communion.

The characteristics not only connected, but an unfixed meaning lends itself to **influences** that are not currently evident in the students of Generation Z. Though Professor Blanche, Professor Edgar, Father Brown, Father Ted, and Arthur influenced the students, by default, the way they influenced invited further influence (see (G) in Figure 21.2). Influence in a postmodern community is not restricted by formal religious rules.

The influence of Father Ted in the classroom highlights this openness. "I teach the students that they will always be in process learning more about spirituality all their lives." Even with an influential default that is open to further influence in the circular movement of the characteristics, the influence of biblical truth was not evident throughout **chapters seven, eight, ten, and eleven.** The **"so what"** of my book is to understand how Communion can function to communicate biblical truth by retelling the redemptive story to students with a postmodern/post-Christian worldview. This understanding will help ministry practitioners to help students interpret their lived experiences and to assist them in finding biblical meaning and an understanding of a biblically described God with whom they regularly connect through the Christian celebration of Communion.

The **"so what"** communicates biblical truth to what already exists in the picture of the postmodern community as seen in the findings and key discoveries of my study. How Communion functions to communicate truth is vital. For example, whatever the church formally or informally taught Sophia, Victoria, Samuel, and William about Communion from the biblical text failed to create meaning for their lived experiences while participating in the celebration. This was particularly highlighted in chapter seven in the experience labelled "Belief" and the key finding of the same chapter: students had to sense or feel something in order for a lived experience to have meaning (see Table 21.2). Communion functioned as a sensory vehicle of communication.

Therefore, a ministry practitioner (F) must work with **what already exists** among the students in the postmodern community (A), as an addition to the influences already present (G), in order to introduce biblical truth into the students of late Millennials and Generation Z (B). The community of individual students (B) already gather together on a regular basis where the religious ceremony of Communion (C) provides for their spiritual connection to a supernatural God (D) in which a lived experience connects with positive elements of community valued by the students providing meaning (E) (see Figure 22.2).

Figure 22.2. Influence of the Ministry Practitioner

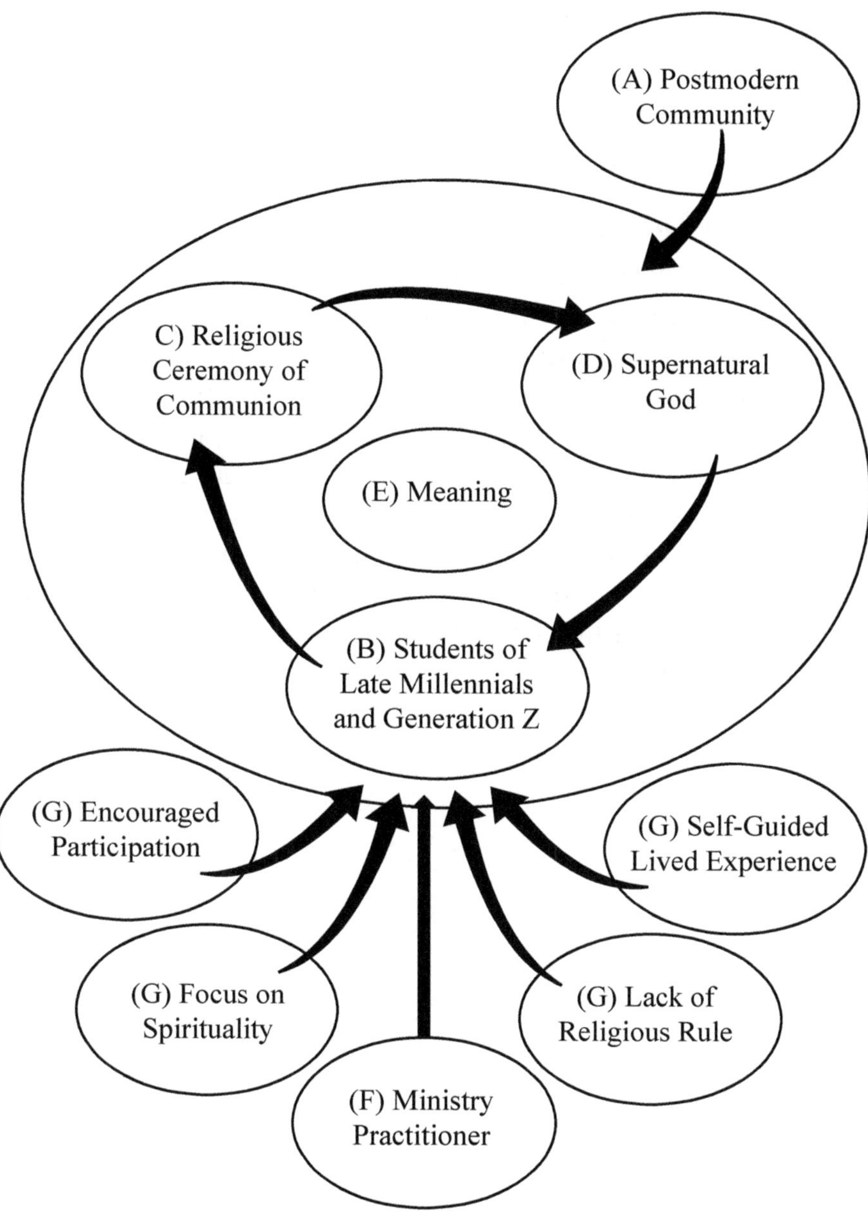

Essential to what is already going on in the postmodern community is Communion (C), described in the key discovery of **chapter eight** as a communication vehicle for the students' lived experiences. The findings in chapter eight showed eight experiences that were being communicated through the sensory vehicle of Communion (see Table 21.2). Ceremony, Community, and Family were necessary experiences as the background for the unique experiences of Presence, Belief, Remembering, Completeness, and Imagination.[108]

Summary Thought

The key discovery in **chapter eleven** showed how those experiences were communicated in the approach of the students to Communion. The students' beliefs approaching Communion shaped what they got out of the ceremony (see Table 21.3). Therefore, Communion not only functions as a sensory vehicle for communication, it also functions as a shaping vehicle for communicating what the students believe. Therefore, Communion can be a **carrier of biblical truth because of its dialectical nature.** The ceremony shapes each student's lived experience as the experience shapes the student.

---

[108] Hans Boersma (2001, 117-118), emphasizes that the theological tradition of gendering God in masculine language does not mean He is male or masculine. However, though Boersma makes this assertion, he does not reduce it to a linguistic issue but states there are theological problems when using inclusive language about God incompatible with the Bible.

CHAPTER 23

THREE SUCCESSIVE STEPS

Continuing to build on the foundation model seen in the connecting characteristics, three successive steps **predict** a number of changes to how a lived experience is informed and may have a causal effect on late Millennials and Generation Z as a postmodern community. Focus is given to the relationship of **common variables** found in the connections of the four characteristics that predict changes. The work of James Jaccard and Jacob Jacoby (2010, 32), helped me determine a concise number of steps for a theoretical model of Communion "so as to yield a theory that is parsimonious yet satisfactory in its level of explanation." Adding extraneous assumptions may run the risk of too many working parts necessary to explain how to bring biblical truth to students who participate in or observe Communion. My hope is that the utility of a theoretical model will generate more empirical research.

The three successive steps are **rooted in the findings and key discoveries** that emerged throughout the book. The steps take into consideration the realities of postmodern spirituality shown at the end of **chapter four** by which the meaning and function of Communion is approached: participation in the ceremony, interpretation of biblical passages, and liturgy used to retell the redemptive story must be inclusive (see Table 21.1).

Each step shows what biblical truth is introduced[109] to late Millennials and Generation Z as a postmodern community; how Communion functions to communicate that truth as a sensory and belief-shaping ceremony; who is involved; the connection between the biblical truth being communicated and ceremony, and meaning making; and how a sub-orthodox interpretation of a lived experience is changed to an interpretation through biblical truth.[110] Those steps are: (1) **an invitation to the table;** (2) **localized theology;** (3) and **creative liturgy.** The causal effect may be collective change on late Millennials and Generation Z.

In **chapter twelve,** personal change through participating in Communion was viewed from both sides. On one side, Nicholls (1996, 451) believed change was not possible because people only had a need to express their own innate spirituality through religious ceremony. On the other side, Kozeny (2004, 125) believed change was possible when personal beliefs and values are involved in that expression. With both sides in mind, data collected in my study showed that personal change did not take place in any of the students as a result of what the church taught them. Their participation in Communion with a community of peers seemed to give an **appearance of change.**

The appearance of personal change was simply an observation of values the students identified in their community of peers that gathered together. My model **predicts a change** in how individual students interpret their lived experiences from sub-orthodox beliefs to biblical truth by working with what already exists in late Millennials and Generation Z as a postmodern community. It also **predicts that continual participation** in Communion could lead to collective change as a community. These predictions are supported by the fact that 67% of the students who were surveyed in my book believed that culture (in this case a postmodern culture) is determined by the beliefs of human beings. Changing individual beliefs based on sub-orthodoxy to beliefs informed by

---

[109] The model generalizes in what biblical truth is introduced.

[110] Deals with an interpretation of a lived experience and not the interpretation of Scripture.

biblical truth has the potential of altering aspects of late Millennials and Generation Z as a postmodern culture.

Two specific challenges to these predictions are seen from the results of the same campus-wide survey. For example, my book supports the Christian view that biblical truth explains a lived experience (or the reality of a lived experience). Nevertheless, 82% of the students who participated in the survey responded by saying no theory of reality can **consistently explain everything,** and 82% believe absolute and certain truth that explains everything is **unobtainable.** As a result, what already exists in the postmodern community at SEU is a **majority position** regarding the reality of their lived experiences.

Nevertheless, 81% in the same survey said that a gap between thinking about something and the thing itself (in this case it would be the reality of a lived experience) requires a **bridge of imagination.** Such a bridge can be viewed as something Turner (2001, 95) uniquely calls **liminality** in the context of a ceremony.[111] Though Turner does not use the term "bridge," he does describe liminality as a moment when all the participants in a ceremony are "betwixt and between the positions assigned" (Turner 2011, 95). Therefore, it would be correct to describe liminality as a type of bridge that requires the use of imagination.

it would be correct to describe liminality as a type of bridge that requires the use of imagination.

Expanding on Turner's idea of liminality, Waaijman (2002, 214) adds that it is a moment in time where the person officiating a ceremony and those who participate play an equal part in an unstructured community. Consequently, liminality is a bridge of imagination **recognizing all those involved** but not recognizing their differing roles. Driver (1991, 213) goes further stating that **liminality is freedom** from formal structure and the roles associated with that structure. Liminality, then, is an important factor

---

[111] In chapter nine, it was noted that Bell (1992, 20-21), Driver (1991, 227-230), and Smart (1996, 86-88) believe Turner's unique view is foundational for ceremonial studies.

in the performance of a ceremony where the majority position of late Millennials and Generation Z as a postmodern community at SEU can be challenged with the consistent and obtainable truth of the Bible unhindered by the formalities of religion, roles, rules, or structure.

CHAPTER 24

—————

STEP ONE: AN INVITATION TO THE TABLE

Throughout **chapters one through four,** gradations of exclusion from Communion were seen in church history that impacted a participant's experience of seeing the empowering actions of Christ[112] and hearing His promissory words.[113] The findings in those chapters showed that inclusion in Communion is typical for late Millennials and Generation Z and a reality of postmodern spirituality (see Table 21.1). Moreover, inclusion in Communion is a biblical truth (see Table 21.5).

Biblical Truth: Present Inclusiveness of God

In **chapters sixteen, seventeen, and eighteen,** an exegesis of biblical passages showed the function of **Communion did not discriminate** among age, gender, or wealth, particularly seen in Paul's rebuke concerning the discriminating behavior found

—————

[112] Empowering actions: "do this [bread and wine] in remembrance of me" (Luke 22:19).

[113] Promissory words: "not drink from this fruit of the vine from now on until that day when I drink it new with you in my Father's kingdom" (Matt. 26:29).

among the Corinthian Christians (1 Cor. 11:17-22). The same cannot be said for the Passover (Exod. 11:6-7), where it was shown that God made a distinction between Israel and Egypt. A distinction was also made at the Wedding Supper of the Lamb (Matt. 22:11-14) where God expelled people from the table who are not appropriately dressed (see Table 21.5).

While Communion connects past and future table celebrations, an exegesis of the biblical passages in **chapters sixteen, seventeen, and eighteen** showed that inclusion is only found at the Communion table. So, the generalized biblical truth introduced in the first step is that God is presently inclusive of all people at the Communion table.

Whether the rhetoric of an **unconditional and radical welcome** to the Communion table is substantiated by concrete theological evidence is not the point of an inclusive invitation. The *why* and *wherefore* are not primarily relevant in the invitation. The first step simply recognizes that a welcome to the Communion table occurs between persons and that interpersonal relations are not motivated by **concrete theological thought.** Rather, as Charles Hefling (2012, 24) points out, interpersonal relations are motivated by feelings. A significant value that late Millennials share with Generation Z is inclusiveness (see Table 12.1). However, Generation Z radically accommodate inclusivism. Cho (Barna 2018, 32) writes, "Code-switching is shifting your language or behavior in order to fit a certain social situation." Cho continues, "Jesus himself was constantly code-switching when interacting with diverse people" (2018, 32).

An unconditional and radical welcome motivated by feeling does not diminish the theological importance of Communion within a Christian community. If this were the case, it would imply that everyone receiving the bread and wine of Communion is really a disconnected and anonymous Christian, which is condescending towards the empowering words (Lk. 22:19) and promissory actions (Matt. 26:29) of Christ. The biblical truth embedded in an exclusive invitation to the Communion table (C) shapes the students (B).

Issues of **discrimination** emerged during the interviews in **chapter ten** and group discussions in **chapter thirteen**. Students were **defensive about any form of discrimination** from the church towards their friends. Therefore, inclusion is not only typical of postmodern spirituality, and a biblical truth, it is also important to late Millennials and Generation Z postmodern who value individuality and inclusivism. In fact, students are far more inclusive than any previous generation with a greater appreciation for difference (Barna 2018, 12).

This was particularly seen in the lived experience Community (see Table 21.2). This may, or may not, be a product of postmodern inclusion, or it may simply be the student's personal attitude towards people at SEU. Either way, the first step not only invites students to an inclusive table celebration, but the invitation itself is embedded in biblical truth that depicts the present inclusiveness of a supernatural God before Christ returns to exclusively celebrate the Wedding Supper of the Lamb.

The first step may sound like the **inclusive invitation has a time limit on it,** but the biblical text actually presents it in this way in order for the Wedding Supper of the Lamb to take place. By default, an inclusive invitation to the Communion table is also an invitation to become part of an exclusive celebration as the redemptive story is performed in Communion (Rev. 19:6-9).

Hefling (2012, 22) believes the idea of an inclusive invitation to the Communion table is relevant today, even though church history reveals gradations of exclusion. The biblical truth that Hefling (2012, 27) associates with an inclusive invitation is the universal drawing of God.[114] If it is God who draws people to Himself, an inclusive invitation is an appropriate way in response to what God may be doing with late Millennials and Generation Z. Anything less than a positive **inclusive invitation without restriction** can possibly hinder God's drawing people to Him.

It may well be a point of cooperating with the drawing of God where sacerdotal power in any form does not presume to set the

---

[114] "This is why I told you that no one can come to me unless the Father has enabled him" (John 6:65).

boundaries for who can, and who cannot, receive the bread and wine of Communion. After all, Generation Z are looking for inclusive, empowering, passionate, and knowledgeable instructors (Seemiller and Grace 2016, 186). A positive inclusive invitation from the students (B) to the Communion table (C) is "full inclusion, radical hospitality, and unconditional welcome" (Hefling 2012, 24).

Communicating Present Inclusiveness through Communion

An inclusive invitation is **rooted in the first, second, third, sixth, and seventh key discoveries.** For example, having received an invitation to the table, whatever the invited students would experience, communicated during Communion, the biblical truth of inclusion would shape the meaning they associate with it (see Table 21.2). Even before the invited students have approached the Communion table to receive the bread and wine, the present inclusiveness of a supernatural God is depicted as expressed in the Bible before Christ returns with an inclusive invitation to the Wedding Supper of the Lamb (see Table 21.5).

Strictly speaking, the present inclusiveness of God is not communicated during Communion, but by an invitation to it. However, Singer (1959 xiii) points out that an invitation is part of ceremonial performance. If so, the invitation itself shapes the student's approach. An inclusive invitation, then, addresses any depiction of a supernatural God that presently excludes from the Communion table that invited students may have already acquired through sub-orthodox beliefs, shaping how they approach the table and what they sense towards meaning making associated with it.

Who Does the Inviting?

In Hefling's (2012, 27) view, an inclusive invitation "is one which has been made, negatively and somewhat mechanically, by insisting on 'no communion without baptism.'" In short, all students are welcome as long as they have been baptized. If this is the case, the way students (B) connect with Communion (C) determines how a supernatural God (D) is depicted and meaning (E) associated with it. A restrictive invitation does not depict the inclusiveness of a supernatural God as expressed in the Bible. Hefling (2012, 24) writes, "Jesus made no such restriction, or for that matter any other restriction. Neither should his followers." As followers of Christ, if the Christian students inviting their peers negatively and mechanically insist on a previous ceremonial requirement (baptism), sacerdotal power is extended through the students (B) regarding Communion (C) depicting a supernatural God (D) as restrictive.

> "Jesus made no such restriction, or for that matter any other restriction. Neither should his followers."

In chapters **one through four,** church history revealed that an invitation to the Communion table largely came from sacerdotal power endorsed by canon law or as a result of reforms and revivals. While the person who officiates matters to the students, an inclusive invitation would primarily come from students already participating in Communion (see Table 21.3). Such a proposition correlates with a central and important characteristic of late Millennials and Generation Z (Seemiller and Grace 2018, 179). For example, in **chapter seven,** I specifically asked the students who it was that invited them to celebrate Communion and how this invitation was understood. Sophia, Victoria, Samuel, and William were invited by their peers to celebrate Communion with two different outcomes.[115]

On one hand, Victoria and Samuel did not understand the invitation as a strictly inclusive one, and they preferred to remain outside the group. On the other hand, Sophia and William understood the invitation as a strictly inclusive one but chose to remain individual within the group. The difference between both outcomes is rooted in the meaning of the lived experience Community. Sameness of faith and practice was essential to Sophia's

---

[115] While Professor Blanche, Father Brown, and Father Ted intentionally welcome everyone to the Communion table, Sophia, Victoria, Samuel, and William were specifically invited by their peers. The emphasis in the first step is peer-to-peer invitation, while the influence of faculty and priests do not obstruct such an emphasis.

and William's understandings of an invitation, shaping how they approached Communion and what they sensed.

Interestingly, all four students did not derive their personal identity from the collective group who celebrate Communion, contrary to the 58% in the campus-survey who said they did. This fact may highlight the difference between Victoria and Samuel and Sophia and William in how they understood an invitation to Communion. Assuming the invited have the same faith and practice, the invitee should also consider that other students may not have the same faith and practice. For example, SEU has forty-nine religious preferences represented in the student body.[116] Nevertheless, the truth that God is presently inclusive at the Communion table and the fact that the invitation is inclusive make no distinction between religious preferences.

An invitee must consider participation in Communion is always with the **observer in mind by performing a set of beliefs** grounded in biblical truth that connect the past and future to the present (see Table 21.5). This would be particularly true for student observers who identify with Islam, Judaism, Buddhism, the Bahia Faith, and no faith preference. After all, Generation Z have no difficulty in associating with people with different religious beliefs (Barna 2018, 12). Therefore, an inclusive invitation to celebrate Communion may be an **invitation to first observe,** especially by those who have a different faith and practice to the Christian invitee. The choice to observe is strictly the decision of the invited student and not the one inviting or the decision of sacerdotal power. A choice made on behalf of the invited student has the potential of depicting a supernatural God in a way the Bible does not portray Him regarding His present inclusiveness at the Communion table.

---

[116] Admittedly, the majority of students identify with some form of Christianity or pseudo-Christianity. However, the students that identify with Islam, Judaism, Buddhism, the Bahia Faith, and no faith preference do not have the same faith and practice as various expressions of Christianity and pseudo-Christianity. In addition, these four religious preferences do not have a ceremony called Communion, or anything similar to it.

Data collected for my book shows that an invitation guarantees students would feel invited as long as it is inclusive and not exclusive, as Victoria and Samuel felt. It does not guarantee students would approach the Communion table in the same way. According to the campus-wide survey, a slight majority derive identity from a collective group, whereas, the four students interviewed did not. Hence, an invitation must be an inclusive invitation shaping the students' approach and/or reshaping any depiction of a supernatural God based on sub-orthodox beliefs or other religious preferences outside the orthodoxy of Christianity.

Liminality does not necessarily occur in the first step because Communion as a ceremony has not commenced, though Singer (1959 xiii) would disagree. There is a connection between the biblical truth of inclusiveness, ceremony, and meaning making in the first step.

Inclusiveness, Ceremony, and Meaning Making

An inclusive invitation connects the Communion table with meaning making in the sense that it creates what Turner (2011, 97) uniquely calls "modelessness" by **rejecting the idea of hierarchy** in a structured and exclusive community. Unstructured does not relate to disorder, but it does temper the pride of those who officiate the bread and wine preventing a posture of appearing "more" than the participants (2011, 96-97). Modelessness views all those involved in Communion equally whether they are observers, participants, or those who officiate. If an invitation to the table is part of the performance of it (Singer 1959 xiii), modelessness is compatible with liminality in the sense that it regards everyone involved in the ceremony as equal.

The issue of equality and inclusivism matter to late Millennials and Generation Z seen in the postmodern community at SEU who celebrate Communion (see Table 21.3). Therefore, an inclusive invitation does not create an environment for an observer to feel **"less"** than those already participating (Turner 2011, 96). Quite the opposite, it creates a public environment of equality. For example, Singer (1955, 27) argues that the **"little traditions,"** or heterogeneity, of those participating or observing a ceremony are framed within a unifying and primary **"great tradition,"** or homogeneity, of the ceremony. This is precisely what Victoria struggled with identifying as Mexican while studying in America (see Table 21.3).

The heterogeneity of Mexican and America traditions came into conflict. Inclusiveness would frame Victoria's heterogeneity in the homogeneity of the Communion table as ceremony without losing her Mexican traditions.

Though Sophia, Victoria, Samuel, and William associate meaning with their lived experiences, it is too ambiguous to predict what precise meaning a student would associate with a lived experience that begins with an inclusive invitation to participate or observe Communion. It does show that meaning is made, and it would be correct to predict the students are shaped by how they are invited. Whether the student participates or observes, Geertz (1973, 93-94) points out the **dialectical nature a ceremony means they would be involved in meaning making.** Meaning is not made for them but with them during a ceremony and, if Singer (1959, xiii) is correct, it includes the invitation.

Summary Thought

The first step of how Communion can function to communicate biblical truth to Generation Z as a postmodern community of college students (A) is an inclusive invitation from students (B) to their peers to celebrate or observe Communion (C) without discrimination rooted in the first, second, third, sixth, and seventh key discoveries. The invitation itself communicates biblical truth depicting the present inclusiveness of a supernatural God (D) shaping the students' approach to the Communion table and what they would sense (see Figure 23.1).

Step one focuses on inclusivism as a common variable found in the connection of the students (B), Communion (C), and a supernatural God (D) within a postmodern community of late Millennials and Generation Z (A). The variable of inclusivism **predicts that biblical truth would change any sub-orthodox beliefs** of the students (B) about Communion (C) and a supernatural God (D) communicated in an inclusive invitation as part of a ceremonial performance. As a result, biblical truth changes the sub-orthodox beliefs of the students (B) regarding Communion (C) and how a supernatural God (D) is depicted by individual students.

The **causal effect** to meaning making (E) is where biblical truth informs meaning associated with a lived experience. As Communion is continually celebrated, a **probable causal effect** is that late Millennials and Generation Z as a postmodern community (A) are also changed from a community that holds to sub-orthodox beliefs to one that in informed by the biblical truth that God is inclusive.

Figure 24.1. Step One: Inclusive Invitation to the Table

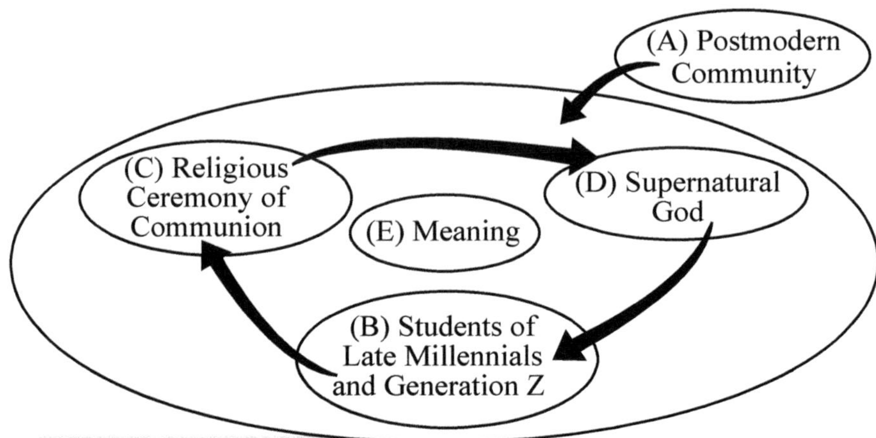

Step One
Focus: inclusivism as a variable in the connection of (B), (C), and (D) within (A).
Predicts: biblical truth changes suborthodox beliefs of (B) about (C), and (D).
Causal effect: change in (E) as a result of change in (B), about (C), and (D).
Probable cause effect: continually celebrating Communion changes (A).
How: biblical truth communicated through an inclusive invitation as part of ceremonial performance.

CHAPTER 25

STEP TWO: LOCALIZING THEOLOGY

In **chapter eight**, a student's typical experience included the ability to **sense God's presence**, a desire to encounter Christ, and imaginative communication with Christ (see Table 21.2). The key discovery in chapter eleven revealed that what the students **believed approaching Communion shaped** what they got out of the ceremony (see Table 21.3). As such, **theology is localized** to the approach and lived experience of the students in how they sense and communicate with God.[117]

Biblical Truth: God Has Revealed Himself in Christ

Students did, indeed, experience Christ when they participated in Communion dependent on their approach. Such an encounter caused all four of the students to feel a sense of completeness (see Table 21.2). While their approaches differed, the result of completeness was the same. **Chapter seventeen** showed that experiencing Christ was also to experience God.[118] Students did

---

[117] As noted in chapter seventeen, God and Christ can be interchangeable in the way students describe their lived experience.

[118] "Anyone who has seen me has seen the Father. How can you say, 'Show us the Father'?" (John 14:9). Also, "Jesus replied, 'Anyone who loves me will obey my teaching. My Father will love them, and we will come to them and make our home with them'" (John 14:23).

connect with a supernatural God, albeit a supernatural God **uninformed by the biblical text.**

Such a description was not surprising when teaching from the Bible unassociated with a lived experience had failed to provide meaning for this connection or a biblical description of a supernatural God (see Table 21.2). So, the generalized biblical truth introduced in the second step is **that the God of the Bible has revealed Himself in Christ.** Consequently, there is a need to focus on biblical passages used in Communion that retell the details of the redemptive story of God within this generalized truth.

Communicating a Revealed God through Communion

In **chapters one through four,** an investigation of church history revealed a pattern that helps in explaining the second step to bring the truth of the revealed God of the Bible to the students' existing connection with a supernatural God. Again, the emphasis is Communion as a communicating vehicle where students sensed or felt God's presence (see Table 21.2). With no particular starting point to the pattern, chapters one through four showed how biblical passages that were used in church history to explain Communion tended to determine how liturgy was used to retell the redemptive story, in a changing environment, which also framed who could and who could not participate in the bread and wine.

The first step modeled an inclusive environment with an invitation to participate or observe Communion. The second step **continues to model that inclusive** environment through biblical passages used in Communion and the use of liturgy[119] that retells the redemptive story of God. Communion communicates the story of God in which **all students are welcome to the table.** Given that Sophia, Victoria, Samuel, and William already acknowledge the story of God, in that, He has been revealed.

However, each student does not use biblical truth, reinforcing that late Millennials and Generation Z have sub-orthodox beliefs about God (Barna 2018, 78). Each student senses God's presence during Communion. Even though the students sense God and have a desire to encounter His Son resulting in a sense of

---

[119] I shall present the use of liturgy in the third step of the theory.

completeness, the way each student communicates with Christ does not appear to acknowledge the complete story of God. The **body and blood of Christ,** represented in the bread and wine, do not seem to play any part in how the students communicate with Christ.

One way of looking at this dilemma is by drawing on the ceremonial system of Geertz (1973, 126-140). The dialectical nature of Geertz's scheme is a performance "of" a lived experience [ethos] and a performance "for" an imagined experience [worldview] (1973, 93-94). **The "of" and "for" shape an experience, as the experience shapes the student.** Key elements of the story of God are absent in how Sophia, Victoria, Samuel, and William communicate with Christ, and those missing elements contribute to the shaping of their approach and lived experience during Communion. The students may acknowledge that God has been revealed in Christ, but the body and blood of Christ play no part in **how and why He has been revealed.**

In **chapter ten,** the ceremonial system of Geertz was used as a lens for analyzing how God was depicted at the Communion table (see Table 21.5). The analysis showed that the Communion table evaluates past forgiveness and senses present and future forgiveness. In short, it is a performance "of" forgiveness and a performance "for" continued forgiveness. Quintessential to the story of God is the **forgiveness of sins because of the body and blood of Christ.**[120]

Despite the lack of acknowledging these key elements in their desire to encounter Christ, all four students **used considerable imagination** to communicate with Him. The sensory desire to interpret a lived experience, and common use of imagination, is fertile ground for involving the students in the interpretation of biblical passages used in Communion that explain the complete redemptive story of God that include the body and blood of Christ.

---

[120] "While they were eating, Jesus took bread, and when he had given thanks, he broke it and gave it to his disciples, saying, "Take and eat; this is my body." Then he took a cup, and when he had given thanks, he gave it to them, saying, "Drink from it, all of you. This is my blood of the covenant, which is poured out for many for the forgiveness of sins" (Matt. 26:26-28).

Who Interprets the Story?

Church history in **chapters one through four** showed that an interpretation of biblical passages was determined for the participant during Communion, and not with them, or by them. However, because postmodernity is full of experimentation (Bird 2014, 24), the realities of postmodern spirituality invite students to interpret biblical passages used during Communion that explain the redemptive story of God (see Table 21.1). In short, localizing theology this way **advocates ethno-hermeneutics**[121] by involving the students to use their own lived experiences to interpret the biblical passages used during Communion.

Walter C. Kaiser and Moisés Silva (1994, 181) point out that the method of ethno-hermeneutics recognizes **three horizons in cross-cultural interpretation.** Those horizons address cultural elements represented in the **biblical text,**[122] the **interpreter,** and the receptor (see Figure 25.1). Caution is needed in localizing theology this way particular to the method itself, and specifically with Generation Z. First, the second and third horizons in the ethno-hermeneutical method must not dictate to the message of the biblical text in the first horizon. Second, the current influence of late Millennials and Generation Z locates all interpretation in a social context by focusing on the students' personal spirituality, self-guidance, participation in Communion, and their intentional reduction of religious rules (see Figure 15.2). In short, the current influences at SEU actually focus on the second and third horizons at the cost of the first. If interpretation of God's redemptive story is measured this way, biblical truth becomes highly subjective to the social context.

---

[121] Ethno-hermeneutics is a unique phrase first used by Larry W. Caldwell (1987, 314-333).

[122] Benno van den Toren (2010, 93), writes, "The Bible itself does not directly present us with this supra-cultural core." However, ethno-hermeneutics is not concerned with a supra-cultural core that can be applied to all readers of the Bible in all cultures. The method of ethno-hermeneutics examines the culture presented in the biblical text itself. For example, Christ was Jewish (Matt. 1:1-16), and he celebrated the Passover (Luke 22:15).

Figure 25.1. Three Intersecting Horizons of the Ethno-Hermeneutics Method

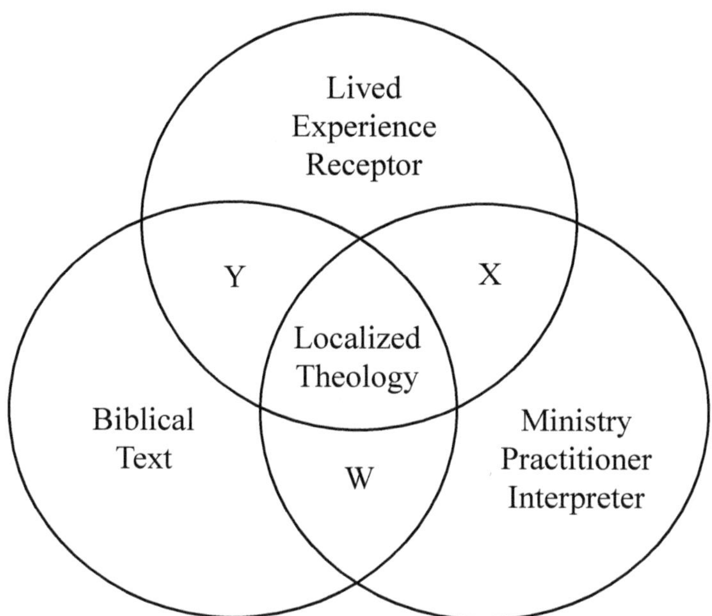

On one hand, data throughout the book consistently shows the biblical text (Y) is not intersecting with a lived experience. On the other hand, the ministry practitioner (priests, faculty, and campus ministry) is intersecting with a lived experience (X). I assume ministry practitioners know the biblical text (W). The goal of ethno-hermeneutics is the intersection of all three called localized theology.

In their collaborative work, Matthew Cook, Rob Haskell, Ruth Julian, and Natee Tanchanpongs (Cook et al 2010, x) believe the idea of **localizing theology is healthy** and biblical in any culture. The Bible must make sense to any culture. The basis for localizing theology must be in the biblical text, understood in a particular culture, and not in a **pre-packaged theological system** (2010, x). Though I doubt they intended to do so, this is what Webber (1999; 2003; 2004; 2006; 2008), Gittoes (2013), Hartman (2011), and Radcliffe (2009) did in **chapter six.** Localized theology involves biblical truth and the culture under consideration, or the biblical text and context in which it is read (Cook et al 2010, 127). Localizing theology addresses the students' lived experiences communicated during the context of Communion and interpreted autonomously of biblical truth.

The students' understanding of a lived experienced not only excludes the biblical text as a basis, it does not include it at any point, pre-packaged or otherwise. Localizing theology does not focus on the single horizon of the students' culture alone, but all three horizons of the ethno-hermeneutical method that include cultural elements represented in the biblical text, the students, and the ministry practitioner. While all three horizons are necessary, I believe a ministry practitioner must begin with the cultural elements of the students lived experience, and not with the biblical text.

> I believe a ministry practitioner must begin with the cultural elements of the students lived experience, and not with the biblical text.

Localizing theology may not always begin with the text, but it can be grounded in the context of a lived experience where the biblical text serves to interpret that experience (Cook et al 2010, xviii). Nevertheless, **context in which the text is read needs dialogue.** This is where the ministry practitioner engages students to discuss their lived experiences in light of the biblical text used during Communion and text not currently used. Therefore, the ministry practitioner "ought to become a pedagogist [teacher] capable of listening more than talking, while guiding the [student] community to reflective action" (2010, 129). Once again, the role **of the ministry practitioner matters.**

The intentional ministry practitioner who intersects with the biblical text (W) is a missing influence needed for good localized theology among postmodern college students called Generation Z at SEU (see Figure 15.2). While the second step encourages students to interpret the biblical text using their own lived experiences as a hermeneutical tool, the vital role of a ministry practitioner is necessary for local theology. He or she must not only be a **good pedagogist** (teacher), but also have a complete biblical grasp of the redemptive story that includes the essential elements of the body and blood of Christ.

The practitioner must "take these eternal truths [body and blood of Christ] originally spoken in a different time and culture and apply them to the similar needs of our culture" (Van den Toren 2010, 93). Without this grasp, Shawn Redford (Cook et al 2012, 5) believes the method of ethno-hermeneutics is left to interpreting the biblical text dominated by worldviews. A ministry practitioner needs to **connect all three horizons** of the ethno-hermeneutical method in the dialectical nature of Communion that evaluates past forgiveness and senses present and future forgiveness (see Table 21.5). Though the truth of forgiveness in Christ was written in the culture represented in the biblical text, the ministry practitioner proclaims the same truth but in a different cultural context (Van den Toren 2010, 93). His or her **influence matters** to the students (see Table 21.3).

The action taken by the community of students in the second step is in light of the truth that has been discovered or revealed in dialogue with the ministry practitioner (Cook et al 2010, 135). The practitioner does not interpret the biblical text for the students, but with them, associating lived experiences with the biblical text, beginning with the context of the students and then the text of the Bible. That reflective action taken by the students from what has been discovered or revealed, guided by the practitioner, is to retell the redemptive story during Communion in a way that makes sense to late Millennials and Generation Z as a postmodern community.

Contextualizing the redemptive story within a postmodern community in light of biblical truth creates a sense of what the story meant when it was first told and what it continues to mean today. If biblical text not currently used during Communion is being discussed, it can create a sense of the Bible as a compilation of smaller stories, or "little traditions" (Singer 1955, 27), within one grand story, or "great tradition" (1955, 27), in which God and human beings integrate and still interact today.

Localized theology in context and text as dialogue between the students and ministry practitioner can shape what the students believe when approaching Communion and can impact what they get out of the celebration. Context and text can also help in depicting a biblically described supernatural God and in helping students to discover meaning for their lived experiences in light of the biblical text. The process of localizing theology in Communion (C) shapes the students (B), depicts a supernatural God (D), and discovers meaning (E) in light of biblical truth.

Interpretation, Ceremony, and Meaning Making

Localized theology means the students would be involved, not only in using ethno-hermeneutics, but also in creating an inclusive celebration of Communion that offers one credible explanation of the redemptive story of God in a way that makes sense to them. In a small way, creating a Communion celebration was particularly evident in the influence of Professor Blanche in chapter fourteen. Her lack of religious rules, emphasis on a Spirit experience, and involvement of her students to create a celebration of Communion show that localized theology, to some degree, is already taking place. The students positively responded to Professor Blanche's influence, becoming involved in creating a celebration to retell the redemptive story, albeit a very small and temporary celebration.

The students already connect with a supernatural God through Communion as a vehicle that communicates their lived experiences. Therefore, involving the students in creating a celebration of Communion also invites them to discuss their lived experiences as a hermeneutic for the biblical passages used in the celebration with a ministry practitioner. He or she **adjudicates between what the students sense or feel and biblical truth.** Interaction of lived experiences, Communion, biblical passages, students, and ministry practitioners are essential for meaning to be grounded in biblical truth. Intentionally discussing lived experiences this way was not evident in Professor Blanche's influence. A Spirit experience did not include the biblical text.

Intentional discussion with a ministry practitioner in step two provides an opportunity for the students to become acquainted with biblical passages used during Communion, and those that are not currently used. They may include passages that describe the ten ways God was experienced as expressed in the Bible in three table celebrations as the redemptive story is explained (see Table 21.5). Once again, involving students in creating a celebration of Communion and discussing their encounters with a supernatural God using the ethno-hermeneutic method addresses any depiction of God revealing Himself through Christ based on sub-orthodox beliefs. Such involvement has the **potential "of" shaping what the students believe approaching the Communion table, and "for" shaping the students' experience** (Shils 1968, 736). It also continues to shape how the God of the Bible is depicted. He is not only inclusive of all people, but He has also revealed Himself to all people because of the body and blood of Christ.

One of the findings in **chapter ten** throws caution over the ministry practitioner's influence (see Table 21.3). For example, William was hindered by his elder because he was given no time to think. Sophia's idea of love differed from her priest's idea of love. Victoria likened her priest to Christ; and Samuel felt distinctly unwelcomed by his priest. A complete biblical grasp of God's story does not automatically qualify the ministry practitioner in the process of localizing theology. He or she must also engage with the family traditions, personal history, beliefs, and values of the students as they discuss their encounters with a supernatural God. His or her role in discussion matters not only theologically but also locally. Localizing theology is not merely a discussion, but an interaction of the biblical text in the context that it is read—a lived experience—so biblical meaning can take place (see Figure 25.1). He or she "ought to become a pedagogist [teacher] capable of listening more than talking, while guiding the community to reflective action" (Cook et al 2010, 129).

The findings in **chapters seven, eight, ten, and thirteen** reveal the students' family traditions, personal history, beliefs, and values, and include how they described their experience of spirituality and religion, the way Communion facilitates an expression of their experience of spirituality and religion, and how they describe a supernatural God. There was no intentional time where a ministry practitioner met with the students to discuss their experiences and descriptions as part of the celebration. Admittedly, campus ministry is very active among the students at SEU. Arthur stated campus ministry was not an educator of the Christian faith, stating, "I believe that we are here to assist the students in their personal faith development and whatever that means for them." Faith did not mean the Christian faith.

Students had a need to meet together to **explore life,** and Communion was a point of attraction for meeting together. There is so much already going on with late Millennials and Generation Z as a postmodern community at SEU that invites a ministry practitioner to facilitate discussion with the students through interaction with their lived experiences and the biblical text in order for biblical meaning making to take place. Though a ministry practitioner has a role to play in localizing theology with postmodern college students, he or she must **take into consideration liminality** when that theology is lived through Communion as a religious ceremony.

Liminality and the Holy Spirit

If liminality is the freedom from formal religious structure (Driver 1991, 213) allowing for inclusion and equality (Waaijman 2002, 214), **meaning making is both reflective and proactive** in step two. It is reflective in the sense that students can discuss what has taken place in Communion with the ministry practitioner. It is also proactive in the sense that students who interpret biblical passages through the method of **ethno-hermeneutics are unrestricted** by formal religious structure. In short, liminality is not accidental but intentional. For example, if God has already revealed Himself in Christ, involving the students to create a celebration of Communion and interpret biblical passages gives them permission to anticipate an encounter with God where liminality takes place within the celebration.

Liminality, then, creates **intentional space for the Holy Spirit** to work in the process of reflective and proactive action with the ministry practitioner. Van den Toren (2010, 100) describes the process of reading a book[123] as something that occupies that space. He suggests the reader brings to the text cultural pre-understandings, and yet not bound by them. "If we read the book humbly and are willing to be challenged, our pre-understanding may be shown to be inadequate" (2010, 100). Such humility allows the reader to **adjust their pre-understandings** to the context of the text. Whereas the three horizons of ethno-hermeneutics bring together the cultural elements of the text, interpreter, and receptor—the process of reading and re-reading in the way that Van den Toren (2010, 100) suggests is a **hermeneutical spiral**[124] "in which our understanding becomes more and more congruent with the content of the book" (see Figure 25.2).

Figure 25.2. The Hermeneutical Spiral

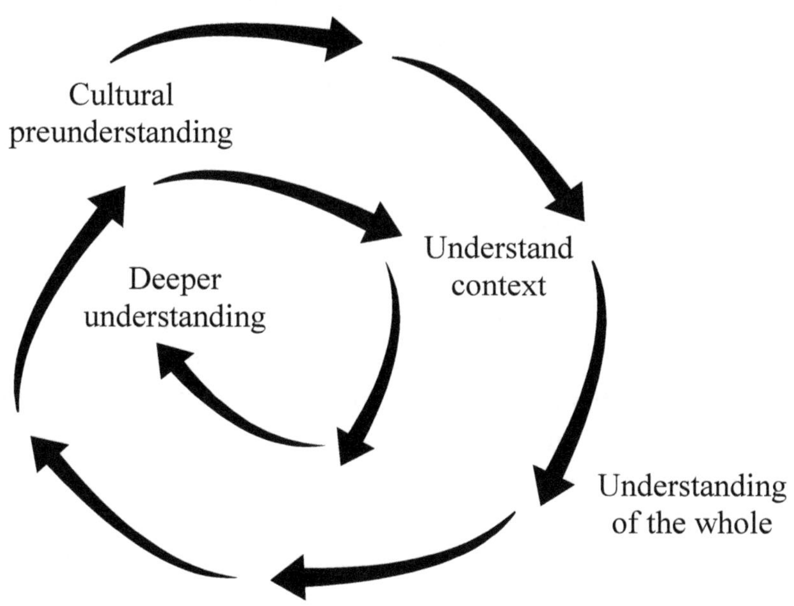

---

[123] Toren (2010, 100) draws on the research of polymath, Michael Polanyi (1975).

[124] Ibid. Adopted the term first used by Grant R. Osborne (1991).

The process of reading and re-reading biblical text accompanies **reflective activity** already going on in late Millennials and Generation Z as a postmodern community at SEU. The students continually celebrate Communion where **meaning is not fixed** (see Figure 21.1). The key discovery in **chapter eleven** shows that beliefs the students already have shape what they get out of Communion as they approach the table of celebration (see Table 21.3). The postmodern community (A) is unstructured (Turner 2011, 97), or modelessness, in order to create a sense of humility. Though an unstructured community highlights the humility of the person officiating Communion, as a participant in the bread and wine Victoria explicitly said, "I feel a lot more humble."

The space that liminality creates is not a place for the church to bring biblical instruction, but a moment where the students' lived experience, the biblical text, and the ministry practitioner enter a dialogue where the **Holy Spirit is at work.** Or, as Driver (1991, 197-198) summarizes in the totality of ceremony, "It goes as far as to ask for transformation—'Pour out your Holy Spirit on us gathered here, and these gifts of bread and wine'—but it does not linger over this. It does not wait for this to happen." **Liminality is the key** to letting the work of the Holy Spirit happen.

Summary Thought

The second step localized theology to the community of students (B) within the postmodern community (A), where celebrating Communion (C) communicates the generalized biblical truth that God is revealed in Christ. The step is **rooted in the first, second, third, and seventh key discoveries** and focuses on storytelling as a common variable specifically found in the connection of Communion (C) and a supernatural God (D) in the approach and lived experiences of the students (B) in Communion (C). The **variable of storytelling predicts** that if the community of students (B) was involved in the interpretation of biblical truth used in Communion (C), it would **change their typical experience** to one that is informed by the biblical text. It also

predicts that involvement in developing a celebration of Communion (C) that made sense to the postmodern community (A), would **enhance their ability to sense God's presence** (D), a desire to encounter Christ, and imaginative communication with Christ. As a result, the **causal effect in meaning making** (E) is shaped by a biblical approach and sensory experience of Communion (C).

The second step also **focuses on ethno-hermeneutics and spiral hermeneutics as a variable** found in the connection of a ministry practitioner (F) and students (B) within a postmodern community (A). The variable of ethno-hermeneutics and spiral hermeneutics **predicts** that the students (B) would localize theology in the biblical text utilizing the **space created by liminality** for the work of the Holy Spirit in order to **adjust to the content of the Bible as truth.** Like step one, as Communion (C) is continually celebrated, a probable causal effect is that the postmodern community (A), or late Millennials and Generation Z, is also changed from a community that holds to sub-orthodox beliefs to one that is informed by the truth of the Bible (see Figure 25.3).

Figure 25.3. Step Two: Localizing Theology

Step Two

Focus: storytelling as a variable in relationship to (C) and (D) in approach and experience of (B) within (A).

Predicts: change to typical experience of (B).

Causal effect: (E) shaped by approach and experience of (C) by (B).

How: biblical truth communicated through intentional involvement of (B) in interpretation of the biblical text and development of a (C) celebration that makes sense to (A).

Focus: hermeneutics as a variable in connection of (F) and (B) within (A).

Predicts: that (F) would localize theology with (B) in ethno-hermeneutics and spiral hermeneutics moored in the biblical text as the Holy Spirit works in (B).

Probable cause effect: continually celebrating Communion can transform (A).

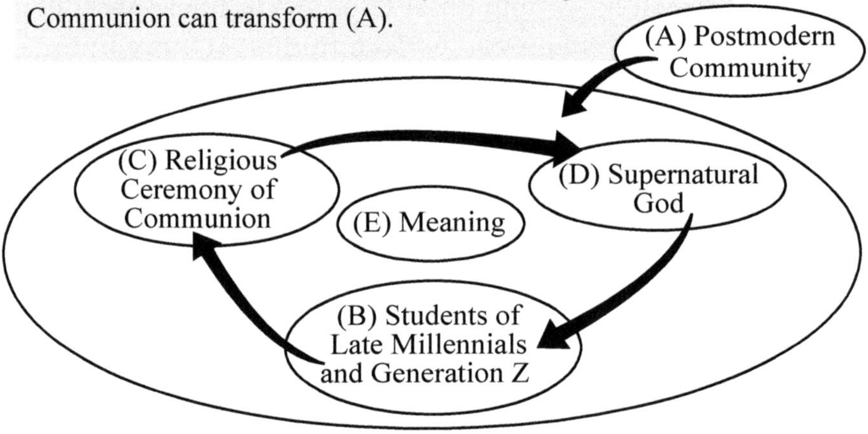

Step One

Focus: inclusivism as a variable in the connection of (B), (C), and (D) within (A).

Predicts: biblical truth changes suborthodox beliefs of (B) about (C), and (D).

Causal effect: change in (E) as a result of change in (B), about (C), and (D).

Probable cause effect: continually celebrating Communion changes (A).

How: biblical truth communicated through an inclusive invitation as part of ceremonial performance.

CHAPTER 26

STEP THREE: CREATIVE LITURGY

The pattern that emerges in an investigation of church history in **chapter one through four** is also applicable to the third step. Biblical passages not only explain the story of God at the Communion table, they also determine how liturgy is used to retell that redemptive story. In many ways, liturgy used during Communion highlights the ceremonial system of Shils (1968, 736) in that biblical beliefs can exist without Communion, but the ceremony of Communion could not exist without beliefs. The realities of postmodern spirituality at the end of **chapter four** indicate how liturgy could be used for introducing biblical truth to late Millennials and Generation Z as a postmodern community. Like the interpretation of biblical passages used in Communion, **liturgy must make sense** to postmodern college students. If step two communicates the generalized biblical truth offering one credible explanation that God is revealed in Christ, step three liturgically communicates in what way He is revealed in Christ.

Biblical Truth: God Incarnate in Christ

Historically, the liturgical reforms of Luther and Zwingli introduced biblical truth that made sense to people who were involved in the **performance or observation of Communion.** Their reforms demonstrated the real agents of Christian worship were not found in sacerdotal power, the Latin language, or the mysteries that surrounded the bread and wine, but in the community of participants (see Table 21.1). Their liturgies were written in the language of the German people so they could be more involved in or observing Communion (Mazza 1999, 239). Liturgies in the language of late Millennials and Generation Z as a postmodern community not only retell the redemptive story, the **language also represents the students as the real agents of worship** in their own postmodern community. The dialectical nature Communion is seen in the development of liturgy used in Communion (Geertz 1973, 112).

Singer's (1955, 27) ceremonial system of participant and observer in **chapter nine** highlights that the involvement of the students in the performance of Communion did, in fact, involve their cultures (see Table 21.3). According to Singer (1955, 27), it is important that a ceremony communicates in a way that identifies not only with the participant but also with the observer. As such, step one inclusively invites students to participate in or observe during Communion. Step two involves students in localizing theology where biblical passages used in Communion offers one credible explanation for the complete story of God.

Step three takes those biblical passages to **liturgically retell the story of God** in language that makes sense to a postmodern community of college students. A liturgical retelling that does not take the observer into consideration has the potential of creating a structured hierarchal community where a student may feel "less" than those participating (Turner 2011, 96). Such a retelling contradicts an inclusive invitation in step one.

Liturgy developed by late Millennials and Generation Z as postmodern college students for the sake of their participating and/or observing peers in language that identifies with their culture demonstrates incarnational truth in that God was incarnate in Christ as a human being who understood the language of the people.[125] Liturgy that identifies with these students goes further

---

[125] "The Word became flesh and made his dwelling among us. We have seen his glory, the glory of the one and only Son, who came from the Father, full of grace and truth" (John 1:14).

than language. It involves delivering what the community of individual students **believe the ceremony promises** in a liturgical retelling of the redemptive story.

Interestingly, Kenda Creasy Dean (2010, 14) identified late Millennials and Generation Z as **moralistic therapeutic deists** with the following tenants: (1) a god exists who created and orders the world and watches over life on earth; (2) God wants people to be good, nice and fair to each other, as taught in the Bible and by most world religions; (3) the central goal of life is to be happy and to feel good about oneself; (4) God is not involved in my life except when I need God to resolve a problem; and (5) good people go to heaven when they die.[126] If these tenants are accurate, the need for liturgy with biblical truth become obvious. **Christ is currently not part of the story.**

Communicating God Incarnate in Christ

The dialectical nature of a ceremony also means Communion has the potential to deliver what the students believe when their beliefs are intertwined with a creative liturgical performance of the redemptive story (Shils 1968, 735-736). Without step two, the students' beliefs would remain uninformed by biblical truth. Step two is vital as a biblical explanation of the redemptive story in order for a retelling in step three. This was particularly highlighted in chapter seven where the meaning attached to the experience Belief showed that formal or informal education from the church failed to form meaning in the students. Beliefs were shaped by experience, and **biblical truth played no part in the shaping process.**

When the students approached the Communion table, they believed certain things that the celebration delivered. For example, Sophia and Victoria depicted God as female believing Communion delivers the nurturing, caring, forgiving, and warm nature of God. Samuel believed a participant must be respectful when approaching the Communion table because God was watching.

---

[126] Quoted by Barna (2018, 81-82) as a good description of Generation Z.

William believed Communion delivered forgiveness and cleansing, but only when he called on God.

Undoubtedly, the current beliefs of the students do exist without the ceremony of Communion. The data collected in this book shows that those beliefs come into play when the students approach the Communion table. Liturgy, then, brings the biblical text in step two into the third step to **examine beliefs that already exist** in light of incarnational truth as expressed in the Bible. For example, do all religions teach that all people should be nice and fair to each other (Dean 2010, 14)? Such an examination does not **reject preexisting beliefs,** but it does **shape or reshape them** in the development of liturgy that intertwines with Communion to retell the story of God. Logically, beliefs not found in the biblical text would produce sub-orthodox liturgy like the tenants of late Millennials and Generation Z (2010, 14). Communion functions to communicate incarnational truth that shapes and/or reshapes preexisting beliefs.

Who Develops Liturgy?

The realities of a postmodern spirituality included experimentation (Bird 2014, 14), creating an opportunity for how the redemptive story could be retold through aspects of community that students value. For example, Paul Hiebert, R. Daniel Shaw, and Tite Tienou (1999, 292) believe retelling a story through ceremony not only **renews the beliefs** and values associated with the story, but it also renews the beliefs and values held by the people involved in the retelling. Similar to step one, a retelling of the redemptive story not only involves the students of Generation Z, it also represents them.

> "For a moment they are Moses, King David, Ruth, or Macbeth"

"For a moment they are Moses, King David, Ruth, or Macbeth" (Hiebert, Shaw, and Tienou 1999, 292). In the redemptive story, the students could be any character represented in the first Passover, first Communion, or Wedding Supper of the Lamb.

Late Millennials and Generation Z, represented in postmodern college students at SEU celebrate Communion in an unstructured community (Turner 2011, 96) removing historical gradations of exclusion. In addition, the faculty, priests, and campus ministry at SEU intentionally reduce religious rules. With these findings in mind, the data collected in this book showed the students valued inspiration, hope, interaction, others, partnership, and love in a community. These values were not just a matter of language, but they were observations that attracted students to the community. Interestingly, all six values would be enriched by an examination of incarnational truth expressed in the Bible towards developing liturgy used during Communion.

If so, the dialectical nature of a ceremony in **chapter nine** (Geertz 1973, 93-94) means the students not only shape a liturgy performance of the redemptive story for the sake of the observer (Singer 1955, 27), but the liturgical performance also shapes students as a postmodern community of individual students in their approaches to the Communion table (see Table 21.3). So, to a lesser degree than step one, a ministry practitioner would be involved with the students in developing liturgy that makes sense to postmodern college students. Involvement is logically less because data collected in chapter four showed that how biblical passages were used determined how liturgy was used, and not the other way around.

Retelling a story through ceremony is a cultural performance that **renews and reshapes people's inner world,** bringing the past into the present and future (Hiebert, Shaw, and Tienou 1999, 293). It reshapes in three ways: at a **cognitive level,** making visible underlying realities; at an **affectionate level,** giving expression of deep feelings; and at an **evaluative level,** revealing values (1999, 293). With these levels in mind, participation in Communion is with the observer in mind, performing a set of beliefs grounded in biblical truth that connects the past and future to the present.

The performance of the redemptive story not only reshapes the inner world of the participant as a continued process, it can also **reshape the observer who has been invited.** From the perspective of Communion, the story looks back to the Passover and forward to the Wedding Supper, focusing on the biblical truth that a supernatural God is inclusive as expressed in the Bible until Christ returns. This focus can reshape underlying realities, deep feelings, and values as the students approach the Communion table as participants or observers.

The redemptive story includes the past and the present and gives ultimate meaning in the conclusion of the story that can be reflected in real life. Meaning is not fixed because students continue to participate in Communion. Meaning deepens not only because the performance is repeated, but because the **dialectical nature ceremony shapes and reshapes the student's inner world.** Hiebert, Shaw, and Tienou (1999, 292-295) show a deepening meaning through identifying in the personal, cultural, and cosmic aspects of a ceremonial retelling of story.

The personal aspect can integrate the student's individual lived experience. The cultural aspect can integrate what students' value about the community or group. The cosmic aspect can integrate the transcendent, where God meets with people, or, as I found, communication with Christ. The process of creating liturgy that retells the redemptive story in Communion (C) shapes and reshapes the cognitive, affectionate, and evaluative levels of the students (B), biblically depicts a supernatural God (D), and discovers in a deepening process for meaning making (E) in light of biblical truth.

Incarnation, Ceremony, and Meaning Making

The first step primarily involved the **students.** Step two involved **the ministry practitioner guiding student discussion** towards localizing theology. Step three also involves the **practitioner, but to a lesser degree,** as the lived experiences of the students find deepening meaning grounded in biblical truth. **Meaning deepens** with continued participation in Communion and subsequent discussion about what it is the students are experiencing, in light of biblical passages that explain and liturgically retell the redemptive story. The three steps are successive and continual. Step three, then, is creative liturgy to communicate incarnational biblical truth in a localized retelling of the redemptive story that makes sense to the students as the real agents of worship where meaning is made in the fact that God revealed Himself in Christ by sending His Son as a human being.[127]

Summary Thought

The third step is **rooted in the first, second, third, and fourth key discoveries.** It particularly focuses on **language as a common variable** in the connection of the community of students (B) approaching Communion (C) regarding the story of God (D) that shapes meaning making (E) with late Millennials and Generation Z as a postmodern community (A). The common variable of language that makes sense to the students (B) regarding Communion (C) as a postmodern community (A) **predicts that localized theology** in step two that offers one **credible explanation** that a supernatural God (D) has revealed Himself in Christ, not only **shapes and/or reshapes beliefs** held by the students (B) in their approach to the Communion table (C), but also in what the students (B) believe Communion (C) promises to deliver.

How the community of students (B) develops liturgy with the ministry practitioner (F) in light of incarnational truth expressed in the Bible to retell the story of a supernatural God (D), ensures that liturgy not only makes sense to the students (B) of late Millennials and Generation Z as a postmodern community (A), but that it represents the students (B) within that community (A) as the real agents of worship. The **causal effect** to meaning making (E) is because the students (B) are involved in the **development of liturgy** that retells the story of a supernatural God (D). Similar to step one and two, as Communion is continually celebrated, a **probable causal effect** is that late Millennials and Generation Z as a postmodern community (A) is also **shaped and/or reshaped** from a community with certain beliefs that holds to sub-orthodox beliefs to one that is informed by the truth of the Bible (see Figure 26.1).

---

[127] "For God so loved the world that he gave his one and only Son, that whoever believes in him shall not perish but have eternal life. For God did not send his Son into the world to condemn the world, but to save the world through him" (John 3:16-17).

Figure 26.1. Step Three: Creative Liturgy

Step Two

Focus: storytelling as a variable in relationship to (C) and (D) in approach and experience of (B) within (A).
Predicts: change to typical experience of (B).
Causal effect: (E) shaped by approach and experience of (C) by (B).
How: biblical truth communicated through intentional involvement of (B) in interpretation of the biblical text and development of a (C) celebration that makes sense to (A).

Focus: hermeneutics as a variable in connection of (F) and (B) within (A).
Predicts: that (F) would localize theology with (B) in ethno-hermeneutics and spiral hermeneutics moored in the biblical text as the Holy Spirit works in (B).
Probable cause effect: continually celebrating Communion can transform (A).

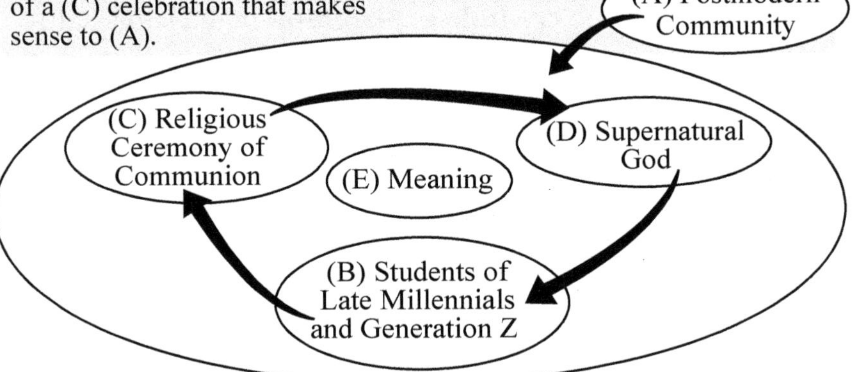

Step One

Focus: inclusivism as a variable in the connection of (B), (C), and (D) within (A).
Predicts: biblical truth changes suborthodox beliefs of (B) about (C), and (D).
Causal effect: change in (E) as a result of change in (B), about (C), and (D).
Probable cause effect: continually celebrating Communion changes (A).
How: biblical truth communicated through an inclusive invitation as part of ceremonial performance.

Step Three

Focus: language as a variable in the connection of (B) approaching (C), regarding the story of (D) shaping (E) within (A).
Predicts: shapes/reshapes beliefs of (B) approaching (C) and what (B) believes (C) promises to deliver as real agents of worship.
Causal effect: shaping/reshaping (E) where (B) is involved in developing liturgy.
Probable cause effect: continually celebrating Communion changes (A).
How: biblical truth communicated through a liturgical retelling of the story of (D).

CONCLUDING THOUGHT

The three steps show how a **ministry practitioner** (F) can bring biblical truth to late Millennials and Generation Z as a postmodern community (A) at SEU as an **additional influence** (G) by working with **what is already transpiring.** The key to this is the religious ceremony of Communion (C). Communion functions as a **communication vehicle** for the individual students' (B) lived experiences, their depiction of a supernatural God (D), and **meaning** (E). Communion (C) is a **carrier of sensory truth** that shapes the beliefs and approach of the students (B) to the Communion table (C), depicting a supernatural God (D), in order to discover **meaning** (E).

Introducing biblical truth in three successive steps makes Communion (C) the carrier of sensory biblical truth for shaping the students (B), depicting a supernatural God (D), and discovering meaning (E). Introducing biblical truth in these three steps has the **potential of transforming late Millennials and Generation Z as a postmodern community** (A). Consequently, Communion (C) is a **carrier of biblical truth that shapes, depicts, and discovers** with the potential of transforming Generation Z as a postmodern community (A) (see Figure 26.2).

Figure 26.2. The Theoretical Model

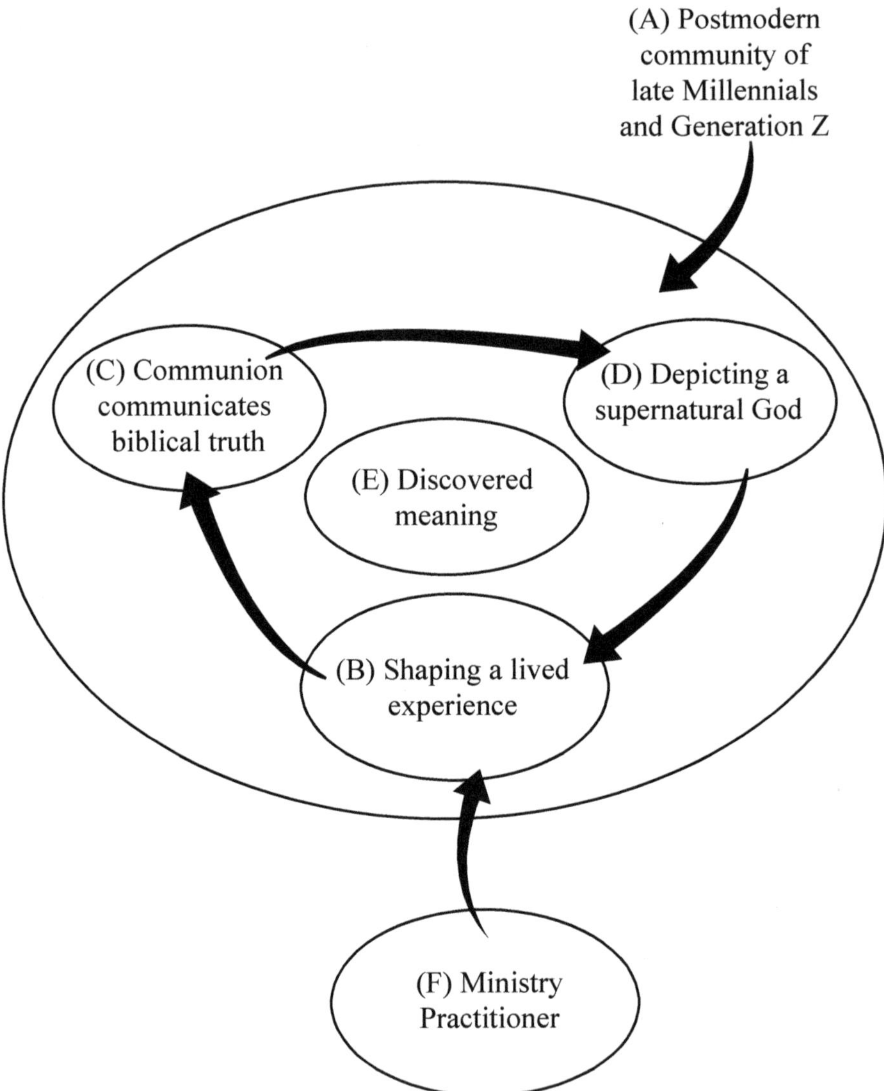

CHAPTER 27

A THEORETICAL MODEL OF COMMUNICATION FOR OUR TIME IN CHURCH HISTORY

An open Communion table is vital if we are to understand how the celebration functions to communicate biblical truth to late Millennials and Generation Z as a postmodern community. Throughout church history, this was not always the case. In the Classical era, **the model in this book may have worked for Irenaeus** who believed in the universal accessibility and inclusive nature of Communion. To a lesser degree, **the model may also have worked for Clement of Alexandria** who believed self-examination was important prior to approaching the Communion table.

By the Middle Ages **the model would have certainly failed** as gradations of exclusion came into effect from the Classical era, endorsed by Canon law, and enacted through sacerdotal power. Also, the intertwining pattern of how biblical passages were used to explain Communion tended to determine how liturgy was used to retell the redemptive story. The model shows that **Communion is a carrier of truth that shapes, depicts, and discovers.** In the Middle Ages, how **Lanfranc and Berengarius, Amalarius, Radbertus,** and **Ratramnus** interpreted biblical passages would shape the participant, depict God, and discover meaning that is not c**haracteristic of current postmodern spirituality.**

Though the model would have failed in the Middle Ages, it **may have gained some credibility** in the era of Modernity. **Luther and Zwingli** wrote liturgies in the language of the people. The fact that liturgy was developed to include people who could not understand Latin is closer to the second and third step of the model than anything else in the Middle Ages. However, **the model would have other challenges** in the era of Modernity. Though the new lights of Puritanism tended to have an open Communion table, the old lights maintained a closed table. Even so, the openness of the new lights was **not as open as the model suggests** for Generation Z as a postmodern community.

The tension of an inclusive or exclusive Communion table was seen in **Stoddard's Half-Way Communion** as an attempt of openness to church members and non-members based on Stoddard's own conversion during the celebration of Communion. The **model is not designed to create tension** between members and non-members of a church. Revivalists like **Wesley** viewed Communion as a **"conversion ordinance."** Other revivalists like **McCready** and **Whitefield** believed that conversion may occur at the Communion table. Revivalist beliefs **tend to come closer to the model** than anything else in the era of Modernity.

Added to the openness of new lights and revivalists, in the era of Postmodernity, the Holy Spirit's work at the Communion table was highlighted by Pentecostalism believing He revealed sin in the participants with their subsequent repentance. The desire of Pentecostals "for the Spirit to function as the Spirit desires on the people and the [Communion] elements" (Alvarado 2013, 188) not only showed an open table with very few restrictions, but also an openness to the work of the Holy Spirit. An open table and openness to the Holy Spirit is where the model works best.

The **model would certainly work** among late Millennials and Generation Z, or "nones," as the fastest growing group of people who value spirituality but not necessarily religion. The ceremonial time and space that liminality creates is the freedom from formal religious structure. It allows for inclusion and equality.

The model gives late Millennials and Generation Z permission to anticipate an encounter with a supernatural God. If the "future [of planting churches] is certainly to be full of experimentation" (Bird 2014, 24), **the model would work** as part of that effort by including people at the Communion table who consider themselves spiritual, but not necessarily religious. Continually including Generation Z not only shapes them, it also depicts the God of the Bible towards a biblical explanation of a lived experience. Most importantly, experimenting with the theoretical model may lead to a conversion experience.

> experimenting with the theoretical model may lead to a conversion experience

The model may not work in all spiritual communities and settings. For example, if the realities of postmodern spirituality are not evident in a community, the act of including and involving the students as seen in the three steps may not be representative of the student body. The realities of modern spirituality must be evident. Investigating the characteristics of a modern community would be a recommendation for further study.

More importantly, the central focus of the model is the celebration of Communion that communicates a lived experience as a carrier of biblical truth. The ministry practitioner may work with late Millennials and Generation Z in a postmodern community where Communion is not practiced. In the absence of Communion there may be the practice of another popular ceremony from a different religion than Christianity. Even so, a ministry practitioner could utilize any one of the four ceremonial systems to convey biblical truth. For example, the system of Singer and Shils particularly help the ministry practitioner utilize the ceremonial aspects of participant, observer, beliefs and the ceremony itself. How a practitioner would convey biblical truth through a religious ceremony other than the Christian celebration of Communion requires further investigation.

A final reason **why the model may not work** with late Millennials and Generation Z in a postmodern community is that in some scenarios the ministry practitioner is the only Christian.

However, it would not be long before a ministry could work with the model, considering the words of Christ regarding His presence, "For where two or three gather in my name, there I am with them" (Matt. 18:20). This implies the suspension of the model until at least two students have become Christians through the grace of God as the fruit of the ministry practitioner's faithfulness.[128] If Communion is not practiced in a postmodern community, at least two Christian students warrant its practice in addition to the ministry practitioner in order to experience the empowering actions and promissory words of Christ.[129]

I collected data representing two years in the life of undergraduate students at SEU. Ideally, collected data would represent the life of a student from freshman to senior year. Such data would not only cover all the college years in the life of a student, but it would paint a picture of what more and deepening meaning looks like. It would also create more time to measure any transformation of late Millennials and Generation Z who participate in Communion. Further study might answer questions such as: In what way can more and deepening meaning be measured when biblical truth is introduced in the life of a student in his or her freshman, sophomore, junior, and senior years? What does more and deepening meaning look like from freshman to senior year as biblical truth is successively introduced? In a similar vein, in what way can the growth of Christianity be measured in late Millennials and Generation Z as a postmodern community through the three steps of the model in the life of a student from freshman to senior year?

---

[128] "For it is by grace you have been saved, through faith—and this is not from yourselves, it is the gift of God—not by works, so that no one can boast" (Eph. 2:8-9).

[129] The minimum required number of people to warrant the practice of Communion was an issue raised in chapter two because multi-site churches are beginning to offer an online Communion. In what way does an individual include/serve him or herself while online? This question is a matter for further study.

In **chapter fourteen**, I discovered that the four characteristics of a postmodern community not only connected, but they moved in a circular fashion as the students repeated the celebration, providing more meaning for their lived experiences. In **chapter twenty-one, the model predicted** that if biblical truth was introduced, continual participation would not only provide more meaning, it would also provide deeper meaning for their lived experiences.

Further research is required to measure the **probable** cause **effect of the model** as a significant outcome: the transformation of postmodern communities represented by late Millennials and Generation Z. I suggest a minimum of four years covering the period of time from freshman to senior at college not only allows for more time, but that time period remains contextualized within college.

The Christian celebration of Communion in its local and universal characteristics throughout church history to the present day has certainly been preserved. Like Pope John Paul II, **perhaps my model will be put into practice** in postmodern communities "in chapels built along mountain paths, on lake shores and sea coasts...on altars built in stadiums and city squares...on the humble altar of a country church...celebrated on the altar of the world." In any of these locations I am sure there are more "Isabels."

CONCLUSION

The purpose of this book involved using the lenses of IPA and ceremonial systems to discover how undergraduate students at SEU experience Christ when they participate in Communion. From my research, I uncovered seven key discoveries. From thirty years in pastoral ministry, I had a suspicion that spirituality, religion, Communion, and meaning were connected. I found the students' spirituality was connected to Communion and their experience of Christ, and they were finding meaning for what they believed and valued. I also found Communion was, indeed, a significant factor in the students' experience as they actively participated in the bread and wine. Students had to sense or feel something in order for a lived experience to have meaning. Communion acted like a communication vehicle for those lived experiences. What the students believed approaching the Communion table shaped what they got out of it.

Active participation in Communion was the environment for understanding how late Millennials and Generation Z as a postmodern community at SEU worked and how it was influenced. The four characteristics of a postmodern community connected in a circular fashion the individual interpretations of a lived experience that began with the student. The influence of faculty, priests, and campus ministry intentionally focused on spirituality, encouraging the students to be self-guided through their lived experiences and reducing religious rules that may hinder that process. Though students were attracted to Communion as a point of gathering together, they were not necessarily attracted to biblical truth that the celebration espouses.

Nevertheless, I found that the biblical text depicted the supernatural God of the Bible in different ways. He was experienced at each table celebration in a set of beliefs grounded in biblical truth, connecting the past and future to the present from the perspective of Communion by ceremonially performing beliefs with the participant in mind, as well as the observer who is not participating informing them of the past and future. It was surprising to me, then, that biblical truth was completely absent in the way students described a supernatural God.

Ultimately, there was an absence of biblical truth in how the students described their experience of spirituality and religion or Communion as a ceremony that facilitated their experiences. This accounts for the fact that late Millennials and Generation Z tend to reject biblical truth, eschewing the church but not the religious ceremony of Communion. It is why students tend to call themselves spiritual, but not religious. My discoveries also account for why most students leave their childhood religion to become unaffiliated. This unaffiliated category has a higher retention rate than most other major religious groups. An increasing student population typically does not become more religiously affiliated, but curiously, they maintain an attraction to the religious ceremony of Communion that provides meaning for their lived experiences.

From my discoveries, I developed a model to help Christian ministry practitioners communicate biblical truth into the spiritual communities of late Millennials and Generation Z in different settings based on my research in the setting at SEU. Because the students have to sense or feel something in order for their lived experiences to have meaning, the model shows Communion as a carrier of experiential biblical truth that shapes the students' lived experiences and their depiction of a supernatural God in order to discover biblical meaning. The model shows Communion is a carrier of truth that shapes, depicts, and discovers, with the potential of transforming a postmodern community.

Church history does reveal that the instructions Christ gave to the disciples during the last days of His life have been preserved, "This is my body...this is my blood" (Matt. 26:26-28). Celebrating

His death, resurrection, ascension, and return by simply doing what He did with the bread and wine has been mystified and, at times, oversimplified, "Do this [bread and wine] in remembrance of me" (Lk. 22:19). Remembering the death, resurrection, ascension, and return of Christ is also to remember a final table celebration He promised. In the upper room with His disciples, Christ promised that He would "not drink from this fruit of the vine from now on until that day when I drink it new with you in my Father's kingdom" (Matt. 26:29).

Until that day, followers of Christ are instructed to make themselves ready (Rev. 19:7), appropriately dressed (Matt. 22:11-14) in righteousness (Rev. 19:8). While celebrating Communion is not required for participation in a final table celebration, regular participation in it helps followers of Christ make themselves ready for it. With my theoretical model, regular participation in Communion can shape the participants' beliefs and values, depict the supernatural God they sense as the God of the Bible, and help them discover a more and deepening meaning to their lived experiences.

It is my hope that others will further develop the model and discover how other Christian ceremonies like weddings, funerals, ordinations, memorials, and baptisms can function to retell the story of redemption.

I have given you, the reader, my thoughts but Christ gave you His body and blood. I have shown you some truth that was discovered through research, but Christ said He is the Truth. I have attempted to help you see the cultural dynamics of late Millennials and Generation Z, but Christ said that seeing Him was also to see the Father. It is my conviction that all 425 students involved in my research are heroes of their generation, but Christ is the Hero for generations. Cross-culturally and interculturally, He is Jesus Christ our Lord and Savior who died on a cross, was buried in a tomb, resurrected on the third day, ascended into heaven, and will return again to drink of the vine. Until them, it is my prayer that you experience Christ in the bread and wine of Communion where the biblical text comes to life in your experience.

GLOSSARY

Agnostic	The existence of God or the supernatural is unknown or unknowable.
Allegorical	A metaphor in which a character, event, object, or location is used to broaden a message or a point.
Anthropology	The study of humans, their societies, cultures, behaviors and developments.
Apotropaic	Supposedly having the power to avert evil influences or bad luck.
	Art Nouveau An international style of art, architecture and applied art, especially the decorative arts.
Baroque	A highly ornate and often extravagant style of architecture, music, dance, painting, sculpture and other arts that flourished in Europe from the early 17th until the mid-18th century.
Canon	A collection of sacred books or scrolls accepted as genuine.
Church:	Western Church.
Communion:	Though many names have been given to Communion as a Christian celebration that include Eucharist, Last Supper, The Lord's Table, and Breaking Bread, I use the term Communion from the Greek noun koinonia, meaning fellowship, participation, and sharing.
Consubstantiation	Christian theological doctrine that describes the real presence in Communion. During

the ceremony, the substance of the body and blood of Christ are present alongside the substance of the bread and wine, which remain present.

Deconstructionism — An approach to understanding the relationship between text and meaning looking for things that run counter to the intended meaning or structural unity of a particular text. It can also apply to all forms of organizational structure, relationships, and authority.

Dialectical — A discourse between two or more people holding different points of view about a subject but wishing to establish the truth through reasoned arguments.

Ecclesiastical — Relating to the Christian Church and its clergy.

Episcopate — The Bishops of the Church

Epistemological — The branch of philosophy concerned with the theory of knowledge or the study of the nature of knowledge, justification, and the rationality of belief.

Eschatology — Part of theology concerned with death, judgment, and the final destiny of the soul and of humankind.

Ethno-Hermeneutics — Interpreting the biblical text in the context of culture.

Exogamous — The social norm of marrying outside one's social group.

Great Awakening — Refers to a number of periods of Christian revival in American history identified as three waves between the 18th and 20th centuries. Characterized by increased religious enthusiasm, spiritual conviction and repentance led by evangelical Protestant ministers.

Great Persecution	The last and most severe persecution of the Church by the Roman Empire between 303AD and 311AD.
Henotheism	The worship of a single god while not denying the existence or possible existence of other deities
Hermeneutics	Branch of knowledge that deals with interpretation, especially of the Bible or literary texts.
Heterogenous	Suggesting that two or more things are unlike in substance or nature.
Homogeneous	Suggesting sameness or alike each other.
Humanism	Prime importance to human rather than divine or supernatural matters.
Ideology	A system of ideas and ideals, especially one which forms the basis of economic, political, or religious theory and policy.
Idiographic	Relating to the study or discovery of particular scientific facts and processes, as distinct from general laws.
Liminality	The quality of ambiguity or disorientation that occurs in the middle stage of a ceremony, when participants no longer hold their pre-ceremonial status but have not yet begun the transition to the status they will hold when the ceremony is complete.
Liturgist	A compiler or composer of liturgy.
Liturgy	Public Christian worship representing a communal response to and participation in the sacred through activity reflecting praise, thanksgiving, supplication or repentance.
Mannerism	A habitual gesture or way of speaking or behaving.

Monolithic	A large, powerful, and uniform church organization.
Monotheism	The doctrine or belief that there is only one God.
Neoclassical	Western movements in the decorative and visual arts, literature, theatre, music, and architecture that draw inspiration from the classical art and culture of classical antiquity.
Nomenclature	The devising or choosing of names for things.
Nominalism	A philosophical view rejecting abstract objects, or rejection of universals.
Nomothetic	Relating to the study or discovery of general scientific laws.
Non-Canonical	Not relating to, part of, or sanctioned by a collection of sacred books or scrolls accepted as genuine (canon).
Ontological	The philosophical study of being or study of concepts that directly relate to being, in particular becoming, existence, reality, as well as the basic categories of being and their relations.
Orthodoxy	Traditional beliefs and values generally accepted as a right or true understanding of truth in Scripture.
Passover	Annual Jewish feast commemorating the deliverance of Israel from their slavery in Egypt.
Pedagogist	The approach to of a teacher to teaching.
Penitentiary	A priest or participant charged with certain incriminating aspects that violate or offend the celebration of Communion.
Phenomenology	The philosophical study of the structures of experience and consciousness founded by Edmond Hurssel in the 19th century.

Pneumatological	Refers to a particular discipline within Christian theology that focuses on the study of the Holy Spirit.
Polytheism	The worship of belief in multiple deities classified as gods and goddesses.
Postmodernism:	While postmodernism represents a rejection of the Enlightenment project and the basic foundational assumptions that it was built on in the eighteenth century, meaning is not inherent in postmodernism therefore everything is open to interpretation.
Postmodernity:	The term postmodernism is a monolithic term, but as a generalization that includes postmodern(s) and postmodernity.
Redemptive story	Activity of God throughout the history of humankind concerning all creation. Retelling the redemptive story is a metanarrative while localized narratives make sense of its historical and eschatological dimensions in the present during Communion. This can incorporate creative ways to utilize Scripture, liturgy, music, song, silence, etc.
Realism	Sometimes called naturalism, the attempt to represent subject matter truthfully, without artificiality and avoiding artistic conventions, or implausible, exotic, and supernatural elements.
Religion	Formal institutionalized system of beliefs and practices that concern a supernatural God.
Rococo	Exceptionally ornamental and theatrical style of architecture, art and decoration which combines asymmetry, scrolling curves, gilding, white and pastel colors, sculpted molding, to create surprise and the illusion of motion and drama.

Romanesque	An architectural style of medieval Europe characterized by semi-circular arches.
Renaissance	The transitional movement in Europe between medieval and modern times beginning in the 14th century in Italy, lasting into the 17th century, and marked by a humanistic revival of classical influence expressed in a flowering of the arts and literature and by the beginnings of modern science.
Sacrament	A Christian rite recognized as of particular importance and significance, in particular the bread and wine of Communion. Many Christians consider the sacraments to be a visible symbol of the reality of God, as well as a means by which God enacts his grace.
Spirituality	Personal beliefs and values by which an individual relates to and experiences a supernatural God.
Sacerdotal Power	Spiritual powers or authority of an ordained priest/pastor/minister/ministry practitioner.
Salvific	Having the intent or power to save or redeem.
Soteriological	Branch of theology dealing with salvation especially as effected by Jesus Christ.
Sub-orthodox	Less than orthodox, not heretical, yet not explicitly aligning with orthodoxy.
Symbiotic	Involving interaction between two different things that live in close physical proximity.
Transmigration	To cause someone or something to go from one state of existence or place to another.
Transelementation	Transformation of the bread and wine of Communion by mystic force attributing that mysticism to the person consecrating them.

Transubstantiation	The change of substance or essence by which the bread and wine in Communion become, in reality, the body and blood of Jesus Christ.
Typological	Holding that things in Christian belief are prefigured or symbolized by things in the Old Testament.
Wedding Supper Of the Lamb	The welcoming and consummating feast that celebrates the marriage of Christ and his Church (Bride) composed of all believers after He has returned for His Church.

COMPLETE BIBLIOGRAPHY

Albrecht, Daniel E. 1999. *Rites in the Spirit: A Ritual Approach to Pentecostal/Charismatic Spirituality.* Sheffield, UK: Sheffield Academic Press.

Alvarado, Johnathan E. 2013. "Pentecostal Epiclesis:" A Model for Teaching and Learning. *Pneuma: The Journal of the Society for Pentecostal Studies* 35, 2: 180–198. Accessed November 8, 2019. doi:10.1163/15700747-12341313.

Arteaga, William L. De. 2015. *Agnes Sanford and Her Companions: The Assault on Cessationism and the Coming of the Charismatic Renewal.* Eugene, OR: Wipf and Stock Publishers.

Austin Stone Community Church. 2019a. "This Matters: Why Do We Take the Lord's Supper? Accessed October 4, 2019. https://austinstone.org/resources/sermons/778--why-do-we-take-the-lord-s-supper

_______________________. 2019b. "Liturgy Archives." Accessed October 4, 2019. https://www.austinstoneworship.com/category/liturgy/

Barker, Robert L. 1999. *The Social Work Dictionary.* Cary, NC: NASW Press.

Barna Group and Impact 360 Institute. 2018. *Gen Z: The Culture, Beliefs and Motivations Shaping the Next Generation.* Ventura, CA: Barna Group.

Batterson, Mark. 2009. *Wild Goose Chase: Reclaim the Adventure of Pursuing God.* New York: Doubleday Religious Publishing Group.

———. 2011. *Soulprint: Discovering Your Divine Destiny.* New York: Doubleday Religious Publishing Group.

———. 2014. *Media.* Accessed November 16, 2019. http://theater-church.com/media.

______. 2014. *The Circle Maker.* Grand Rapids, MI: Zondervan.

Beale, G. K. 1999. *The Book of Revelation.* Grand Rapids, MI: Wm. B. Eerdmans Publishing Co.

Bell, Catherine. 1997. *Ritual: Perspectives and Dimensions.* New York: Oxford University Press.

___________. 1992. *Ritual Theory, Ritual Practice.* New York: Oxford University Press.

Bingham, Joseph. 2010. *Origines Ecclesiasticæ: Or, the Antiquities of the Christian Church.* Vol. 1. Farmington Hills, MI: Gale ECCO, Print Eds.

Bird, Warren. 2014. "Leadership Network/Generis Multisite Church Scorecard Faster Growth, More New Believers and Greater Lay Participation." Church Growth and Leadership. Dallas, Texas: Leadership Network/Generis, Accessed October 16, 2019. http://leadnet.org/wpcontent/uploads/2014/03/2014_LN_Generis_Multisite_Church_Scorecard_Report_v2.pdf.

Bock, Darrell L. 1994. *Luke.* Baker Exegetical Commentary on the New Testament 3. Grand Rapids, MI: Baker Books.

Boersma, Hans. 2001. *Living in the Lamblight: Christianity and Contemporary Challenges to the Gospel.* Vancouver. B. C., Canada: Regent College Publishing.

Bradshaw, Paul F., and Maxwell E. Johnson. 2012. *The Eucharistic Liturgies: Their Evolution and Interpretation.* Collegeville, MN: Liturgical Press.

Bullis, Ronald K. 2013. *Spirituality in Social Work Practice.* Bristol PA: Taylor & Francis.

Burns, JoAnn. 2016. "Communion." February 3. Accessed October 14, 2019. https://bay182.mail.live.com/?tid=c-mT2c1wY7K5RG4UgAiZMJIyA2&fid=flinbox.

Bussing, Arndt. 2019. *Measures of Spirituality/Religiosity* (2018). Basel, Switzerland: Mdpi AG

Caldwell, Larry. 1987. "Third Horizon Ethnohermeneutics: Re-Evaluating NT Hermeneutical Models for Intercultural Bible Interpreters Today." *The Asian Journal of Theology 1*, no. 2: 314-333. http://www.newadvent.org/cathen/02487a.htm

Canda, Edward R., and Leola Dyrud Furman. 2010. *Spiritual Diversity in Social Work Practice: The Heart of Helping*. New York: Oxford University Press.

Carroll, John T. 2012. *Luke: A Commentary*. Louisville, KY: Westminster John Knox Press.

Cascio, T. 1998. "Incorporating Spirituality into Social Work Practice: A Review of What to Do." *Families in Society* 79, no. 5: 523–32.

Catholic Advent. 2019. "Berengarius of Tours." Accessed September 28, 2019.

Celebration Church. 2019a. "Beliefs Celebration Church." Accessed October 1, 2019. http://celebrationchurchtx.com/about/beliefs/.

__________. 2019b. "Message Archives." Accessed October 4, 2019. https://celebration.church/media/archives

Chance, J. B. 2011. "The Journey to Emmaus: Insights on Scripture from Mystical Understandings of Attachment and Detachment." *Perspectives in Religious Studies* 38, no. 4: 363–82.

Chezelle, Celia. "The Eucharist in Early Medieval Europe, 205-250," in *A Companion to the Eucharist in the Middle Ages*, edited by Ian Christopher Levy, Gary Macy, and Kristen Van Ausdall. Boston: Brill. Accessed October 8, 2019. http://dx.doi.org/10.1163/9789004221727.

Clydesdale, Tim and Kathleen Garces-Foley. 2019. *The Twentysomething Soul: Understanding the Religious and Secular Lives of American Young Adults*. New York, NY: Oxford University Press.

Cook, Matthew A., Rob, Haskell, Ruth Julian, and Natee Tanchan-pongs. 2010. *Local Theology for the Global Church: Principles for an Evangelical Approach to Contextualization.* Pasadena, CA: William Carey Library.

Craigie, Peter C. 1976. *The Book of Deuteronomy.* 2nd ed. Grand Rapids, MI.: Wm. B. Eerdmans Publishing Co.

Creps, Earl. 2002. "Disciplemaking in a Postmodern World." *Enrichment: A Journal for Pentecostal Ministry.* 7, no. 4:54-59.

Dean, Kenda Creasy. 1994. *Almost Christian: What the Faith of Our Teenagers is Telling the American Church.* New York, NY: Oxford University Press.

Derrida, Jacques. 2016. *Of Grammatology.* Baltimore, MA: John Hopkins University Press.

DeKoven, Marianne. 2004. *Utopia Limited: The Sixties and the Emergence of the Postmodern.* Durham, Duke University Press.

Derezotes, David. 1995. "Spirituality and Religiosity:" Neglected Factors in Social Work Practice. *Arete 20*, no. 1: 1-15.

Diamant, Anita. 2007. *The New Jewish Wedding, Revised.* New York: Simon and Schuster.

Donaldson, Robert. 1999. *Ante-Nicene Fathers: Fathers of the Third and Fourth Centuries.* Vol. 7. Peabody, MA: Hendrickson Publishers.

Drescher, Elizabeth. 2016. *Choosing Our Religion: The Spiritual Lives of America's Nones.* New York, NY: Oxford University Press.

Driver, Tom F. 1991. *The Magic of Ritual: Our Need for Liberating Rites That Transform Our Lives and Our Communities.* San Francisco: HarperSanFrancisco.

Dryer, George H. 2005. *History of the Christian Church Part One.* Whitefish, MT: Kessinger Publishing, LLC.

Etheria, M.L. McClure, and C.L. Feltoe. 1919. "The Pilgrimage of Etheria." Society for Promoting Christian Knowledge. Accessed October 2, 2019. http://www.ccel.org/m/mcclure/etheria/etheria.htm.

Fee, Gordon. 2014. *The First Epistle to the Corinthians.* Rev. Ed. Grand Rapids, MI: Wm. B. Eerdmans Publishing Co.

Foley, Edward. 2009. *From Age to Age: How Christians Have Celebrated the Eucharist.* Rev. ed. Collegeville, MN: Liturgical Press.

Fowler, James W. 1995. *Stages of Faith: The Psychology of Human Development.* New York: HarperCollins.

Fowlds, Sean. 2015. "A Return to Liturgy." *Ministry Today Magazine.* Accessed October 12, 2019. http://ministrytodaymag.com/index.php/ministry-today-archives/198-words/13675-a-return-to-liturgy.

Foucault, Michel. 1980. *Power/Knowledge: Selected Interviews and Other Writings,* 1972-1977. Edited by Colin Gordon. Translated by Colin Gordon, Leo Marshall, John Mepham, and Kate Soper. New York, NY: Pantheon Books.

France, R. T. 2007. *The Gospel of Matthew.* Grand Rapids, MI: Wm. B. Eerdmans Publishing Co.

Gadamer, Hans-Georg. 2013. *Truth and Method.* New York, NY: Bloomsbury Academic.

Geary, Patrick. 2010. *Readings in Medieval History.* Guelph, ON: University of Toronto Press.

Geertz, Clifford. 1973. *The Interpretation of Cultures: Selected Essays.* New York: Basic Books.

Gehring, Roger W. 2009. *House Church and Mission: The Importance of Household Structures in Early Christianity.* Peabody, MA: Hendrickson Publishers.

George, L. K., D. B. Larsen, H. G. Koeing, and M. E. McCullough. 2000. "Spirituality and Health: What We Know, What We Need to Know." *Journal of Social and Clinical Psychology* 19. no. 1: 102–16.

Giddens, Anthony and Christopher Pearson. 1998. *Conversations with Anthony Giddens: Making Sense of Modernity.* Redwood City, CA: Stanford University Press.

Gittoes, Julie. 2013. *Anamnesis and the Eucharist: Contemporary Anglican Approaches.* Farnham, UK: Ashgate Publishing.

Gotterer, R. 2001. "The Spiritual Dimension in Clinical Social Work Practice: A Clinical Perspective." *Families in Society* 82, no. 2: 187–93.

Green, Chris E. W. 2012. *Toward a Pentecostal Theology of the Lord's Supper: Foretasting the Kingdom.* Cleveland, TN: CPT Press.

Greenway, Kimberly. 2006. "The Role of Spirituality in Purpose in Life and Academic Engagement." *Journal of College and Character* 7 (6). Accessed October 9, 2019. http://www.tandfonline.com/doi/pdf/10.2202/1940-1639.1212.

Grenz, Stanley J. 1996. *A Primer on Postmodernism.* Grand Rapids, MI.: William B. Eerdmans Publishing Co.

Grimes, Ronald L. 2010. *Ritual Criticism: Case Studies in Its Practice, Essays on Its Theory.* Place of Publication: CreateSpace Independent Publishing Platform.

Groeschel, Craig. 2010. *What Is God Really Like?* Grand Rapids, MI: Zondervan.

Groeschel, Benedict J., and James Monti. 1997. *In the Presence of Our Lord: The History, Theology, and Psychology of Eucharistic Devotion.* Huntington, IN: Our Sunday Visitor Publishing.

Gruen, Erich. 2002. *Diaspora: Jews Amidst Greeks and Romans.* Cambridge, MA: Harvard University Press.

Halsall, Paul. 2015. "Medieval Sourcebook: Twelfth Ecumenical Council: Lateran IV 1215." *Fordham University.* Accessed October 6, 2019. http://legacy.fordham.edu/halsall/basis/lateran4.asp.

Hartman, Laura M. 2011. *The Christian Consumer: Living Faithfully in a Fragile World.* New York: Oxford University Press.

Hay, Eldon. 2012. *Covenanters in Canada: Reformed Presbyterianism from 1820 to 2012.* Montreal: McGill-Queen's Press.

Haynes, N. Stephen, and William Hayes. 2000. *Principles and Practices of Behavioral Assessment.* New York, NY: Kluwer Academic/Plenum Publishers.

Hefele, Charles Joseph. 2007. *A History of the Councils of the Church: From the Original Documents, to the Close of the Second Council of Nicaea A.D. 787.* Eugene, OR: Wipf and Stock Publishers.

Hefling, Charles. 2012. "Who is Communion for?" *Christian Century* 129, no. 24: 22-27.

Heidegger, Martin. 1962. *Being and Time.* Oxford, UK: Blackwell.

Hellmann, Helman. 2006. A Brief Look at the Recent History of NATO's Future, in Peters, I. (ed). *Transatlantic Tug-Of-War: Prospects for US-European Cooperation*, Munster: Vit. Verlag.

Hendriksen, William. 1998. *More Than Conquerors: An Interpretation of the Book of Revelation.* Grand Rapids, MI: Baker Books.

Hendriksen, William, and Simon Kistemaker. 2002. *New Testament Commentary.* Grand Rapids, MI.: Baker Book House.

HERI. 2003. "The Spiritual Life of College Students: A National Study of College Students' Search for Meaning and Purpose." Washington, DC: Higher Education Institute. Accessed November 2, 2019. http://spirituality.ucla.edu/docs/reports/Spiritual_Life_College_Students_Full_Report.pd.

Hiebert, Paul, Daniel Shaw, R., and Tienou, Tite. 1999. *Understanding Folk Religion: A Christian Response to Popular Beliefs and Practices.* Grand Rapids, MI. Baker Books.

Higgins, Dick. 1978. *The Post-Cognitive Era: Looking for the Sense in it all.* Dick Higgins.

Hunsinger, George. 2014. *Conversational Theology: Essays on Ecumenical, Postliberal, and Political Themes, with Special Reference to Karl Barth.* New York: Bloomsbury Publishing.

Hurtado, Larry W. 1999. *At the Origins of Christian Worship: The Context and Character of Earliest Christian Devotion.* Grand Rapids, MI: Wm. B. Eerdmans Publishing Co.

Husserl, Edmund. 2012. *Ideas: General Introduction to Pure Phenomenology.* New York: Routledge.

Izbicki, Thomas. 2015. *The Eucharist in Medieval Canon Law.* Cambridge, UK: Cambridge University Press.

Jaccard, James, and Jacob Jacoby. 2010. *Theory Construction and Model-Building Skills: A Practical Guide for Social Scientists.* New York: Guildford Publications.

Jameson, Frederic. 1991. *Postmodernism, Or, The Cultural Logic of Late Capitalism.* (Durham, Duke University Press.

Jencks, Charles. 2011. *The Story of Post-Modernism: Five Decades of the Ironic, Iconic, and Critical in Architecture.* Southgate, Chichester: John Wiley and Sons.

Jensen, Irving L. 1990. *Revelation—Jensen Bible Self Study Guide.* Chicago: Moody Publishers.

Jeremias, Joachim. 1966. *The Eucharistic Words of Jesus.* Norwich, UK: SCM Press Limited.

Kaiser, Walter C., and Moisés Silva. 1994. *An Introduction to Biblical Hermeneutics: A Search for Meaning.* Grand Rapids, MI.: Zondervan Publishers.

Keener, Craig. 2009. *The Gospel of Matthew: A Socio-Rhetorical Commentary.* Grand Rapids, MI: Wm. B. Eerdmans.

Kereszty, Roch A. 2004. *Wedding Feast of the Lamb: Eucharistic Theology from a Historical, Biblical, and Systematic Perspective.* Chicago: Liturgy Training Publications.

Killen, Andreas. 2006. 1973 *Nervous Breakdown: Watergate, Warhol, and the Birth of Post-Sixties America.* New York, NY: Bloomsbury.

Khoo, Lorna Lock-Nah. 2005. *Wesleyan Eucharistic Spirituality: Its Nature, Sources and Future.* Adelaide, Australia: ATF Press.

Kozeny, Geoph. 2004. "Dancing with Dogma: The Fine Line Between Religion and Spirituality." *Communities* no. 124 (Fall): 72–71.

Kurlansky, Mark. 2005. 1968: *The Year That Rocked the World*. New York, NY: Random House.

Lanfranc. 2009. *On the Body and Blood of the Lord; On the Truth of the Body and Blood of Christ in the Eucharist*. Trans. Fr. Mark Vaillancourt. Washington, DC: CUA Press.

Lantz, Joe. 2007. *My Yacad: Who Am I? What Am I? And Why?* Bloomington, IN: AuthorHouse.

Lenski, Richard C. 2001a. *Commentary on the New Testament: The Interpretation of St. Luke's Gospel*. Peabody, MA: Hendrickson Publishers.

——————. 2001b. *Commentary on the New Testament: The Interpretation of the Acts of the Apostles*. Peabody, MA: Hendrickson Publishers.

——————. 2001c. *Commentary on the New Testament: The Interpretation of St. John's Revelation*. Peabody, MA: Hendrickson Publishers.

Lévinas, Emmanuel. 1995. *The Theory of Intuition in Husserl's Phenomenology*. Evanston, IL: Northwestern University Press.

Levy, Ian Christopher, Gary Macy, and Kristen Van Ausdall. 2012. *A Companion to the Eucharist in the Middle Ages*. Leiden; Boston: Brill. Accessed September 19, 2019. http://dx.doi.org/10.1163/9789004221727.

Life.Church. 2019a. "You Can Take Communion at Home or Just About Anywhere." Accessed October 4, 2019. https://leaders.life.church/you-can-take-communion-at-home-or-just-about-anywhere/

——————. 2019b. "Pray." Accessed October 4, 2019. https://open.life.church/resources/2054-pray?search_id=7030079

Lipka, Michael. 2015. "Millennials Increasingly Are Driving Growth of 'Nones.'" *Pew Research Center*. Accessed October 12, 2019. http://www.pewresearch.org/fact-tank/2015/05/12/millennials-increasingly-are-driving-growth-of-nones/.

Lipka, Michael, and David Masci. 2016. "Americans May be Getting Less Religious, but feelings of Spirituality are on the Rise." *Pew Research Center.* Accessed October 7, 2019. http://www.pewresearch.org/fact-tank/2016/01/21/americans-spirituality/

Long, Kimberly. 2011. *The Eucharistic Theology of the American Holy Fairs.* Louisville, KY: Westminster John Knox Press.

Macy, Gary. 2005. *The Banquet's Wisdom: A Short History of the Theologies of the Lord's Supper.* Akron, OH: OSL Publications.

Marcus, Ivan G. 2013. *The Jewish Life Cycle: Rites of Passage from Biblical to Modern Times.* Seattle, WA: University of Washington Press.

Marion, Jean-Luc. 2002. "'They Recognized Him; and He Became Invisible to Them.'" *Modern Theology* 18, no. 2: 145–52.

Marshall, I. Howard. 1998. *Luke: Historian & Theologian.* 3rd ed. Downers Grove, IL: InterVarsity Press Academic.

Meeks, Wayne. 2006. "Social and Ecclesial Life of the Earliest Christians, 145-175," in *Cambridge History of Christianity,* edited by Mitchell, Margaret M., Frances M. Young, and K. Scott Bowie. Cambridge, UK: Cambridge University Press.

Milavec, Aaron. 2003. *The Didache: Text, Translation, Analysis, and Commentary.* Collegeville, MN: Michael Glazier.

Mazza, Enrico. 1999. *The Celebration of Eucharist: The Origin of the Rite and the Development of Its Interpretation.* Translated by Matthew J. O'Connell. Collegeville, MN: Pueblo Books.

McBride, Alfred. 2006. "Eucharist A Short History." *Catholic Update* (October): 2.

McHale, Brian. 2015. *The Cambridge Introduction to Postmodernism (Cambridge Introductions to Literature).* New York, NY: Cambridge University Press.

McConnell, Scott, and Ed Stetzer. 2009. *Multi-Site Churches: Guidance for the Movement's Next Generation.* Nashville, TN: B&H Publishing Group.

McDowell, David Paul. 2012. *Beyond the Half-Way Covenant: Solomon Stoddard's Understanding of the Lord's Supper as a Converting Ordinance.* Eugene, OR: Wipf and Stock Pub.

Merleau-Ponty, Maurice. 1962. *Phenomenology of Perception.* London, UK: Routledge.

Miller, W. R., and C. E. Thoresen. 2003. "Spirituality, Religion, and Health: An Emerging Research Field." *American Psychology* 58, no.1: 24–35.

Nicholls, William. 1996. "Saints and Fanatics: The Problematic Connection Between Religion and Spirituality." *Judaism* 45, no. 4: 446–58.

Nolland, John. 2005. *The Gospel of Matthew.* Grand Rapids, MI: Wm. B. Eerdmans Publishing Co. Community Church. 2019a. "Communion." Accessed October 4, 2019. https://theaterchurch.com/media/ritual/communion

—————————————. 2019b. "Media". Accessed October 4, 2019. https://theaterchurch.com/media

Northpoint Community Church. 2019a. "Messages." Accessed October 4, 2019. https://northpoint.org/messages

—————————————. 2019b. "Andy Stanley." Accessed October 4, 2019. https://open.life.church/speakers/andy-stanley

O'Connor, James T. 2005. *The Hidden Manna: A Theology of the Eucharist.* 2nd ed. San Francisco: Ignatius Press.

Osbourne, Grant. 1991. *The Two Horizons: New Testament Hermeneutics and Philosophical Description with Special Reference to Heidegger, Bultman, Gadamer and Wittgenstein.* Downers Grove. IL.: IVP.

Outreach Magazine. 2014. "America's Largest Churches, 2014." *OutreachMagazine.com.* Accessed September 20, 2019. http://www.outreachmagazine.com/2014-outreach-100/outreach-100-largest-churches-america.html.

Parales, Heidi Bright. 1998. *Hidden Voices: Biblical Women and Our Christian Heritage.* Macon: GA: Smyth & Helwys Publishing, Inc.

Parks, Sharon Daloz. 2011. *Big Questions, Worthy Dreams: Mentoring Emerging Adults in Their Search for Meaning, Purpose, and Faith.* San Francisco, CA: John Wiley & Sons.

Pargament, Kenneth I. 2001. *The Psychology of Religion and Coping: Theory, Research, Practice.* New York: Guilford Press.

Plante, Thomas G., and Allen C. Sherman. 2001. *Faith and Health: Psychological Perspectives.* Guilford Press.

Pelikan, Jaroslav. 1985. *The Christian Tradition: A History of the Development of Doctrine, Volume 4: Reformation of Church and Dogma* (1300-1700). Chicago: University of Chicago Press.

Peterson, David. 2009. *The Acts of the Apostles.* Grand Rapids, MI: Wm. B. Eerdmans Publishing Co.

Polanyi, Michael, and Harry Prosch. *Meaning.* Chicago, IL.: University of Chicago Press.

Radcliffe, Timothy. 2009. *Why Go to Church?: The Drama of the Eucharist.* New York, NY: Continuum Publishing.

Redford, Shawn. 2012. *Missiological Hermeneutics: Biblical Interpretation for the Global Church.* Eugene, OR.: Pickwick Publications.

Rickman, H. P. 1979. *Dilthey Selected Writings* (1979-04-30). Cambridge, UK: Cambridge University Press.

Roberts, Alexander, James Donaldson, and A. Cleveland Coxe. 1999a. *Ante-Nicene Fathers: The Writings of the Fathers Down to A.D. 325. Volume VII – Lactantius, Venantius, Asterius, Victorinus, Dionysius, Apostolic Teaching and Constitutions, 2 Clement, Early Liturgies.* Peabody, MA: Hendrickson Publishers.

———. 1999b. *Ante-Nicene Fathers: The Writings of the Fathers Down to A.D. 325. Volume I—The Apostolic Fathers, Justin Martyr, Irenaeus.* Peabody, MA: Hendrickson Publishers.

———. 1999c. *Ante-Nicene Fathers: The Writings of the Fathers Down to A.D. 325. Volume II—Fathers of the Second Century: Hermas, Tatian, Athenagoras, Theophilus, and Clement of Alexandria (Entire).* Peabody, MA: Hendrickson Publishers.

———. 1999d. *Ante-Nicene Fathers: The Writings of the Fathers Down to A.D. 325. Volume III—Latin Christianity: Its Founder, Tertullian I. Apologetic; II. Anti-Marcion; III. Ethical.* Peabody, MA: Hendrickson Publishers.

———. 1999e. *Ante-Nicene Fathers: The Writings of the Fathers Down to A.D. 325. Volume V—Hippolytus, Cyprian, Caius, Novation, Appendix.* Peabody, MA: Hendrickson Publishers.

Robson, Colin. 1993. *Real World Research: A Resource for Social Scientists and Practitioner-Researchers.* Oxford, UK: Blackwell.

Rosenburg, Roy. 1994. *The Concise Guide to Judaism: History, Practice, Faith.* Salinas, CA: Meridian Publishers.

Rothenbuhler, Eric W. 1998. *Ritual Communication: From Everyday Conversation to Mediated Ceremony.* Thousand Oaks, CA: Sage Publications.

Rouwhorst, Gerard. 1997. "The Quartodeciman Passover." *Katholieke Theologische Universiteit.* Accessed September 20, 2019. http://www.academia.edu/7808976/The_Quartodeciman_Passover.

Sartre, Jean-Paul. 1948. *Existentialism and Humanism.* Translated by P. Mairet). London, UK: Methuen.

Schaff, Philip. Wace, Henry. 1999a. *Nicene and Post Nicene Fathers: A Selected Library of the Christian Church Volume 2—Augustine: City of God, Christian Doctrine.* First Series. Peabody, MA: Hendrickson.

———. 1999b. *Nicene and Post Nicene Fathers: A Selected Library of the Christian Church Volume 14—The Seven Ecumenical Councils.* Second Series. Peabody, MA: Hendrickson.

———. 1999c. *Nicene and Post Nicene Fathers: A Selected Library of the Christian Church Volume 1—Eusebius: Church History, Life of Constantine the Great, and Orations in Praise of Constantine.* Second Series. Peabody, MA: Hendrickson.

Schleiermacher, Friedrich. 1998. *Hermeneutics and Criticism and Other Writings.* Translated by A. Bowie. Cambridge, UK: CUP.

Seemiller, Corey, and Meghan Grace. 2016. *Generation Z Goes to College.* San Francisco, CA: John Wiley and Sons.

__________. 2019. *Generation Z: A Century in the Making.* New York, NY: Routledge.

Segger, Glen J. 2008. *Petition for Peace: A Theological Analysis of Richard Baxter's "Reformed Liturgy" in Its Ecclesiological Context.* Drew University, New Jersey. ProQuest.

SEU. 2015. "Mission." *Mission of St. Edward's University.* Accessed November 2, 2019. https://www.stedwards.edu/mission.

Shils, Edward. 1968. "Ritual in Crisis." *The Religious Situation.* Donald Cutler, ed. Boston: Beacon Press.

Singer, Milton B. 1955. "The Cultural Pattern of Indian Civilization." *Far East Quarterly* 15: 23–36.

———. 1959. *Traditional India.* Structure and Change. Philadelphia: American Folklore Society.

Smart, Ninian. 1996. *Dimensions of the Sacred: An Anatomy of the World's Beliefs.* Berkeley: University of California Press.

Smith, D. E. 1981. "Meals and Morality in Paul and His World." *Society of Biblical Literature Seminar Papers*, no. 20: 319–39.

Smith, Jonathan. 2011. "Evaluating the Contribution of Interpretative Phenomenological Analysis." *Health Psychology Review* 5, no.1: 9–27.

Smith, Jonathan A, Paul Flowers, and Michael Larkin. 2013. *Interpretative Phenomenological Analysis: Theory, Method and Research.* Los Angeles: CA: SAGE Publications.

Sokolowski, Robert. 1994. *Eucharistic Presence: A Study in the Theology of Disclosure.* Washington, D.C.: Catholic University of America Press.

Speck, Bruce W., and Sherry L. Hoppe. 2004. *Service-Learning: History, Theory, and Issues.* Westport, CT: Praeger Publishers.

Sri, Edward, Curtis Mitch, Peter Williamson, Mary Healy, and Kevin Perrotta. 2010. *The Gospel of Matthew.* 2nd in a series of 17 ed. Grand Rapids, MI: Baker Academic.

Stark, Rodney. 1996. *The Rise of Christianity: A Sociologist Reconsiders History.* Princeton, NJ: Princeton University Press.

Stetzer, Ed. 2014. "Multisite Churches Are Here, and Here to Stay." *The Exchange: A Blog by Ed Stetzer.* Accessed October 5, 2019. http://www.christianitytoday.com/edstetzer/2014/february/multisite-churches-are-here-to-stay.html.

Stone, Darwell. 2014. *A History of the Doctrine of the Holy Eucharist.* Vol.1. Place of Publication: CreateSpace Independent Publishing Platform.

Streib, Heinz, Astrid Dinter, and Kirstin Soderblom. 2008. *Lived Religion – Conceptual, Empirical and Practical Theological Approaches: Essays in Honor of Hans-Gunter Heimbrock.* Boston: Brill.

Surratt, Geoff, Greg Ligon, and Warren Bird. 2009. *The Multi-Site Church Revolution: Being One Church in Many Locations.* Grand Rapids, MI: Zondervan.

Thiselton, Anthony C. 2000. *The First Epistle to the Corinthians: A Commentary on the Greek Text.* Grand Rapids, MI: Wm. B. Eerdmans Publishing Co.

Thomas, John Christopher. 2005. The Spirit of the New Testament. Dorset, UK: Deo Publishing.

Throntveit, Mark A. 1997. "The Lord's Supper as New Testament, Not New Passover." *Lutheran Quarterly* 11, no. 3: 271–289.

Toren, Benno van den. 2010. *Reasons for My Hope: Responding to Non-Christian Friends.* New York, NY: T&T Clark.

Tozer, A. W. 2009. *Jesus, Our Man in Glory: 12 Messages from the Book of Hebrews.* Chicago: Moody Publishers.

Turner, David L. 2008. *Matthew (Baker Exegetical Commentary on the New Testament).* Grand Rapids, MI: Baker Academic.

Turner, Victor W. 2011. *The Ritual Process: Structure and Anti-Structure.* Piscataway, NJ: Transaction Publishers.

Waaijman, Kees. 2002. *Spirituality: Forms, Foundations, Methods.* Walpole, MA: Peeters Publishers.

Wandel, Lee Palmer. 2005. *The Eucharist in the Reformation.* New York: Cambridge University Press.

Windelband, Wilhelm. 1921. *An Introduction to Philosophy.* Translated by Joseph McCabe. T. London, UK: Fisher Unwin Ltd.

Webber, Robert. 1999. *Ancient-Future Faith: Rethinking Evangelicalism for a Postmodern World.* Grand Rapids, MI.: Baker Books.

———. 2003. *Ancient-Future Evangelism: Making Your Church a Faith-Forming Community.* Grand Rapids, MI: Baker Books.

———. 2004. *Ancient-Future Time: Forming Spirituality through the Christian Year.* Grand Rapids, MI: Baker Books.

———. 2006. *The Divine Embrace: Recovering the Passionate Spiritual Life.* Grand Rapids, MI: Baker Books.

———. 2008. *Ancient-Future Worship: Proclaiming and Enacting God's Narrative.* Grand Rapids, MI: Baker Books.

White, James Emery. 2017. *Meet Generation Z: Understanding and Reaching the New Post-Christian World.* Grand Rapids, MI: Baker Books.

White, Susan J. 2006. *Foundations of Christian Worship.* Louisville, KY: Westminster John Knox Press.

Whitt, Keith and French Arrington. 2012. *Issues in Contemporary Pentecostalism.* Cleveland, TN: Pathway Press.

Williamson, Peter S. 2015. *Revelation.* Edited by Peter Williamson and Mary Healy. Grand Rapids, MI: Baker Academic.

Windelband, Wilhelm. 1921. *An Introduction to Philosophy.* Translated by Joseph McCabe. T. London, UK: Fisher Unwin Ltd.

Wright, Christopher J.H. 2006. *The Mission of God: Unlocking the Bible's Grand Narrative.* Downers Grove, IL: IVP Academic.

Yardley, Lucy. 2000. "Dilemmas in Qualitative Health Research." *Psychology & Health* 15, no. 2: 215.

Young, Howard. 2005. "Pentecostal Ministry in a Postmodern Culture." *Enrichment: A Journal for Pentecostal Ministry.* 10, no. 1:33-38.

SCRIPTURE INDEX

Oxford Publishers is pleased to announce
another book from Andrew K. Fox in 2020-21.
The following is a brief overview of the concept, questions,
and responses that tell and retell the story:

THE TALE OF REDEMPTION THROUGH THREE TABLES

Introduction

Something during the adult life of a man called David, this Israelite king penned one of the most endearing Psalms. Within the twenty-third Psalm, David has enemies, he knows deathly danger, yet is writes about lacking nothing, with goodness and mercy always with him. His singular desire above everything else is to dwell in the presence of God. It is within this alluring and captivating Psalm that David writes, *"You prepare a table for me"* (Ps. 23:5).

The idea that David conveys is more than a simple food and drink. It is a table set with the very best of everything, much like the table of celebration set before the Prodigal Son on his return (Lk. 15:11-31). Old Testament Scholars are divided on the background of where David's table idea comes from. Some say it was inspired by the courts of King Saul where David was invited to feast at his table. Others disagree referring to the family table of Jesse his father. Either way, there is meaning in this singular verse: God prepares an intimate table for you.

There are three significant table celebrations in the Bible that God gives specific instruction to prepare: (1) **the Passover table;** (2) **the Communion table;** and, (3) **the Wedding Banquet table.**

I am not suggesting that David had all three tables in mind when he wrote the twenty-third Psalm. However, the meaning in this singular verse is applicable to all three tables: God prepares an intimate table. All three tables interconnect in a way that tells the story of redemption.

There are two ways of looking at these tables to understand this story. First, beginning with the Passover, each table progressively moves forward to the third table of celebration. Second, beginning with the Communion table, we look back historically to Passover and forward eschatologically to the Wedding Banquet table. Either way, these tables are linked together that tell the story of redemption.

Three questions must be asked about each table of celebration: (1) **who is invited to the table;** (2) **how does the table explain the story of redemption;** and, (3) **why does the Communion table significantly matter today?**

Who is Invited to the Table?

Though the three tables are linked together, they are unique in terms of who is invited.

The Passover Table

The Passover table is largely exclusive. *"No foreigner may eat it. Any slave you have bought may eat it after you have circumcised him, but a temporary resident or hired worker may not eat it"* (Exod. 12:43-45). An invitation to the table was dependent on the preparedness of those who participated, *"...for the generations to come you shall celebrate it as a festival of the Lord – a lasting ordinance"* (Exod. 12:14). Up until the fourth century Christians were in dispute over whether they should celebrate the Passover. Gentiles in particular were called *Quartodecimans* (meaning fourteeners) because Passover was celebrated on the fourteenth day of the month. Irenaeus in *Against Heresies* and Eusebius in his *Letter to Victor* write that Polycarp was an advocate of Passover. This carried great weight with the early church. In his *Sermon on the Passover*, Melito the Bishop of Sardis insisted all Christians should celebrate the Passover. However, at the First Council of Nicaea 325 AD, Passover was officially replaced with Easter. So, in summary, the **Passover Table was largely exclusive**.

An invitation to the Communion table is dependent on what God has done through Christ.

The Communion Table

Communion is absolutely inclusive. *"While they were eating, Jesus took bread, and when he had given thanks, he broke it and gave it to his disciples, saying, 'Take and eat; this is my body.' Then he took a cup, and when he had given thanks, he gave it to them, saying, 'Drink from it, all of you. This is my blood of the covenant, which is poured out for many for the forgiveness of sins. I tell you, I will not drink from this fruit of the vine from now on until that day when I drink it new with you in my Father's kingdom'"* (Matt. 26:26-29).

An invitation to the Communion table is dependent on what God has done through Christ. *"I will not drink from this fruit of the vine from now on until that day when I drink it new with you in my Father's kingdom"* (Matt. 26:29). The Apostle Paul reminds us that the Communion table invites an anticipation of Christ celebrating it with us, *"...you proclaim the Lord's death until he comes"* (1 Cor. 11:26). So, in summary, the Communion table is absolutely inclusive.

The Wedding Banquet Table

The Wedding Banquet is absolutely exclusive. *"For the wedding of the Lamb has come, and his bride has made herself ready. Fine linen, bright and clean, was given her to wear... Blessed are those who are invited to the wedding supper of the Lamb!"* (Rev. 19:7-9)

An invitation to the table is dependent on the preparedness of the Bride. *"But when the king came in to see the guests, he noticed a man there who was not wearing wedding clothes. He asked, 'How did you get in here without wedding clothes, friend?' The man was speechless. 'Then the king told the attendants, 'Tie him hand and foot, and throw him outside, into the darkness, where there will be weeping and gnashing of teeth'"* (Matt. 22:11-13).

Is this a one-time event, and how long does the table celebration last? The imagery that John uses is a Jewish wedding banquet that would typically last approximately one week. The Wedding Banquet of the Lamb appears is a celebration of announcement and proclamation. Storytellers would say, 'happy ever after.' So. In summary, the **Wedding Banquet table is absolutely exclusive**.

What this means for us today is that the Communion table explains the past and the future from the present reality.

What this means for us today is that the Communion table explains the past and the future from the present reality. It is therefore a table to remember what God has done and a place for the curious to hear about what God has done.

How Does Each Table Celebration Explain the Story of Redemption?

Redemption as a pragmatic narrative embedded in the Jewish imagination and therefore in the Christian imagination. The narrative has four characters in a reoccurring story throughout human history. From the perspective of the Communion table each character is foreshadowed at the Passover table, fully realized at the Communion table, and finalized at the Wedding Banquet table.

Walter Bruegermann refers to the four characters: (1) **the oppressor**; (2) **the oppressed**; (3) **God**; and (4) **the deliverer.** Each time we participate in the Communion table we reenact the redemptive story that was fully realized in Christ.

Redemptive Story at the Passover Table

We must remember that the first Passover was different to successive Passovers. There was no Pharaoh, ten plagues, or Red Sea in successive Passovers.

The oppressor was **Pharaoh**, uncaring and full of greed. In a time of famine, Pharaoh purchased all the land, property, and even the Jewish people. Inheritance for the next generation is lost. Pharaoh was not just a god in Egypt's eyes, but the surrounding nations also saw him as a deity. However, the one who has oppressive power but does not have God is the most irrational. So, Pharaoh increased the workload of the Jews, and at the same time murders all the Jewish baby boys who would be his future workforce. Power without God creates destructive policies that contradict the needs of the oppressor.

The oppressed were the **Jews** reduced to an undifferentiated people with no name or face. They were enslaved. They even forfeited their own bodies. Oppressed people never benefit from their own hard labor because they are in the service of the rebellious ambition of the oppressor.

Pharaoh dies and another god-like king takes his place. It is here that the oppressed find their voice. Remarkably, **God** does not respond until the people cry out. But they did not cry out to God. They simply cried out in their oppression. *"The Israelites* *groaned in their slavery and cried out, and their cry for help because of their slavery went up to God"* (Exod. 2:23). We must be careful not to paint a picture of an uncaring God who does not respond until he hears the cries of the oppressed. God strides into the narrative directly from Genesis where He had made certain promises to Abraham, Isaac, and Jacob. Into a pluralistic Egyptian world, the monolithic God of the Jews responds.

Almost all the time, a deliverer comes from the people who are oppressed. This is certainly true in the case of the exodus. **Moses** notices a Jewish man being exploited by the oppressive policies of Pharaoh and intervenes. Again, we must be careful not to paint a picture of God's deliverer as a freedom fighter, anarchist or terrorist. These do not represent God. As a result of his actions, Moses spends half a lifetime detached from the alluring power of Pharaoh until he is ready to challenge the oppressor with no desire for power.

Redemptive Story at the Communion Table

Like the first Passover, we must remember that the first Communion was different. Christ was present with his disciples, the crucifixion had not happened, therefore the resurrection had not occurred. We must also remember that the idea of an oppressor, the oppressed, God, and a deliverer was very familiar in the imagination of the Jews. Therefore, it was no coincidence that Christ chose the Passover to introduce Communion. The same characters are in play, but this time it is not localized to Egypt and the surrounding nations. It is cosmic and universal to every human being from every culture, language, and nation.

The **devil** is the oppressor. He is a thief and a liar who takes the inheritance of successive generations. He destroys families, cities, and nations through his puppet oppressors filled with greed and no regard for people.

The Bible paints a picture of **humanity** enslaved to sin. Adam's work was a delight because he served the purposes of God. You could say he had a solid theology of work. However, sin will always cause work, career, or occupation to be unsatisfying as Solomon clearly stated that *"everything is meaningless"* (Eccl. 1:1-11). A spouse becomes unsatisfying. If we want to measure how much humanity is oppressed, look into the pharmaceutical world, the therapist's office, and prisons. More people are classified as refugees and immigrants than all of recorded human history mostly because of oppression.

God remembered His promises to Abraham, Isaac, and Jacob. For instance, the precision of God's response to the cry of the oppressed was *"In the fullness of time"* (Gal. 4:4-7). It is no surprise that God precisely chose a time in human history where Judea was occupied by the Roman Empire. It not only tells the story of redemption; it joins the branches of other nations to the Root of David.

In the genealogies of the Bible, Mary was a direct decedent of King David. But where was her property and land? The oppressor had consumed it all. So, out of a town recognized by Nathanael as a place from the other side of the tracks comes the deliverer who is Christ. A man of the people from the people. Christ said, *"For God so loved the world that He gave His only begotten Son"* (Jn. 3:16).

Redemptive Story at the Wedding Banquet Table

The Wedding Supper of the Lamb is not a reenactment of the redemptive story. It is the culmination of it.

The oppressor has been destroyed forever, and by default, all his puppet oppressors with him.

The oppressed are washed, dressed, given a new name, known and recognized. God gives **absolute identity** to a once undifferentiated people those at the Banquet.

The oppressor character has never recognized human dignity. However, at the Wedding Banquet table all the redeemed will hear something the oppressor could never say, *"Well done, good and faithful servant"* (Matt. 25:21).

The most remarkable aspect of **Christ** as our deliverer is that he is still human. He is not flesh and blood, but flesh and bones (Luke 24:39). A. W. Towzer refers to Him as the man in glory. Even in eternity, He is like us as we shall be like Him.

> **The most remarkable aspect of Christ as our deliverer is that he is still human.**

Why Communion Matters Today

The Passover table is largely exclusive, as the Wedding Banquet table is absolutely exclusive. However, the Communion Table is absolutely inclusive. It is this inclusiveness that has attracted attention throughout church history.

For example, reformers like Martyn Luther and John Calvin admitted the Communion table could be the **means for conversion**. Puritans like William Prynne and John Humfrey believed the Communion table could do the same. The Judd manuscripts during the Great Awakening contain a record of Solomon Stoddard's conversion while at the Communion table. As a result of his conversion, he built a great congregation in Northampton around something he called a Halfway Communion. The diaries of John Wesley contain similar records. Revivalists like George Whitefield and Jonathan Edwards preached the Communion table could be the **point of conversion**.

Today, contemporary scholars from many branches of the church are focusing on the work of the Holy Spirit at the Communion table. The focus is not on the bread and wine, but on the participant as a significant character in the redemptive story. Robert Webber's *Ancient Future* series brings to light how **college students have become attracted to the Communion table**. Pentecostal scholar Simon Chan believes the Communion table is impoverished without understanding its natural appeal for salvation. The body and blood of Christ will always set people from the oppression of sin and death.

For more information about this, and other publications:
www.drandrewfox.com
andrew@drandrewfox.com

Lightning Source UK Ltd.
Milton Keynes UK
UKHW020821100321
380099UK00015B/1466